Sephardic House
2112 Broadway
New York, NY 10023
(212) 496-2173

D1686454

HAHAM GAON
MEMORIAL VOLUME

HAHAM GAON MEMORIAL VOLUME

Edited by

RABBI MARC D. ANGEL

Published by

SEPHER-HERMON PRESS, INC.

FOR

SEPHARDIC HOUSE, INC.

HAHAM GAON MEMORIAL VOLUME

Copyright © 1997 Sephardic House, Inc.

Published by:
Sepher-Hermon Press, Inc.
1265 46th Street, Brooklyn, NY 11219

ISBN 0-87203-148-9

Library of Congress Cataloging-in-Publication Data

Gaon, Solomon.
   Haham Gaon memorial volume / edited by Marc D. Angel,
      p.   cm.
   Contains sermons and lectures by Solomon Gaon and essays by colleagues and students.
   Includes bibliographical references.
   ISBN 0-87203-148-9
   1. Jewish sermons, English. 2. Judaism- -Sephardic rite- -Sermons. 3. Sephardim. 4. Jews- -Attitudes toward Israel.   I. Angel, Marc. II. Title.
BM740.2.G36 1997
296.4'7-dc21
                                                                               97-4970
                                                                                   CIP

The preparation and publication of this volume were assisted by grants from The Memorial Foundation for Jewish Culture (New York City) and The Doron Foundation (Jerusalem).

We also thank the following contributors to the Haham Gaon Memorial Volume:

SPONSOR
Consulate General of Spain

FRIENDS
Karen Erani
(In Memory of Raymond Erani)
Nessim D. Gaon
Mr. and Mrs. Leon Levy
Jack Rudin
Sephardi Communities Department of the World Zionist Organization, Jerusalem
Vicky and Michael Turek
Mr. and Mrs. Morrie Yohai
(In Memory of Mary Yohai)

SUPPORTERS
The Braka Family
Dr. Nicole Cohen-Addad
(In Memory of Simon Cohen-Addad, Henri Chamak, Germaine Cephal and Mme. Namia)
HH The Exilarch, Mr. Naim Dangoor, The Exilarch's Foundation, London
Alvin Deutsch
Andy Gluck
Dr. and Mrs. Jose A. Nessim
(In Honor of Mrs. Regina Gaon and Family)
Jack and Margo Schwartz
(In Honor of Uncle Morrie Yohai)
**Women's Division,
the Central Sephardic Jewish
Community of America**

DONORS
Rita and Joshua Angel
Mr. and Mrs. Victor Capelluto
Mr. and Mrs. Donald Cooper
Ide and David Dangoor
Eva and Simon Haberman
Leon L. Levy
Joe Maleh
The Sofaer Foundation
(In Memory of Rick Scheuer)

CONTRIBUTORS
Mark Aaron
Rabbi Elie Abadie (In Memory of Haham Abraham Abadie)
Jose Abady (In Memory of Shabatai Abraham Abady)
Liza Abraham
 (In Memory of Joseph H. Abraham)
Mordechai Arbell
Isaac Azose (In Memory of Jack Azose, Salem Shemia and Habiba Shemia)
Julius Barnathan
Isaac Barrocas
Carole L. Basri
Els Bendheim
Marc & Lori Ben-Ezra (In Memory of Isaac & Elvira Amir and Max & Rebecca Ben-Ezra)
Henri Bengualid
Abraham Beniso
Jim & Ruth Blumberg

Jack, Gwen, Solara & Sarah Calderon
Joseph Calev
Felix & Fortuna Calvo-Roth
(In Memory of Isaac & Rose Calvo)
Abe Capon
Dr. & Mrs. Morris N. Capouya
(In Honor of Capouya Family)
Mordechai Chetrit
Louise Defez
Rachel El Hassid
Martin Elias
Zohra Gefitte Elkaim
(In Memory of Corinne Elkaim)
Mr. and Mrs. Albert Franco
Hillel J. Franco
Joseph Franco
Mimi and Alan Frank
(In Honor of Elsi and Leon Levy)
Robert Franklin
(In Honor of Franklin Family)
Samuel Gabai (In Honor of Rabbi Albert E. Gabbai, Congregation Mikveh Israel, Philadelphia)
Clement Galante
Esther & Solomon Garazi
Shaar Hashamayim Synagogue, Gibraltar
Jack Greenberg
(In Memory of Mary Zellin)
Andre & Maggie Guenoun
Gershon & Rena Harris (In Honor of Yonah, Tehila, Moriah, Akiva, Gamliel & Aderet Harris)
Emile Harrosh (In Memory of Joseph & Hanina Harrosh)
Rosa & Salomon Helfgot
Rabbi and Mrs. S. Robert Ichay
Kehila Kedosha Janina
Bonita Nahoum Jaros

Mr. and Mrs. Stuart Marks
Solomon and Meira Max
Avraham Isaac Menashe, Haifa
Jonathan de Sola Mendes
United Congregation Mikve Israel - Emanuel, Curacao
E. Sherry Miller
David and Sydelle Mitchell
Henry and Rose Moskowitz
Victor Mushabac
David & Rebecca Nathan
Mr. and Mrs. Edgar J. Nathan 3rd
Melvin and Deborah Neumark
(In Memory of Sylvia Kramer)
Susan and Avery Neumark
Ernest S. Nounou
Carol Olivar
Marcia C. Pinchas
(In Memory of Raphael Pinchas)
Marlon and Susan Portes
Sheldon Reaven (In Honor of the 50th Wedding Anniversary of Saul and Glorie Reaven)
Porfessor Charlotte Russel (In Memory of Joseph Sananes and Marguerite Saltiel Sananes)
Nathan and Daisy Saatchi
Linda Gale Sampson
Herman and Doris Schwarz
Sephardic Federation of Palm Beach
Foundation for the Advancement of Sephardic Studies and Culture
(In Memory of Louis N. Levy)
Sandi Knell Tamny
Dr. Henry Toledano
Turkish Sephardi Federation
Norris & Judith Wolff
Dr. David Zakai (In honor of Mrs. Zakai)

TABLE OF CONTENTS

Introduction, *Rabbi Marc D. Angel*	XI
An Appreciation of Haham Gaon, *Dr. Herbert C. Dobrinsky*	XIII
Illustrations	XXIV

Sermons and Lectures by Haham Gaon

The Development of Jewish Prayer	1
Sermon on the Occasion of His Induction as the Haham	17
Sermon in Honor of Consecration of Girls	23
The Priestly Blessing	27
On Revitalizing Sephardic Life	33
Religion and Culture	37
Planning for the Future	41
Sephardim and Zionism	45
The Need for Inspired Leadership	51
The Idea of Charity	55
Message to a Bar Mitzvah	63
Sermon for Youth	67
The Religious Significance of the State of Israel	71
Material and Spiritual Progress	75
The World Sephardi Federation and the Bibliographical Exhibit	79
On the Re-opening of the Bevis Marks Synagogue	89
Israel Independence Day Address	93
Israel: Dream and Reality	97
Report on Sephardim of America	101

HAHAM GAON MEMORIAL VOLUME

Repentance	117
Raising our Religious Level	121
Report of the Haham for the Year 1970/71	127
Message for Passover, 1979	129
Israel and Spain	131
The Present Condition of Sephardi Life	137
Acceptance Speech	145

Essays in Memory of Haham Gaon

Tzeniut: A Universal Concept, *Norman Lamm*	151
Elleh Toledot: A Study of the Genealogies in the Book of Genesis, *Hayyim Angel*	163
Rabbi Israel Moshe Hazzan on Music, *Edwin Seroussi*	183
The Attachment of Moroccan Jewry to the Land of Israel According to Rabbinic Literature, *Henry Toledano*	197
Architecture and Visual Arts of the Spanish and Portuguese Synagogue of New York City, *Ronda Angel*	223
A History of the Jews of Bosnia Based on the Notes of Dr. Solomon Gaon, *M. Mitchell Serels*	235

"Dr. Gaon, who has been associated with Yeshiva University as Director of the Sephardic Studies Program over the past three years and who has brought to these shores a calibre of outstanding international rabbinic leadership, has won the love, respect and admiration of his colleagues and of the entire community in this short period. His warmth of personality, his untiring and dynamic efforts in behalf of the enrichment of Sephardic life in America have helped to unite and strengthen our Sephardic brethren in every corner of the North American continent. His selfless and consecrated service which the Haham is rendering in order to assure the survival and preservation of Sephardic religious life in America is at the price of great personal and familial sacrifice. I am certain, however, that in the history of Jewish life in America, these noble efforts will have, in large measure, helped shape the destiny and vitality of the Sephardic traditions in Jewish learning and Jewish living which might otherwise fall into oblivion."

Dr. Samuel Belkin, President
Yeshiva University

(Excerpted from a letter dated September 3, 1965)

INTRODUCTION

Haham Dr. Solomon Gaon was one of the outstanding rabbinical figures of the twentieth century. From his humble beginnings in the Sephardic community of Travnik, he went on to become the Haham of the Spanish and Portuguese Congregation of London, the Haham of the World Sephardi Federation, Professor of Sephardic Studies at Yeshiva University and an international lecturer on behalf of Sephardic culture, Zionism and Orthodox Judaism.

I first met Haham Gaon shortly after I began my studies at Yeshiva College in September 1963. I had the privilege of studying with him, and it was he who influenced me to become a rabbi. Indeed, I was the first rabbinical graduate of the Sephardic Studies Program established through the efforts of the late Dr. Samuel Belkin, President of Yeshiva University, and Haham Gaon. During my years of service as a rabbi, I always looked to the Haham as a mentor and guide, and as a genuine friend.

Those of us who were privileged to know him will remember him as a man of profound faith in God and enthusiastic devotion to Jewish tradition in general and Sephardic tradition in particular. He was generous beyond measure to his family, students, congregants, colleagues - to the entire community. He was one of those rare human beings who truly rejoiced in the success of others, a man of generous spirit.

Haham Gaon was one of the last representatives of the old country Ladino-speaking Hahamim for whom God was a steady presence and a friend. Among Sephardim, a rabbinic leader was revered not only for being learned and analytical, but for being a Godly person who could pray to God with simple sincerity and honesty, with a pure and spiritual soul. Haham Gaon was this type of spiritual personality. His deep trust in God made him an optimist about life. In spite of the many difficulties and hardships which he endured, his spirit was not only unbroken, but was radiant with hope and kindness. All of us remember his enthusiasm, his ubiquitous smile, his love of song. He had the unique gift of making each person feel special.

Haham Gaon felt a keen responsibility towards the traditions of his parents and ancestors. He felt that he was in some sense a guardian for all Sephardim, for all Jews, for the State of Israel. He traveled, lectured, gave classes, consulted with people throughout the world. He worked with an intense degree of energy, fueled by his sense of personal responsibility for his community and his people. He gave of himself freely and tirelessly in order to help meet the needs and interests of the community.

I thank Mrs. Regina Gaon for having made available to me copies of sermons and addresses given by the Haham over the years. The selections included in this volume have, with few exceptions, not been published before. They are reflective of the concerns and ideals which animated Haham Gaon's rabbinic leadership. Sermons and lectures, of course, are meant for oral- rather than written- presentation. Nevertheless, in reading through the sermons of Haham Gaon, we sense his enthusiasm and seriousness of purpose. We remember Haham Gaon's impressive manner of speaking, we almost hear his voice and see his face.

A number of colleagues and students have contributed articles to be included in this volume in memory of Haham Gaon. The Haham had a way of inspiring Jewish learning during the course of his lifetime; and he continues to inspire Jewish scholarship even after his death.

His memory will continue to serve as a source of inspiration to his family, colleagues and students for many years to come. He lived a good life as a devoted son of his people. He was able to transmit his love of God, Torah, Israel and humanity to his generation, and his memory will be a source of blessing for generations to come.

Rabbi Marc D. Angel
Hanukkah, 25 Kislev 5757

AN APPRECIATION OF THE HAHAM RABBI DR. SOLOMON GAON AS A MAJOR BUILDER OF NORTH AMERICAN SEPHARDIC JEWRY

by Dr. Herbert C. Dobrinsky
Vice President for University Affairs, Yeshiva University

The Haham, Rabbi Dr. Solomon Gaon, one of my most cherished friends in life, was undoubtedly one of the truly dynamic and multifaceted rabbinic personalities of the twentieth century. As an international rabbinic leader of the Sephardic Jewish community in the diaspora, he had no peer. His charisma and charm, his animated and sincere concern for his colleagues, friends, and brethren throughout the world, was all embracing. In him one found the modern day synthesis of prophet and priest, for he was zealously committed to a specific sacred mission and goal, yet totally concerned with the need for harmony and cooperative endeavor among all segments of world Jewry, and within Sephardic Jewry, in particular. His talents and strengths are precisely what is needed in the Jewish world today, where we are faced with so many dilemmas borne of disunity, inability to communicate and a zealotry which has raised its head on both ends of the spectrum.

Perhaps one of the greatest privileges and satisfactions that have come my way in my professional career as a Rabbi in Israel and as an administrator of a great Jewish university, Yeshiva University, has been the honor granted me in working with the Haham throughout his more than 30 years of association with our institution. Mine was the sacred task to work with him in developing what would become the world's first bona fide Sephardic studies and Sephardic community program under the auspices of a recognized university as the founding Director of Sephardic Community Activities at Yeshiva University.

To be with this gentle giant of a man was to see that one is measured not by one's height but by one's stature. Dr. Gaon's role as an international Jewish leader spanned the entire world. He was revered in Asia, Africa, Australia, North and South America and throughout Europe. Wherever there were Sephardic communities that required guidance or inspiration, they would bring their problems to the attention of the Haham, Dr. Solomon Gaon, then serving as Chief Rabbi of the Sephardic Congregations of the British Commonwealth. He would endeavor to respond to their needs with wise counsel and spiritual direction. Indeed, in matters of Halakhah and public policy his opinions were sought by communities throughout the world. Where necessary, in dealing with truly complex issues, the Haham would consult with other Sephardic rabbinic sages to provide a response that would be comprehensive, authentic and acceptable. His breadth of knowledge in both sacred and worldly matters made him unique among his rabbinic colleagues. Unlike many other great rabbinic teachers, he had the ability to communicate in many languages. He could navigate from one to the other with a grace and swiftness that made his comprehensive grasp of diverse cultures seem natural and easy. His fluency in English, Hebrew, Ladino, German, Slavic languages, Spanish and French, and his working knowledge of Arabic, enabled him to maintain a rapport with a wide array of congregants, community leaders and international personalities, all of whom sought his wise counsel and advice. He was at home with royalty and the common man. The Haham's beloved wife, Regina, is as regal as her name and it is thanks to her wonderful cooperation and selfless concern, which she shared for the world's Sephardim, that he was able to accomplish all that he did.

Most impressive about the man was that he was a *mensch* in the classic sense. An aristocratic and refined gentleman, his radiant countenance and embracing smile, coupled with his special dignity, imbued all those who had contact with him with a deep feeling of his genuine warmth and friendship.

AN APPRECIATION OF HAHAM GAON

The Haham walked into my life and changed it radically in 1963 when he first came to Yeshiva University. Brought to America for a three month visit to New York by the late Ivan Salomon, of blessed memory, Dr. Gaon was soon invited to serve as a Visiting Professor of Practical Rabbinics in The Rabbi Isaac Elchanan Theological Seminary by the late, revered Dr. Samuel Belkin, then President of Yeshiva University. It was through that connection that I first met the Haham.

Seemingly there was a problem within one of the newly founded synagogues in Queens that had been nurtured by Mr. Ivan Salomon. Its congregational leadership heard that Dr. Gaon was at Yeshiva University and called upon him to resolve the situation. As the member of the staff of the Max Stern Division of Communal Services in charge of servicing Queens and Long Island, it was my pleasant task to accompany the Haham to this meeting. That was my first encounter with the Sephardic community and because of the Haham's adept ability in dealing with the matters at hand, it was a most memorable and meaningful one. Many Sephardic community leaders began to come to his office at Yeshiva University for him to advise them and to encourage them. Dr. Samuel Belkin, of blessed memory, asked him to come back from England to Yeshiva University in order to establish a Sephardic program to educate the Rabbis, Hazanim and teachers which the Sephardic community sorely needed: Dr. Gaon agreed to do so, providing that he would not be paid a salary (only his expenses were provided) and that I would be assigned to work with him. He could only spend one month per year or at best one month per semester as the head of this urgently needed program while still preserving his important role in England. Dr. Belkin agreed immediately and appointed me to this new post and asked that I give up some of my other activities to start a Sephardic Studies Program under the tutelage and direction of Dr. Gaon. My life has never been the same since, a fact I state with pride and pleasure. I was destined to have the good fortune of working under the direction and inspiration of Dr. Gaon as my mentor. His sincerity of purpose infused within me a deep love and respect for the Sephardic community to which he was so totally dedicated. I felt genuinely privileged to espouse that commitment. To this day, the zeal and love for the Sephardic community to which I have dedicated myself, is still a major part of my life. It carries forth the far reaching vision of that great and expansive future for Sephardic Jewry, which the Haham uniquely was able to perceive in 1964.

It was not long before I understood the intrinsic urgency in the Sephardic community in America to develop a comprehensive educational program to preserve its heritage and destiny. In 1964, shortly after Dr. Gaon first arrived in New York and began teaching at RIETS, an article appeared on the front page of the New York Times, which boldly stated Sephardic Jewry On The Brink of Extinction. The headline reflected the self description of the Sephardic community leaders. They were in a state of despair and saw little hope for the continuity of their heritage on these shores.

Dr. Gaon's mandate to us at Yeshiva University was to work in a selfless partnership with the Sephardic community and to overcome the ennui, to revitalize Sephardic heritage and, through an educational program, to reach out to the entire Sephardic community. This mandate would require traveling from community to community throughout the land, to recruit Sephardic students, to create an awareness in the communities of the pressing need for cultural revitalization, and to raise the necessary funds to implement a meaningful, ongoing program that would sustain Sephardic Jewry's intellectual and communal needs for many years to come. In this sacred and noble endeavor, the Haham and I became virtual brothers in spirit, mind and deed. His boundless energy and complete commitment to the goals of enabling Sephardic Jewry to nourish and nurture its own academic and communal program within Yeshiva University, was exciting to share and emulate. Thus, Yeshiva University, an Ashkenazi institution, had opened its arms to enable the Haham to accomplish what others had tried, but failed to achieve in the past. With full confidence in his ability and leadership skills, Yeshiva University offered its full range of services to Dr. Gaon and the Sephardic Jewish community.

Many had been the attempts on these shores to create a united Sephardic community but each failed in short order. Parochialism and issues of turf prevented the Central Sephardic Jewish Community of America (which had earlier unsuccessfully turned to Yeshiva University for help) from achieving this goal. Now, under the umbrella of Yeshiva

University and with Dr. Gaon as its Sephardic spiritual guide, the Sephardic leaders came forth to cooperate and to work in harmony. Thus, due to Dr. Gaon, Yeshiva University was able to achieve the first cooperative effort of all segments of the Sephardic community including the Syrian, Spanish and Portuguese, Ladino, Iraqi and North African communities which, at that time, comprised the vast majority, if not almost the complete totality, of Sephardic Jewry in North America. In later years, there was an influx of many Jews from Iran, Bukhara, and other countries of the Middle East. Their needs are also currently being answered by Yeshiva University as a result of the Haham's efforts.

Through his activities on behalf of communities scattered across the United States and Canada, through the Yeshiva University Sephardic Studies Program, Dr. Gaon was exposed to even larger numbers of Jews, Sephardim and Ashkenazim alike. They all recognized his leadership qualities and cherished his affable personality. His travels (in which I joined him) from one corner of this country to the other, put him in contact with virtually every Sephardic community in North America and gave him widespread recognition throughout this continent. The fame and respect that he had earned and enjoyed in other parts of the world, were now shared by North American Jewry. His prestige and the esteem in which he was held, encouraged many Sephardic lay leaders from all the communities to join his effort at Yeshiva University to encourage young men and women within their communities to attend Yeshiva University. Starting with only five Sephardic students, Yeshiva University now claims some 350 Sephardim (250 undergraduates) , representing one in seven students on the undergraduate level which provides the dual programs of Jewish and general studies at Yeshiva College, Stern College for Women and The Sy Syms School of Business. Over the years some 800 Sephardic alumni have studied at Yeshiva University schools. This achievement has far exceeded the dreams of anyone, most of all the skeptics. The far reaching vision of Dr. Gaon made him realize that if he trained Sephardic Rabbis, educators and Hazanim, who would bring to their congregational constituencies the high level of general and Jewish education for which Yeshiva University is known, Sephardic Jewry in North America could better prosper and flourish. That dream has already been more than partially fulfilled.

Today the vast majority of North American Sephardic congregations receive their spiritual and educational leadership from Yeshiva University graduates. The renaissance of Sephardic culture that took place following the founding of Yeshiva University's Sephardic Programs under Dr. Gaon, on which we worked together, are programs that emulate his pioneering work. The American Sephardi founded in December 1966 by Yeshiva University's Sephardic Studies Program soon became a respected journal of Sephardic scholarship which encouraged other publications throughout the Sephardic world. Dr. Isaac J. Lévy and I, as co-founders of The American Society of Sephardic Studies, organized and attracted a group of academicians of all religions interested in Sephardic Jewry in its broadest parameters. The ASOSS was successfully initiated with the Haham, Dr. Solomon Gaon, as its founding president. His reputation in academic circles attracted scholars from all precincts to come to Yeshiva University each year for a full day of lectures on Sephardic topics. Many of those lectures were subsequently published in The Sephardic Scholar, an ASOSS publication founded to preserve and distribute the proceedings of these intellectually stimulating conferences. The Annual Sephardic Synagogue Leadership Conferences initiated at Yeshiva University and conducted by our Sephardic Community Activities Program involved several hundred lay and rabbinic leaders to discuss the need for a curriculum for Sephardic schools; to train them in Synagogue leadership skills; and to develop synagogue programs for youth and sisterhoods. We also established an Off Campus Sephardic Faculty Lecture Bureau, to provide the Jewish community with a host of outstanding lecturers to discuss a variety of topics of interest to Sephardic and Ashkenazic congregations and organizations interested in learning more about the Sephardim. These and the Adult Home Study Groups initiated by the Sephardic Community Activities Program brought the vision of the Haham for a revitalized Sephardic heritage into the homes and communities of Sephardim. The founding of some thirty new Sephardic congregations, helped by the Sephardic Community Activities Program of Yeshiva University, stand among the Haham's glorious achievements.

The later establishment of the Jacob E. Safra Institute of Sephardic Studies brought added lustre to YU's academic credibility in the

Sephardic world. It became regarded and remains as the prime academic resource for the academicians and synagogues. Its fostering of Sephardic intellectual growth gradually had an impact upon world Jewry that was soon to be recognized by universities and institutions throughout the world.

Our Sephardic Community Activities Program later inaugurated an annual Sephardic Cultural Festival at Yeshiva University which brought the artistic and creative talents of Sephardic men and women to public attention. This has now been expanded and transformed over the last many years as the excellent Semana Sepharad Programs conducted in synagogues throughout the United States and Canada by my successor, the Director of Sephardic Community Programs, Rabbi Dr. M. Mitchell Serels, who also serves as Associate Director of the Jacob E. Safra Institute of Sephardic Studies, a post he has held since 1973 when I became a Consultant to the Sephardic Programs and assumed senior administration duties. As one of the first two graduates of Yeshiva University's Sephardic Program, Dr. Serels, a protégé of Dr. Gaon, has become world renowned as a respected scholar who brings the message of Sephardic Jewish culture to communities the world over. His academic research is uncovering and rediscovering the treasures of the ancient Sephardic past in Spain, Morocco, and elsewhere. His teaching of a wide variety of Sephardic courses at Yeshiva University has infused many students, Sephardim and Ashkenazim, with an expanded appreciation of the rich diversity of Jewish life.

Under Dr. Gaon's inspiring leadership, Yeshiva University undertook in the early years of the Sephardic Programs to establish youth activities for Sephardic teenagers. Later, under Dr. Gaon's direction, Yeshiva University was joined by the World Sephardi Federation in hosting international Sephardic rabbinic conferences on campus at the University beginning in March 1967. These conferences are held every few years and have been attended by Sephardic rabbis from throughout North and South America. They have been joined by several Sephardic Chief Rabbis of Israel beginning with Rabbi Ovadia Yosef, and later with Rabbi Mordecai Eliahu and Rabbi Eliyahu Bakshi-Doron. Each Rishon Lezion (Chief Rabbi) of Israel delivered Talmudic lectures and stirring addresses, first in the presence of the late Dr. Samuel Belkin, the second

President of Yeshiva University and later in the presence of Dr. Norman Lamm, the third President of Yeshiva University, who, since his tenure began some nineteen years ago, has given much added strength and prominence to the Sephardic programs and the role of Sephardim at Yeshiva University. The first Chief Rabbi of Israel to visit Yeshiva University under the auspices of the Sephardic Program was the Rishon Lezion, Rabbi Yitzhak Nissim, who was welcomed by Dr. Samuel Belkin, both of blessed memory. Chief Sephardic Rabbis of Holland and many Israeli cities also came to lecture at Yeshiva University. Dr. Gaon, in turn, often delivered keynote addresses at the major Sephardic conferences conducted in Israel, beginning with the world's first Conference of Ashkenazi and Sephardi Synagogues in 1968 and later at the Hebrew University's Misgav Yerushalayim conferences at which Dr. Serels and I also lectured on topics of Sephardic interest representing Yeshiva University's Sephardic Program.

The four annual Sephardic Synagogue Leadership Conferences at Yeshiva University convened by the Haham following the founding of the Sephardic Program featured such speakers as Rabbi Dr. Jacob M. Kassin, of saintly memory, then Chief Rabbi of the Syrian Sephardic Jewish Community of Brooklyn and Mr. Eliahu Eliachar, President of the Sephardic Jewish Community in Jerusalem. These conferences involved rabbis and lay leaders from congregations throughout America.

Because of the wide respect for Dr. Gaon's leadership, major collections of Sephardic manuscripts, books, newspapers and other memorabilia were donated to Yeshiva University. Housed in the Sephardic Reference Room established by Dr. Gaon's devotee, Ronald P. Stanton, a Yeshiva University trustee, and a prominent lay leader of the Spanish and Portuguese Synagogue in the City of New York, who endowed the library room in memory of the late Ivan Solomon and Edgar J. Nathan, Jr., this library became a central resource for many scholars and graduate students working on their degrees and was regarded as the world's third largest Sephardic collection.

Dr. Gaon s contagious enthusiasm compelled devoted leaders among the Sephardic community's most outstanding philanthropists to join hands in establishing the world's first endowed Professorial Chair in

AN APPRECIATION OF HAHAM GAON

Sephardic Studies at Yeshiva University. Professor Hayyim J. Cohen of the Hebrew University was the first chair holder. Subsequently the Haham Dr. Gaon himself held the Sephardic Chair from 1976 until his retirement.

The Haham and I encouraged and supported the establishment of the American Sephardi Federation from its inception. We immediately and voluntarily relinquished holding our annual synagogue leadership conferences so as to enable the American Sephardi Federation to successfully launch its national program and to hold its conventions without a duplication of effort. Having succeeded in helping bring about a renewed interest in Sephardic life, Dr. Gaon understood the importance of nurturing the development of new vital dynamic organizations that would help carry on Sephardic life in all precincts of the community. Thus, in his capacity as Director of Yeshiva University's Sephardic Programs; Professor of Sephardic Studies; the Sephardi Rosh Yeshiva at RIETS; as well as President of the Union of Sephardic Congregations; Haham of the World Sephardic Federation; and Chairman of its Committee on Jewish Education, Dr. Gaon mentored and encouraged new organizations to help them develop and flourish. He served as their spiritual guide and counselor both publicly and privately.

The Haham was especially proud of Rabbi Dr. Marc D. Angel, another of his protégés, spiritual leader of Congregation Shearith Israel in the City of New York for more than 27 years, and a world respected author, thinker and rabbinic leader, (who was the other of the first two graduates of Yeshiva University's Sephardic Program), who helped create, with others, Sephardic House, as a resource organization for the informational and cultural expression of the Sephardic community. Its efforts, which were initially nurtured and hosted by the Spanish and Portuguese Synagogue, are currently conducted elsewhere and have always worked in cooperation with Yeshiva University's Sephardic Community Program. A similar harmonious relationship continues between those administering Yeshiva University Sephardic programs and the American Sephardi Federation, with Yeshiva University serving as the major intellectual, spiritual and service resource, assisting whenever and wherever called upon.

Similarly, the Syrian Jewish community today is blessed with two outstanding young Sephardic rabbinic leaders who were educated at Yeshiva College and ordained at Yeshiva University's affiliated Rabbi Isaac Elchanan Theological Seminary. Rabbi Ezra Labaton, in West Deal, New Jersey, and Rabbi Raymond Harari in Brooklyn will play a significant future role in the enrichment of Jewish education and synagogue life for Syrian Sephardim in New York, and environs. Their success brought Dr. Gaon great satisfaction.

The following is a listing of most of the rabbinic students of the Haham who are RIETS and YU graduates who serve the Sephardic Community as rabbis with distinction:

Rabbi Dr. Elie Abadie, M.D., Rabbi Hayim Angel, Rabbi Dr. Marc D. Angel, Rabbi David Arzouane, Rabbi Manuel Behar, Rabbi Avraham Benhamu, Rabbi Daniel Bouskila, Rabbi Victor Delouya, Rabbi Raymond Harari, Rabbi Jeff Ifrah, Rabbi Meir Kadosh, Rabbi Hayyim J. Kassorla, Rabbi Ebrahim Kohan, Rabbi Herve V.B. Krief, Rabbi Ezra Labaton, Rabbi Yamin Levy, Rabbi Samuel Mellul, Rabbi Moises Nahon, Rabbi M. Mitchell Serels, Rabbi Yaacov Shemaria, and Rabbi Ralph Tawil. Other Yeshiva University graduates serving the community are Rabbi D. Aryeh Greenberg, and Rabbi Harold Sutton. Many other Yeshiva University alumni serve as Hazzanim, Jewish educators, and Jewish communal leaders. Many Sephardic women, Stern College for Women alumnae, serve in Jewish education and the professions.

All of the foregoing overview attests to the unique leadership role that one man successfully enacted. He inspired others to join forces with him in building and strengthening a self-respecting, independent and self-confident Sephardic community in North America. It may have a way to go but Sephardic Jewry in North America has overcome, with giant steps, the hurdles that were present in 1964. To a large degree those challenges have been met through the herculean efforts of the man whose memory we honor, the Haham, Rabbi Dr. Solomon Gaon. May we continue his legacy of love for the Jewish people and fulfill his long range hope and vision for an ever stronger and expanded Sephardic community. May the Sephardic community remain steadfast in its efforts to maintain the integrity of its respective and varied traditions, while living in harmony, understanding and mutual respect with each other, and within the larger Jewish community. This will cause the Haham's memory to remain in our midst as a source of enduring blessing for the benefit of Jews throughout the world. This was his dream.

It was indeed appropriate that the heir to the throne of Spain, Prince Felipe I, should present to Dr. Gaon the Prince of Asturias Prize in Oveida in May, 1990 on behalf of the Sephardic Communities of the World. For as we can see, Dr. Gaon, more than any other Sephardic leader on the world scene, had successfully brought international recognition, respect and admiration for Sephardic culture in its broadest sense.

Alas, on December 21, 1994, the Haham, Rabbi Dr. Solomon Gaon, Professor Emeritus of Sephardic Studies at Yeshiva University was called to his eternal reward to find everlasting repose in his celestial abode in the Academy on High. From his window in heaven he will continue to look down upon the Jewish community with his countenance and smile and as a *melitz yosher* - a righteous pleader for the well-being of our people.

LIST OF ILLUSTRATIONS

1. Haham Gaon with Rabbi Papo and Mr. K. Rosen, President of the synagogue in Rhodesia, 1951.
2. Haham Gaon with Prime Minister Golda Meir, 1967.
3. Haham Gaon with President Katzir of Israel, when Mr. Katzir visited London and was a Shabbat guest of Haham and Mrs. Gaon.
4. Haham Gaon with the Queen of Holland and other dignitaries, at a reception in the Portuguese Synagogue of Amsterdam in 1975.
5. Haham Gaon officiating at the dedication of the synagogue in Madrid in 1968.
6. Haham Gaon greeting Dr. Norman Lamm, in the presence of Rabbi Herbert C. Dobrinsky, at a reception held on December 2, 1976 at Congregation Shearith Israel in New York, welcoming Dr. Lamm as the newly elected President of Yeshiva University.
7. Haham Gaon with the Chief Rabbis of Israel, Rabbi Mordechai Eliyahu and Rabbi Abraham Schapira at Yeshiva University, November 8, 1994.
8. Haham and Mrs. Gaon.
9. Haham Gaon planting a tree in Jerusalem. He visited Jerusalem for the opening of Hechal Shelomo, and was invited to participate by Sir Isaac Wolfson.
10. Haham Gaon congratulating Rabbi Marc D. Angel on having been elected President of the Rabbinical council of America, at the installation ceremony in Jerusalem, July 1990.

1

2

3

4

5

6

7

8

XXVIII

9

10

SERMONS AND LECTURES
BY HAHAM GAON

THE DEVELOPMENT OF JEWISH PRAYER

*A lecture delivered on Sunday, March 27, 1949
at Congregation Shaar Hashamayim in London.*

In writing of the development of Jewish Prayer, one must at the outset differentiate between prayer in general and the order of prayers as it is found today in our prayer books and as used in all the congregations of Israel. Prayer as such is as old as man himself. We find in the book of Genesis (Ch. IV, v. 26) that, already at the time of Seth, man began to call upon the Name of God. This is the first reference in Jewish literature to prayer, but thence onwards we find many such references. Our ancestors, Abraham, Isaac and Jacob, all prayed to God. It is significant that Abraham's most moving prayer was not for himself and his family, but for the doomed cities of Sodom and Gomorrah. Isaac prayed for his wife when she was childless; and Jacob prayed when on his way to Laban, as well as when he was to meet Esau on his way back to Canaan. The children of Israel, when in the bondage of Egypt, prayed to God and cried to him from the midst of their oppression.

In connection with Moses, we find many prayers; and some of them have been embodied in our present liturgy. When praying for the Children of Israel after they had sinned with the golden calf, Moses finished his prayer with the words: "...and pardon our iniquity and sin and take us for Thy inheritance" (Exodus, Ch.XXXIV, v. 9). This sentence is repeated very often in the confessions of the Penitential Days and the Day of Atonement. From Moses onward all the outstanding figures of the Bible prayed to their God; and their prayers were not merely repetitions of some stereotyped form of prayer, but real outpourings of the heart. We have only to mention the Psalms. The prayers of many prophets, like those of Jeremiah, Daniel and Ezra, have also been incorporated in our prayer book.

While it is easy to ascertain the development of prayer in general in Israel, it is rather difficult to be sure about the time when prayers began to take definite form and so to be recited. There is sufficient evidence that the Ten Commandments and the Shema were recited, if not in the first, then certainly in the second Temple in Jerusalem. There is also evidence that there were formal prayers which were recited while the sacrifices were carried out not only in the Temple in Jerusalem, but even in the desert Sanctuary. We find that persons who committed sin were not only commanded to make restitution and bring a sin offering, but also "that they should confess their sin, which they have done" (Numbers, Ch.V, v. 7). The High Priest also confessed the sins of the Children of Israel when he made his sacrifice for them on the Day of Atonement. There is no doubt that, while these confessions were made according to the feelings of each individual, there was probably a general formula to which these confessions conformed; and especially must this have been so in the case of the Confession made by the High Priest for all the people on the Day of Atonement. This statement can be confirmed by the fact that in the Bible we have precise forms of confession, as is clear from the confessions which were prescribed for people who bought their first fruits to the Temple and who had put aside the tithes for the priests and the Levites. As regards the first fruits, there was a long confession on the history of Israel, which ended with the words, "and now, behold, I have brought the first of the fruit of the ground, which Thou, O Lord, hath given me." When the tithe had been drawn, the Israelite was commanded to recite the following: "I have put away the hallowed things out of my house, and also have given them to the Levite, and unto the stranger, to the fatherless, and to the widow, according to all Thy commandments, which Thou hast commanded me; I have not transgressed any of Thy commandments, neither have I forgotten them." (Deuteronomy, Ch. XXVI, v.13.)

This shows that confession was the first definite form of prayer to be found in our history. This is no way surprising when we realize that confession was the form of prayer used by all the nations at their most primitive stage.

The next stage after confession in the general development of prayer is always "song." The Song of Moses was sung not only by him but also by all the Children of Israel (Exodus, Ch. XV, v. 1). When the children of Israel found water in the desert, they sang: "Spring up, O well, sing ye unto it, the well which the princes digged, which the nobles of the people delved, with the scepter and with their staves" (Numbers, Ch. XXI, v. 17-20). The Children of Israel were also commanded that on their feasts and at the beginning of their months they should blow with their trumpets over their burnt offerings and sacrifices (Numbers, Ch. X, v. 10); and our Rabbis say that if this music was not performed then the sacrifices were not valid.

We also find that when the Children of Israel saw that the sacrifice was consumed before the Lord they shouted with joy and fell on their faces (Leviticus, Ch. IX, v. 24).

Deborah commemorated her victory with a song to the glory of God. We know that in the Temple of Jerusalem there were special levitic choirs, which beautified the service in the Temple and stirred the emotions of the nation. From the earliest days people joined in the service, not only by singing, but also through responses. Thus, when the Levites intoned some of the psalms, the people often joined in with "Hallelujah." When the Shema was recited, as well as when the priests in their blessings mentioned the name of the Lord, the people joined in with the response, "Blessed be the Name of the Glory of His Kingdom for ever and ever." One of the most usual responses was "Amen."

We have evidence from the prophets that side by side with the sacrifices, prayers were also offered by the people of God. Thus Isaiah says: "When ye spread forth your hands, I will hide mine eyes from you; yea, when ye make many prayers I will not hear, for your hands are full of blood (Ch. I, v. 15).

The prophet Amos tells his people in the name of God: "Take thou away from Me the multitude of thy songs, for I will not hear the tunes of the viols" (Ch.V, v. 23). Indeed, as the prophets objected to sacrifices which were brought without sincerity and without the decision of the individual to mend his ways, so they objected to prayers which did not come from a pure and sincere heart and which were not the expression of a perfect harmony between God and man, a righteous relationship between man and man.

Jewish prayer did not develop from a sacrificial cult as is the case with other religions; but from the Bible we see that prayer existed before sacrifices were introduced- according to Maimonides- as a concession to the pagan instincts of Israel; and even then prayer was often offered independently from the sacrifices.

It is relevant here to draw a distinction between the sacrifices offered by the pagan nations and those brought by the Israelites to the Temple to be sacrificed to the glory of God. The sacrifice of the Israelite was never accepted unless it was the expression of a determined effort to mend his ways towards God and towards his fellow-men. The sacrifice was not a means whereby he sought to appease a deity, as was the case with other nations, but a symbol through which in those primitive days the Israelite could convince himself that his sins had been pardoned rather than his God should be appeased. So the sacrifice in Israel was indeed a source of prayer made in a material form to satisfy the pagan inclinations to which he was subject through contact with the peoples about him and also to educate him towards a finer and more spiritual form of service. For this reason, it was not difficult for Judaism to free itself from the shackles which the Temple and its sacrifices imposed upon its spiritual strivings; and, indeed, when these material limitations were removed through the destruction of the Temple, many Rabbis secretly rejoiced at it and even in some measure gave expression in their sayings to their feeling of contentment. We can agree with the scholar (Elbogen, "The Development of Prayer and Divine Service in Israel") who said that Jewish prayer was the first prayer to free itself from sacrificial rites and to become purely the prayer of the heart, the service which every individual could offer to his Heavenly Father.

There are many names for prayer. The one most commonly used is tefilla; but the name tefilla was not always applied to all the prayers, and different prayers had their own names. In Talmudic times as well as in the Gaonic period careful distinction was made between the names of one kind of prayer and another, but in later ages these names became entirely confused. In the Talmud the name tefilla is applied to the Amida. The name tefilla originally referred to asking for God's mercies. It was closely connected with the noun פלילים which means "judges." God was appealed to as the judge of all humanity. In later times, however, this name began to be applied to all prayers in general.

The first form of post-biblical prayer with a definite form is the beraha, which we commonly call "the blessing." It comes from the root ברך from which the noun "bereh," meaning "knee," derives. It means literally "to kneel." We find this name beraha in the Bible in Chronicles II, Ch. XX, v. 26, as well as in Nehemiah. Later on beraha was applied not only to supplication, but also to praise and to prayer in general, especially to those prayers that began and ended with a blessing.

The name seder also sometimes refers to prayer. In the Talmud, in the Tractate Rosh Hashana, we find that it refers to the arrangement of the wording of a single prayer; and in later ages it was applied to the order of prayers in general.

At first, prayers were short. The contents in general were known, but the arrangements of these and the form in which they were expressed were entirely left to the readers, to those people of learning and inspiration who were usually asked by the congregation "to come before the Ark" and to lead the community in prayer. Thus, the Amida consisted at the beginning of very short prayers each with a benediction: for instance, the prayer for health consisted only of the first few words: "Heal us, O Lord, and we shall be healed," and the benediction at the end. The prayer for forgiveness was: "Our Father, cause us to turn to Thy Law," and the benediction. And it can be generally stated that all prayers in the Shemone Esre at first consisted merely of the first words which we find in the present blessings, with the final benediction, and only through the ages were additions made which are incorporated in its present form. This can be confirmed if we know a little of the history of the Amida, as the editor of which the Talmud (Ber. 28b) names Simeon Hapakoli (c. 100. C.E.), who was at the Academy of R. Gamliel II, at Jabneh. This, however, does not mean that these benedictions were not known before that date, for in other passages of our literature this prayer is ascribed to the first wise men, among whom there were prophets, as well as to the men of the Great Synagogue, of whom Ezra was one. In order to reconcile these discrepancies, the Talmud gives as explanation that the Amida had fallen into disuse and R. Gamliel had reinstituted it. R. Gamliel II, who undertook to give the service a definite form and to fix the times for worship, requested Simeon Hapakoli to edit the blessings of the Shemone Esre and to give them a definite form which would be binding for all the Israelites who were at that time already scattered in many parts of the world.

At first prayers were not allowed to be written down. In the Tosefta we find the saying that those who write the blessings down are considered as though they were burning the Torah. Only after the Talmud had been concluded and the times forced the Rabbis to write it down did prayers begin to be collected and written down.

At long last the Rabbis realized that a definite form should be given to all the prayers, and they found encouragement in doing this from the saying of R. Meir, that every man should recite a hundred blessings daily: and so the first compositions of prayers were arranged on the basis of these hundred blessings. The first such known composition is that of R. Natronai Gaon (c. 860), and this is entitled Mea Berahot- Hundred Blessings. This collection was found only about the beginning of the present century.

One of the oldest prayer books is that sent by R. Amram Gaon (C. 875), to the communities of Spain at the request of their religious leaders. Thenceforward every prominent Rabbi tried to compose his own prayer book. The best known of these collections is the Mahzor Vitry of R. Simha the son of Samuel (who lived at the beginning of the 12th century), who was one of the students of Rashi. In this prayer book the liturgical customs of France are put on record.

These collections of prayers were either called sidur or mahzor. Sidur comes from the noun "seder," which means, as previously stated, "order," but originally it meant "collection," and we find this noun used with this meaning in the Jerusalem Targum. The name mahzor was applied originally to a period of 19 years called mahzor katan, and mahzor was applied to the book dealing with the calculations of the calendar. The name mahzor as applied to a prayer book is first found in the Christian Church of Syria, where the prayer book was called "the Mahzarta." Probably, the first calendars were called mahzorim and in time different prayers and different rules governing prayers were introduced into these mahzorim. Although there is not a great difference between sidur and mahzor yet we should know the difference between these two types. The sidur is the ordinary prayer book containing only the main prayers and excluding the hymns, whereas the mahzor contains all the prayers and the hymns and, very often in addition, many rules and regulations of the Rabbis as well as their instructions concerning the different prayers.

From the 5th century onwards new additions were made to the prayers, and these especially consisted of piutim (hymns) composed by different poets, the literary merit of which varies from excellent to very bad indeed. Also new local customs- minhagim- were introduced. We find that one and the same country did not have a uniform liturgy, but different provinces- and even different towns- had their own customs and usages. This is well reflected in the present community of Gibraltar where the four synagogues have not a uniform service but each of them has differences due to the fact that their founders belonged to different parts of Europe and Africa.

The Cabbalists, the Jewish mystics, also left a deep mark on our prayers by their special additions, but these were removed, especially in the 19th century, by Mendelssohn and his school. Many Sephardi communities hardly ever accepted them in their entirety, as is the case with our own congregation. Yet there are many prayers which have remained in our liturgy as a reminder of this Cabbalistic influence. It is sufficient to mention the Kedushah and the En Kelohenu.

In Jewish prayer not only petitions to God and praise of Him are found, but also the ethical ideals of Judaism, as well as the philosophic conceptions of the Jew concerning God, the world and the relations of man to both. Jewish prayer is also a mirror in which the history of our people is often faithfully reflected. Our liturgy is perhaps the only liturgy in the world that has grown with the people. There are minor additions which were introduced by individuals merely as the fruits of their inspiration, but these additions, even when introduced by poets and

Rabbis, were usually the reflection of the times and the conditions then existent.

While prayer is as old as man himself, the Jewish form of prayer is closely connected with the oldest religious institutions of Israel. Many prayers recited today are mentioned in the Talmud as the prayers recited in the Temple in Jerusalem. Thus we know that the psalm of the day, as we have it in the present prayer book, was recited by the Levites in Sanctuary. The Levites also sang the Hallel and other appropriate psalms. The reading of the Shema with its appropriate preceding and subsequent blessings also took place in the Temple as well as the priestly blessings and the reading of the Torah with its appropriate blessings. We see, therefore, that the main elements of our present form of prayer go back to our earliest religious history and that our prayers developed with our history. The earliest discussions and disagreements of Rabbinic Judaism with the Samaritans and other Jewish sects are well reflected in the opening passages of the Shemone Esre, where the resurrection of the dead is found as one of the tenets of Judaism, as well as in the following blessings, where we pray for the rebuilding of Jerusalem and to the Lord "Who breakest the enemies and humblest the arrogant." The same events are also mirrored in the blessings of the Haftarot, where we acknowledge God as "King of the Universe Who hath chosen good prophets and delighted in their words which were delivered in truth."

All this becomes living history if it is realized that the Samaritans, as well as other sects near to the Jews, rejected the ideas of resurrection, of Jerusalem as the centre of divine holiness, and the teachings of the prophets, and did not hesitate to invite even the enemies of Israel to break not only the political freedom of the Jew but also his faith and beliefs.

There are some who believe that the words: "for they worship vain and worthless beings and make supplication to a god that cannot save" refer to the early Christians; and in fact the Christians took these words as an insult to themselves. They forced many communities to eliminate these words from the Alenu, with the consequence that they are today not to be found in the Ashkenazi rite, although they have been retained by the Sephardim. It is, however, difficult to imagine, if this prayer had been directed against the Christians, that it would have been retained by the

Sephardim, who lived for so long in Christian Spain. Moreover, although the Jews never accepted Christianity as a religion on an equal basis with that of its mother religion- Judaism- yet they did not think of it in the same light in which they regarded paganism, against which these words of the Alenu appear to be directed.

The announcement of the new moon in the synagogues on the Shabbat preceding Rosh Hodesh is a remnant of the days when great and fateful discussions took place between Rabbinic Jewry and the Karaites, who insisted that the months should be consecrated only if the new moon had been seen, as was the case in ancient Israel, whereas the Rabbis insisted that the new calculations inaugurated by them should be binding for all. To make this manifest to the whole House of Israel it was decided in the Gaonic days that the new month should be announced according to the calculations of the Rabbis, that is, even before the new moon was seen.

The opening blessings in the morning prayers, where God is blessed as the "King of the Universe who forms light and creates darkness," is directed against the belief in dualism, namely, that there are two deities, one of the light and goodness and the other of evil and darkness. When this religion was dominant in Persia and its adherents endeavored to suppress Judaism, the Jews were not allowed to recite the Shema; and for that reason it was recited very early in the morning, hence the Shema found in the Zemiroth.

Jewish prayer seems to have tended to develop from private devotions to public and organized divine service. There are some scholars who assert that Jewish prayer was in its very origin a spontaneous expression of the whole community of Israel, as is found in the Shira sung by Moses and all Israel. This theory is difficult to accept because it is known from the Bible that prayer began with the individual. This was not only the case with the Jews, but also with the all other religious communities. It was only after the fate of the individual Jew became the fate of the whole people, that the greater emphasis was laid on public prayer and the Rabbis went so far as to assert that prayer is accepted only in the synagogue (Ber. 6a). This obligation to attend organized public service three times daily was not immediately accepted by all the Rabbis and met with considerable opposition. Thus it is said of Rav Kahana (3rd century) that he neglected to attend the public service in the synagogue (Ber.7b). Of Rav Jehuda it is reported that he would pray publicly only once in 30 days (Rosh Hashana 35).

In this desire to make prayer an expression of the whole community the Rabbis went as far as to re-arrange in the plural prayers which are found in the Bible in the singular. For example, the words of Jeremiah: "Heal me O Lord and I shall be healed; save me and I shall be saved, for Thou art my praise," were changed in the Amidah, as we find them today, into "Heal us O Lord and we shall be healed; save us and we shall be saved, for Thou art our praise." Even the Shemone Esre, which is considered a private prayer and which many people think is first recited silently for that reason, the Rabbis looked upon as a public prayer; to which only the petitions and the prayers of the individual to God could be added, and it was recited silently not because of its private nature, but because when confessing their sins sinners should not be embarrassed as they would be if they recited it aloud (Sota 32b).

During the Mishnaic and Talmudic periods, prayers were not allowed to be written down, probably because of the fear that the sectarians- among whom the Christians were included- might misuse them and insert some of their own ideas. On account of this prayers were memorized only and it is natural, therefore, that very often different wordings of the same prayers were retained among different groups. We find discussions on these differences in the Talmudic days (Ber. 33a and 34a), but gradually these differences developed and became traditional with some congregations. The latest variants known were those that existed both in Palestine and Babylon. This does not mean that in either of these two places all prayers were uniform. On the contrary many places and communities had their own versions. Thus we find that Rav himself, the organizer of liturgy in Babylon, was more than once amazed to find in different sections of the country so many liturgical variants and customs.

The differences that existed between the Palestinian and Babylonian traditions were not merely textual, but were very often of a deeper character. Thus, in Palestine, the reading of the Torah was completed in three years, whereas in Babylon this was done in one year. Consequently a difference arose concerning the celebration of Simhat Torah, which festival was kept in Palestine only once in three years whereas in Babylon it was celebrated every year. In Palestine, when people were called up to the Torah, they read their own portions, while in Babylon the portion was read by the Reader. In Palestine, the Kedushah was recited only on Shabbat and festivals, whereas in Babylon it was recited every day. In Palestine, six adult men were sufficient to constitute a quorum for public service, but in Babylon ten adult men were required. Altogether 73 differences are supposed to have existed between the religious customs of Palestine and those of Babylon.

The differences existent between these two main centers of Judaism were transmitted to all other parts of the diaspora; and in various communities of Europe, of Asia and of Africa, additional glosses were made to the prayers, so that local uses assumed great importance. Out of those uses we can differentiate two main branches in the liturgy, the Sephardi and the Ashkenazi orders of service. To these could be added many other uses, among which the most important are the Italian ritual and the ritual of Rumania (the Byzantine Empire).

Zunz, who wrote the first comprehensive work on the development and history of Jewish liturgy, assumed that the Sephardi ritual was the one practiced by Babylonian Jews and that the Ashkenazi was the ritual of Palestine. In support of this view he adduced the fact that some communities in Spain turned first to Natronai Gaon and then to Amram Gaon to send them the order of prayer which should be the definite form of prayer for all the Jews of Spain. The book of Amram is the first prayer book in the real sense of the word; and, as the practices contained in that book were sent to the Jews of Spain, there was no doubt in the mind of Zunz that they became the basis of the liturgy of the Sephardi Jews. In addition to support his view, he cited the piutim which were introduced into the Palestinian liturgy by Kalir, but which are not found in the ritual of the Spanish Jews, who adopted the piutim written by the great Spanish poets, Gabirol, Jehuda Halevi, Abraham and Moses Ibn Ezra. In the words of a Jewish scholar (see article on Sephardim in Jewish Encyclopedia), the Sephardi liturgy originated in part with the Geonim. It is more natural and elevating than the Ashkenazi and also less burdened with piutim. The Sephardim admitted into their liturgy only the piutim of

Spanish poets, which are characterized by Rappaport as mediators between the soul and its Creator while the Ashkenazi piutim are the mediator between the nation and its God.

This view of Zunz that the Sephardi ritual originated in Babylonia and the Ashkenazi in Palestine was taken for granted from his time onwards. When the late Haham of this congregation- Dr. Moses Gaster- advanced in his introduction to our present prayer book an entirely new theory it created a great stir as it completely controverted the assumptions of Zunz, which were at that time generally accepted by Jewish scholars.

According to Dr. Gaster, the fact remained that, although the text of Rav Amram was brought to Spain, where it may well have influenced the Sephardi liturgy to some extent, yet this text is much more in keeping with the Franco-German than with the Spanish ritual. As to Kalir, he maintained that long before the time of this poet, the older portions of the Palestinian prayer book had been brought to Spain. He compared our Sephardi order of Service with Saadia Gaon's prayer book, embodying the rite of Egypt, and with the Yemenite ritual- both of which were Palestinian in origin- and came to the conclusion that it agreed much more with those than with the book of Rav Amram.

It must also be mentioned that it is difficult to ascertain the correct text of Rav Amram's Sidur because his Sidur remained in manuscript for a thousand years and was copied in various countries and at different times; and when copies were made there is no doubt that the customs and usages of the particular country were also introduced, as is seen from the existence of texts of the Sidur suffering considerably from each other.

In the texts of Rav Amram's book, the editors, A. Marks and L. Ginsberg, made thorough investigations of the various texts in order to establish which was correct, and we find that the Ashkenazi rite is nearer to that of Amram than is our own. It should be added that Amram himself did not entirely reflect the Baylonian usage, as can be proved from the Talmud, but introduced some of his own compositions. It was not the Spanish Jewish Community as a whole who appealed to Amram for a prayer book, but only one section; and as there already existed in Spain many local minhagim, differing greatly from each other and jealous of their own traditions, there is no doubt that the influence of Rav Amram's book may well have been limited to one or at most a very few Spanish communities.

The best known Spanish rituals are those of Castile, Aragon and Catalonia. The most surprising thing is that the minhag of Catalonia is nearer to the minhag of Provence that to the Spanish rite proper; and it may have been that part of Spain that Amram's Sidur exercised a great influence.

Not only did these differing usages exist in Spain, but even after the Jews were expelled, the exiles coming from different parts of that country retained their own usages, and in the synagogues which they organized in the new countries of their adoption, they introduced their own minhagim. Thus we know that in 1540 there existed in Salonika 14 congregations with different rituals, and among these there were the Castilian, the Aragonese, the Catalonian and the Portuguese synagogues. The continuation of the distinctive rituals often led even to physical conflicts. It was only at the end of the 16th and the beginning of the 17th centuries that some sort of uniformity was introduced into the ritual of the Sephardi synagogues of the East.

As to the poetry of Kalir and its absence from the Spanish ritual, Dr. Gaster seems also to be correct. Views differ as to the date and the native land of Eleazar Ha-Kalir, one of the most prolific liturgical poets. His date has been given variously between the end of the 7th and the end of the 10th centuries of the Common Era; and Italy, Babylonia, Mesopotamia and Palestine have been claimed by different scholars as his native land. Scholars now agree that he probably was born in Palestine and flourished nearer to the 10th than the 7th century; and by then the major forms of the Spanish liturgy were well established.

Dr. Gaster, limited as he was by space in his introduction, could not amplify and cite all the proofs mentioned by him; and probably it is owing to the absence of citation in his introduction that many scholars as yet do not accept his view. The late Haham certainly indicated a new path for research in Jewish liturgy and showed future students of our prayer book the way in which research could prove both exciting and illuminating. It would be interesting to collate all the existing manuscripts of the Yemenite liturgy as well as those of the Egyptian and of Rav

Amram's prayer book on the one hand and the Franco-German manuscripts of prayer books on the other and compare them with the present day Sephardi and Ashkenazi liturgies.

The original so-called Castilian ritual was printed for the first time in Venice in 1522, and from then onwards has been reprinted and amplified from different manuscripts. The first translation of our prayer book into Spanish appeared in 1552 in Ferrara and in 1618 in Amsterdam, eight years before the Hebrew original was printed there. In 1740 a Spanish version of part of our prayers was published by the Rev. Isaac Nieto.

The fact that the prayers were translated in Amsterdam, before even the Hebrew text was printed there, indicates that the Spanish Jews, although they possessed many prominent Rabbis, did not possess great knowledge of Hebrew. This is supported by the fact that the correspondence between the Geonim in Babylon and the authorities in Spain was always carried on in Arabic. Consequently, I think we can safely assume that many prayers in Spain were translated not only for private use, but also for public recitation. Dr. Gaster mentions a manuscript, which he believes to derive from Spain, in which the rubrics of the Haggada are written in Spanish. In the Sephardi communities in the East it was a well established custom to read different parts of the prayer, especially on Rosh Hashana and Kippur, in Spanish. Remnants of this custom are still preserved in our own community where the Haftara on Tisha Beav is read in Spanish, and, in days gone by, the Haftara of the preceding Shabbat was also read in the same language. This can be ascribed to the Sephardi codifiers and especially to Maimonides, who maintained that many parts of the prayers should only be recited in the language the individual who offered them could understand. Maimonides himself exercised an immense influence on the formation of the liturgy; and his rulings have been generally accepted by all the Sephardi communities. He was in addition concerned about the impression made by the Jew on his neighbor when worshipping God. He observed that, having recited the Amida in silence, worshippers behaved in the most undignified manner during the repetition, thus exciting the comment and contempt of their Moslem neighbors. Consequently, he decided that the Amida should only be recited aloud even though it was against the rule laid down by the Talmud. Indeed, it can be said that the attitude of the

Sephardi codifiers to Jewish life in general and to prayer in particular was always much governed by the conditions of the time. Hence came the practice to read portions of the prayer in the vernacular, a custom which was retained in the Spanish communities in the Balkans, until these communities were destroyed in the last war. These translations were not merely servile translations of the Hebrew text but were free renderings by great and inspired people. Frequently these translations were very free indeed and seemed to put the main emphasis not merely on the meaning of each word but on the whole idea which the prayer contained, on the impression it was intended to convey and on the sentiments it meant to stir.

It was quite otherwise with the Ashkenazi ritual, because Yiddish included so many Hebrew words that it was not so difficult for them to understand at least the main ideas of the prayers. The first modern translations of the Hebrew prayers came with Mendelsohn and his pupils, who were later labeled as the originators of Reform Judaism: hence the allegation that translation in prayer is closely connected with attempts to reform Judaism. Such an allegation, however, could not apply to the Sephardi translations, which probably originated in Spain or soon after the exile and were motivated by a desire not to reform Judaism but to preserve it in all its essentials. These translations were also prompted by the desire to make the ideas and ideals of Judaism available to the masses of Jewry who were not always able to master the Hebrew language properly.

And so we come once again to the idea of prayer as an expression of the yearnings of the individual for his God and for his Creator, as was the prayer of our ancestors, Abraham, Isaac and Jacob.

SERMON ON THE OCCASION OF HIS INDUCTION AS THE HAHAM

Sermon delivered on October 25, 1949 in the synagogue at Bevis Marks of Congregation Shaar Hashamayim, London.

Who shall ascend the mountain of the Lord, and who shall stand in His holy place? (Ps. xxiv).

The psalmist envisages the approach of man to his Creator in two stages. First comes the ascent, the effort to climb the mountain of the Lord; when this desired goal has been reached, man cannot relax in his endeavors. All his energies must be devoted to the task of maintaining his position, a task which challenges all his intellectual faculties and puts to a severe test all his moral integrity.

In reaching the heavenly heights, man is helped by the advice and guidance of his parents, teachers, friends and well-wishers. But having scaled the peak, he must be left to prove his worth alone. He must show himself religiously, morally, socially and intellectually worthy of standing - or rather, dwelling - as Ibn Ezra remarks, in God's own place. "He that hath clean hands and a pure heart, who hath not lifted his soul unto vanity, nor sworn deceitfully," (ibid v. 3) - the qualities, required by the psalmist for the man aspiring to make his abode in the place where the presence of the Lord resides, are beyond the reach of an ordinary human being. In the words of our Rabbis, Moses alone, the prophet of prophets, was endowed with them all.

The Rabbi who is translated to the high and holy office of spiritual leader of a community can maintain his position only by striving, through spiritual exercise and religious and social endeavor, to acquire some of these qualities. He has been called by the prophet "the messenger of the Lord of Hosts," (Malachi ii. 2) at whose mouth the people should seek the Law. In interpreting the words of the prophet, our sages point out that only "if the religious head is really the messenger of the Lord, should they seek the Law at his mouth," otherwise they should not. How exacting are the demands made by God and man upon one such as myself!

Who shall ascend the mountain of the Lord? On this day I assume the high and honorable office of Haham of the Spanish and Portuguese Jewish Community of England, the most ancient Jewish community in the British Empire, whose history has become venerable through three centuries of noble endeavor for the glory of God, for the well being and prosperity of this great and freedom-loving country and for the honor of Israel. Its sacred traditions have hallowed its long existence.

My ascent has been made the easier by the inspiration of my martyred parents, by the guidance of my teachers, in my native land and here, and by the help of the leaders and members of this congregation, which has become my second home. To God Almighty and to them all, to the memory of the martyred and of the dead and to those who are with me today, I offer my grateful thanks, praying that I may be given wisdom and understanding to walk in the footsteps of my revered predecessors, who by their erudition and piety have lent grace and glory to the office of the Haham. There were men of integrity and learning, like David Nieto and Moses Gaster; there were men of piety and eloquence, like Benjamin Artom. This day, their mantle falls upon my shoulders; and I realize that neither my learning nor my ability can stand comparison with the qualities of any of those giants of the spirit who were the religious heads of the community. All I can offer is readiness to learn, willingness to obtain experience, and eagerness to serve my God, my country, my people Israel and my fellow-men. All that I have to give, I shall give with all my heart, with all my soul and with all my might.

Over thirty years have elapsed since the last Haham of this congregation, Dr. Moses Gaster, of blessed memory, retired. The interregnum has been ably filled for many years by the devoted services of the scholarly Ab Beth Din, Rabbenu Shemtob Gaguin, whom I have the honor of numbering among my teachers.

The lack of continuity in the office of Haham will undoubtedly give rise to special problems and difficulties in my work, but, with God's guidance and blessing, I know that I can rely upon the forbearance, patience and help of the Mahamad, Elders, Yehidim and Yehidot of this congregation.

Having been elevated to this high and sacred office, I become aware that I have reached the second stage, of which the psalmist speaks - "who shall stand in His holy place?" God Almighty having granted me this exalted position, it is now my task to maintain it. I realize that 300 years of history look upon me at his moment. History and posterity will not, I know, judge me merely by the results of my efforts, but above all by the sincerity and devotion with which I shall undertake them and carry out my task.

It would be wandering into the realm of useless speculation to try to put forward here today a precise plan according to which I intend to act in the future. The work of a Rabbi is too varied and many-sided to fit into any pre-arranged pattern or to be accomplished along predetermined lines. He does not deal merely with situations which can be envisaged, but above all with the complex phenomena of the human soul, which, assume different expression in each individual and cannot be predicted.

The Rabbi is not - and should not be - a leader who gives orders, instructs and directs, while standing aloof from the ordinary man and his everyday problems. On the contrary, he must be easily accessible to all. He must be ever ready to succor every individual of his flock with practical help, advice and comfort. This I consider to be of such paramount importance that my first prayer to God is that my house may always be as was the house of Abraham our Father, where, according to the traditions of our Rabbis, all guests - friends and strangers - were equally and ever welcomed. I say to you, the door of my house is ever open, by night and day, to each and every one of you, man and woman, young and old, and last but not least, to the children of the community. My time is yours and such ability as I possess is devotedly at your service.

I am aware that, although my appointment in some respects restricts my activities to the Spanish and Portuguese Community of this country, I still have responsibilities, duties and obligations towards Anglo-Jewry as a whole. The Spanish and Portuguese Jews, though heirs to distinct traditions, social and religious, have always keenly co-operated with their Ashkenazi brethren in different countries for the unity of action and purpose of the community of Israel in those lands. An ancient Rabbi once compared the House of Israel to a cluster of rubies. It is the variety of colour and form of the individual stones that lend special beauty to the cluster as a whole. It is its different communities with their peculiar histories and customs that are the source of the spiritual opulence of Israel.

It is these liturgical and traditional differences that should bring us together and not divide us. If I can in any way contribute towards the strengthening of the unity of Anglo-Jewry, I shall strive to do so; and in these efforts, I pray that I may be guided by the spirit of the great spiritual leaders of Sepharad, who know how to distinguish between tolerance and licence, who, while following the path of genuine and enlightened authority, were uncompromising in their attitude to fanaticism.

As the Anglo-Jewish Community is the only great Jewish community left in Europe, so is this Sephardi community now one of the best organized in the Sephardi world. This imposes upon us special responsibilities towards those of our brethren who are unable to enjoy that equality of advancement and opportunity which this England, land of freedom, has for centuries made the birthright of all its citizens, regardless of race or religion. Many are there still of our brethren who need our help in the rebuilding of their shattered lives in new lands, or in the reborn state of Israel, of which the great poets of ancient Sepharad so longingly sang and within the boundaries of which may the prophetic visions of humanity's salvation find spiritual and material fulfillment. This is the earnest prayer of every Jew.

The Torah has commanded us to educate our children. It is on them that the destiny of our community rests. During the past years some progress has been made in this field, but much still remains to be done. It is only by bringing up our children in the spirit of our sacred Torah and in the spirit of the teachings of our Rabbis that we shall be able to make of them good men and good Jews. The only way to do this is by a planned program of education, carried out by the best available teachers.

Even as far back as the first century of the current era, organized classes for children, where they could receive proper instruction, were arranged by the High Priest Joshua, son of Gamla. It is only by making our younger generation aware of their heritage and its vital importance that we shall be able to fit them for a useful and fruitful life as far as their community and their country are concerned. The tragedy to-day is that there are many young people with great spiritual potentialities, who are unable to use them because of the lack of a thoroughly organized system of Jewish education.

Furthermore, education is incomplete if it is given in the classes alone; only through the closest co-operation between parents and teachers can this task be fulfilled. The home - the Jewish home has always been the source of our strength, and I appeal to you to make the home once again a reality in our community, a reality for yourselves and for your children. It is for this reason that I realize that my efforts in the field of education must not be limited merely to the children and to the young. My aim is also to create a laity, imbued with the spirit of Judaism and proficient in knowledge of the most important branches of Jewish learning. The impression which is unfortunately gaining strength in the community, is that the function of the Rabbi is in particular the resolving of religious questions; but this conception of the duty of the Rabbi is not in accordance with the spirit of our Faith. It is for the Rabbi to guide and to help, but among the laity he must also have supporters and friends in learning. Our sages say that the words of the Torah have been compared to a fire; and, as a fire cannot burn unless it is fed, so the words of the Torah cannot be imbibed by oneself, but in the company of friends. It is these friends that the Rabbi must seek in his community.

Before I conclude I must thank the Lord Mayor, the Sheriffs, and Aldermen of this great and ancient City in which we dwell for the honor they have done us by their presence. I thank the Chief Rabbi of the Ashkenazi sister community, who was one of my teachers, for coming to give me his moral support. And I thank too those men of distinction in church and public affairs, who have done me honor by their attendance. I shall not be misunderstood if I single out the representative of the great Dutch people, ever our friends, in whose land our history is writ large, and the Minister of Israel, the youngest of States, the homeland of our people.

I would ask you all to join in prayer with me: My God, and God of my Fathers, on this day, I promise, in the words of the prophet (Hab. ii. I) "I shall stand upon my watch," for the good of the community, for the welfare of Israel, of all men. Today I dedicate myself and all my life to the service of this holy congregation, to Sha'ar Hashamaim. I turn my eyes to Thee, to guide me in the difficult task that lies before me, for Thou alone makest my work prosper.

Grant Thou me, O Lord, the blessing of wisdom, that I may be of service to those who are in need of help, and that I may comfort those who are in need of consolation!

Grant Thou, O Lord, peace to all men so that they may faithfully serve Thee and live with each other in love and understanding!

SERMON IN HONOR OF CONSECRATION OF GIRLS

Sermon delivered at Congregation Shaar Hashamayim, London on May 21, 1950

You are privileged to be the first girls to be consecrated in this synagogue. It is an honor which is no way diminished by the fact that such consecration ceremonies have been held in the past in other Sephardi synagogues in England and abroad as well as in Ashkenazi congregations.

As this ceremony is taking place for the first time in our Congregation, I am sure it will not be out of place to say a few words to you about its meaning and purpose, although you yourselves, through your work in the Religion classes and through your religious preparation for this ceremony, must have become, to a great extent, aware of its significance.

This Consecration ceremony is a milestone in your lives. Today, you undertake to fulfill all the duties of Jewish womanhood. You have been instructed in some of these duties and have promised to acquire all the further knowledge necessary to fit you to be a credit to Jewish womanhood. Jewish woman have, from the earliest days of our history, played their part, together with the men, in the realization of that great message which was given to all the children of Israel at the foot of Mount Sinai.

So that there should be no confusion, I should perhaps say straight away that there is no connection whatsoever between the Bar Mitzvah ceremony of the boys and this ceremony, in which you are taking part today. Your ceremony is a ceremony of its own, a ceremony of which the main aim is to ensure that the young girls of this Congregation shall be encouraged to prepare themselves for their adult lives by learning the duties which will fall to them as Jewish women. This ceremony is not intended to relate your duties in Judaism with those of men, but, on the contrary, to emphasize your duties as Jewish women in Israel and to show you that the Jewish religion- as you are surely aware by now- in no way relegates the women to an inferior position, but apportions to men and women their own spheres of activity: these for which they are best suited.

I am fully aware that the fact that women do not take an active part in our public worship is wrongly construed by many people as an inferiority imposed upon the Jewish woman. Yet if we read through our sacred and rabbinic literature, we shall find that the contrary is the case, and that the tasks allotted to the Jewish woman are of such significance and importance that she was exempted from all duties connected with public worship and other obligations for which a specific time was laid down. Thus, the woman was freed from wearing a Talith and from being present at morning and evening prayers, because these had to be performed at certain times of the day. She was also freed from saying the blessing on the Lulab, again because this duty is performed at a certain time of the year. Hence, the rabbinic saying that women are freed from duties connected with specific times or seasons.

The reason for this is that after the destruction of the Temple, the home of the Jew, in the words of our sages, became the Sanctuary, and the running of the home with a distinctive Jewish atmosphere was left to the woman. To the woman was also left the duty of educating her children, for the Jewish child receives real education- as you know yourselves- not in the Sunday classes, not in the schools, but in the home.

This, indeed, does not mean that the woman is relegated to the four walls of her home; but that, through the home, she is able to influence the life of the Jewish community and shape the destinies of the Jewish people as a whole.

Our rabbis say that it was because of the righteous Jewish women in Egypt that the people of Israel were saved from the Egyptian bondage. It was the women who adhered zealously and faithfully to their tasks. They imbued their children with love of their faith and their God. It was also they who continued to remind their husbands of their allegiance to the God of Israel, the only Ruler of Heaven and Earth, for, indeed, men subjected to slavery as harsh as they were in Egypt, might easily have neglected their religious duties under the strain of their physical sufferings.

We also read in the Midrash that on the eve of Israel's departure from Egypt, Moses was very worried because he was unable to locate the place where Joseph was buried. Joseph had commanded the children of Israel to take his remains with them when they left. The Egyptians were aware of this and they buried Joseph in the depths of the Nile, knowing that the people of Israel would never leave Egypt if it meant breaking the trust that Joseph had laid upon them. And it was a woman who led Moses to the place where Joseph was buried.

Indeed, it was the women who continued to be concerned with the spiritual welfare of Israel and who cared for the future, while the men under the rigors of the Egyptian slavery, had forgotten their past and became indifferent towards the future.

These two stories clearly indicate that the woman was, if anything, regarded as intellectually and morally stronger than the man. Far from being his inferior, she was the one to whom the soul of the Jewish people was entrusted- the education of the youth. By faithfully fulfilling the commandments and the laws of our religion, by kindling the lights on the eve of every Shabbat and on the eve of the Festivals, by creating an atmosphere of happiness and contentment of the Shabbat days and on the Holy days, she keeps alive the Jewish spirit throughout the ages and does not allow it to die even under oppression and persecution.

It is significant that it was the mother, and not the father, who in olden days took her young child to the Rabbi to learn the law of the living God. She continued to be interested in her children's progress at school.

In the Torah we read that the Almighty commanded Moses to instruct the children of Israel in the laws and ordinances which they had to fulfill. "Now these are the ordinances which thou shalt set before them." Our Rabbis state the words "before them"- lifnehem- indicates that men and women equally were commanded concerning these laws, thereby making them equally responsible for the preservation of our holy Faith. Their duties have been allotted to them, and Judaism can only survive and gather strength if each one adheres faithfully to his or her duty and finds that great inspiration which only comes to us when we know that in addition to doing our duty, we are acting in a spirit which brings us nearer to our God and to our fellowman.

Today, my dear friends, you have pledged yourselves to carry high the banner of Jewish womanhood; to fulfill those laws and commandments which God in His mercy and goodness has given to us and which have fallen to your lot to carry out. Your duties are great and fine.

You have great examples to follow, examples of Jewish women in the Bible, in the Talmud, and, indeed, throughout Jewish history. Sarah, our mother, played as great a part as Abraham himself in the shaping of Jewish morals and ways of conduct. Deborah was endowed by the Almighty with the gift of leadership and judgement. And there is no period in Jewish history where one woman or another did not play a prominent part in the fortunes of our people. Stories are still told of the forbearance and encouragement which mothers gave to their children and wives to their husbands in the concentration and death camps in Europe during the last war. Stories are told of husbands losing their faith, of children afraid of death; but it was the mothers of Israel who kept their faith to the last, who kept untarnished, through their devotion to God and to their people, the dignity of Israel. From your Bible and your history you can know that on you, even more than on the men, depends the future of the people, for our future has always been based on the sanctity and the stability of the Jewish home, which is your kingdom, the kingdom where the Jewish woman reigns supreme. It was so in the past. It is so in the present, and it will be so in the future.

THE PRIESTLY BLESSING

Sermon delivered at Willesden Synagogue, May 27, 1950.

Speak unto Aaron and unto his sons saying: In this wise will they bless the children of Israel.

It was in almost identical terms that God addressed Moses concerning Aaron - as we read a few weeks ago in the Parasha Emor - when Aaron and his sons were commanded in the laws of their defilement as regards the dead. They were not allowed to defile themselves for the dead among their people, except for those who were their kin and who were near unto them. Here, in today's Parasha and in almost the same terminology, they are commanded as regards the way in which they are to bless the children of Israel.

Some commentators, in comparing these two instances, draw certain conclusions as to the mission and duties of the priests. Among many nations of old - and even in some of the religions today - the priests were considered the representatives on earth of the Almighty Himself. They were able to bestow pardon upon sinners, if it was considered that they had shown themselves worthy of being granted forgiveness before the Lord. These priests took this duty upon themselves because they considered that they were invested with a special power and authority and that their word and decision was in fact the word and decision of the Almighty Himself.

Judaism, however, has different ideas concerning its priests and ministers. Although the Kohanim were set apart by God to minister in the Sanctuary, they had none of that authority which would entitle them to consider themselves in any way different in nature from the rest of the people. They were not endowed with any authority to consider themselves as direct representatives of the Divine power. They merely constituted a group of men who had specific duties allotted to them for the welfare of the nation. The priests were only the teachers who interpreted the Law of God and taught its principles to the children of Israel. As such, they were given the privilege of pronouncing the blessing over the people of Israel. Our Rabbis point out that even in this role the priests were not thought of as a special sect, but only as agents who fulfilled the command of the Lord.

As we read in today's Parasha, Speak unto the children of Israel - Tebarekhu - thus shall ye bless the children of Israel. The priests were instructed merely to pronounce the blessing and they had no authority to change it or vary it as they thought fit, and the blessing did not come from them. It was not an expression of their goodwill towards the people. It was not bestowed through their own generosity of heart and mind. The blessing itself originated from the Almighty, as He clearly implied at the end of the sentence - Vaani Abarekhem - "and I will bless them."

True that in the Gemara Hulin we find that Rabbi Simeon says that the words "and I will bless them" refer not to the children of Israel, but to the priests: that, having blessed the children of Israel, they in turn will be blessed by God Himself. Rabbi Akiba, however, disagrees with this opinion, and says that these words refer not to the Kohanim, but to all the people of Israel.

The priest will pronounce the blessing, but it will be God Himself who will bring about the realization of the blessing. He will bless His children with happiness in their spiritual and material lives and He alone will grant them that peace which comes from contentment in both those aspects of life.

In addition, the priests, in pronouncing this blessing, were to some extent fulfilling their duty as the teachers of the people. The blessing, as our rabbis interpreted it in the Pesikta and in the Midrash, conveys in itself an instruction to the children of Israel, and its meaning reveals to them the way in which they may find contentment and happiness in their lives.

"The Lord bless thee and keep thee." This blessing, our sages say, refers to the material welfare of the nation. The Lord bless thee with prosperity, but may He also keep thee from evil inclinations. May prosperity not become a cause for pride and arrogance on your part, but may the Almighty keep you from such evils, so that you may use your prosperity for the good of your fellow-men in order that you may be able to serve you God without anxiety and fear and serve your fellow-men with friendship and devotion!

The second blessing - "The Lord make His face shine upon thee and be gracious unto thee" - refers to the spiritual welfare of the people. The Torah has been compared to a light. May God enlighten your life through the knowledge and understanding of the Torah, but - so that you may not use this knowledge for self-glorification - may He "be gracious unto thee" in granting that you find grace and love among your fellow-men! May your fellow-men be inclined kindly towards you so that you may be able to spread among them that knowledge which you have obtained from the Torah and the happiness which that knowledge brings with it!

The third blessing: "The Lord lift His countenance upon thee," is one that, according to our sages, refers to both aspects of our life - material prosperity and spiritual well-being. "May He turn His countenance upon thee in pardon." However strong we may be, still we sin in some way or other - are blinded by and so fall victim to temptation. Then we need God's pardon, His mercy and His loving-kindness so that we may be forgiven our transgressions and be allowed to achieve that inward peace which comes from harmony between our spiritual and physical selves, and through which alone we can work effectively for peace between man and God and man and his fellow-men.

The priest, in pronouncing this blessing, was, as the prophet called him, the messenger of the Lord of Hosts and such "his lips should keep knowledge so that the people could seek the law at his mouth." His task was limited to the instruction of the people. That instruction was to be given with courage "for the law of truth was in his mouth and unrighteousness was not found on his lips."

And this brings to us the the Parasha Emor, where a command was given to Aaron in almost identical terms. The command with regard to the blessing was a command in keeping with their task as instructors of the people and messengers of the Lord. Thus their duty was connected with life and with the preparation of the people for life. Their task as the teachers of the people could in no way be connected with the dead, and for this reason they were commanded not to defile themselves by coming into contact with the deceased because this was entirely outside their main mission in life.

In the Gemara Nedarim, we find a discussion as to whether the Kohanim, when bringing a sacrifice for an individual, are considered as the representatives of the one who brings the sacrifice - or whether they themselves receive the sacrifice on behalf of the Almighty, and thus become His emissaries.

The Tosafot point out that the representative of an individual must be in the same position as the individual, namely, he can only do those things and fulfill those tasks which individual may perform. But as not every individual, unless he is a priest, can perform the sacrificial rites in the Temple, the Tosafot derive that the priest could hardly be considered as the representative of the individual, but as the representative of the Almighty.

In this instance, too, the priests are merely the messengers of the Almighty, performing a duty which has been commanded to them, and they are in no way considered as receiving the sacrifice in the place of God. They should not act in any way which is not in keeping with the precise instructions given to them in connection with the performance of their duty. In no way do we see them here as representing God's authority on earth, but as the teachers of the people, as the mediators between the Almighty and His nation, in the same way as they appear when bestowing the priestly blessing in Israel.

And as the blessing ends with the exalted idea of peace, there must be a special place where love, brotherhood and harmony can find full expression. Could there be any better place than the Sanctuary - the place consecrated to the service and to the glory of the Almighty? And as the Parasha, immediately after the priestly blessing, speaks about the consecration of the Sanctuary, our rabbis say in that connection, that it was mainly in the Sanctuary where the influence of the priests was to be most felt and where it could be administered in the most beneficial manner. This does not mean that the priest's influence did not extend outside the walls of the Sanctuary, that his influence did not penetrate even within the circle of the family. But the Sanctuary - the House of God - was the place where he could make his voice heard and give his instruction to the whole community; where he could see their reactions and judge the effect his words had on the people. In this way the priest and the Sanctuary became almost one institution, together symbolizing the ideals and strivings of the people of Israel, as, indeed, can be said today, that the minister and the synagogue stand as a symbol of the same ideals.

The community must learn, and learn soon, if it is not to become merely an organization without a heart and soul, that the minister, its spiritual leader, must be given an opportunity of guiding its destinies and must be allowed to express freely the message which the Lord Himself dictates to him, as He did in the days of old to the priests in the Sanctuary.

Today's Parasha took us to the days when Israel had its Sanctuary, when, surrounded by the glory of the Almighty, the priest with outstretched hands, said the blessing over Israel.

May the Almighty in His infinite mercy, as in the days of old, grant His blessing to this holy congregation, to those who worship within the walls of this synagogue of God, and to all the children of Israel.

ON REVITALIZING SEPHARDI LIFE

Sermon delivered Friday evening, June 22, 1951 to the Sephardi community of Salisbury, Rhodesia.

In the Talmud Shabbat, we read that God said: "I have a precious gift in My treasury, and its name is Sabbath." This saying, combined with the 4th commandment which deals with the Sabbath rest and the injunction to hallow it, gives us the idea of Judaism as regards this fundamental ordinance in Jewish life. This idea is concerned not merely with the sanctification of the Sabbath, but with the beauty which it imparts to the life of the Jewish people and the enjoyment which in turn the House of Israel derives from it. We find a discussion in the Gemara Pesahim, as well as in Betza, whether the Sabbath day should be devoted only to prayer to God and to the study of Torah, or to eating and drinking which are also part of the enjoyment of this earthly life. Our sages of blessed memory came to the conclusion that both aspects are necessary.

In this argument we find not only the concept which the Jewish people hold as regards the day of rest, but also a principle which underlines Jewish life and Jewish teaching in general. Our Torah has warned us that we have no right to withdraw from life, to deny ourselves the legitimate pleasures which life is capable of affording us. But, at the same time, we have no right to allow this enjoyment to develop into license, and thus forgetting entirely the spiritual side of our being. The combination of both spiritual exercise and meditation on the one side and of gladness and cheer, which are the expression of the physical life, on the other, have always been the Jewish ideal. This ideal has found its most worthy expression in the day of Shabbat. Consequently, its sociological importance has been great not only for the Jew, but for the world in general. Shabbat proclaims that every person must be given the opportunity of resting body and soul once in the week, thus enabling one to reach through his soul to God and at the same time to dwell upon his relations with his fellow-man.

It is, therefore, not surprising that the Sabbath day has been one of the most unifying factors in the life of Israel throughout the ages. It brought comfort and hope to the persecuted Jews and gave them strength to withstand the trials of life, and an opportunity to derive through prayer a new confidence for the future.

There is a saying that, as much as the Jewish people have done for the Sabbath, the Sabbath has done more for the preservation of the Jewish people. It is not merely the symbol of the special covenant between God and His chosen people, but is also the symbol of the unity of Israel.

This unity of our people has been a decisive influence not only in the fortunes of the House of Israel, but in the destinies of the world. This unity could exercise such an influence because it rested on solid foundations and was made up of smaller loyalties and unities. It sprang from the unity of the Jewish family, and the unity of Jewish communal life. The Jew's loyalty to these unities was the fountain-head from which sprang the larger loyalty of the Jew to Kellal Yisrael, to the House of Israel.

It is in this concept of Jewish unity that we find the explanation why the unity of Sephardi Jews throughout the ages has never been regarded as an act of separatism, but, on the contrary, as a valuable contribution towards the advance of the Jewish spiritual heritage. It has been recognised that by virtue of their history and of the special characteristics which the rabbis and savants attached to the development of Jewish thought, the Sephardi Jews - those who came from the Iberian Peninsula - have a special and specific contribution to make to the general treasure of Judaism.

It has been one of the great tragedies of the Jewish people that during the past centuries, owing to lack of communal organisation, and for many other causes, the Sephardi Jews have not played as important a part in Jewish life as their history would have entitled them to do.

Today, it is not only the Jews of Sephardi origin, but the Jewish communities throughout the world, that consider the organisation of the Sephardi communities in the world as one of the very pressing necessities for the progress of the whole of the Jewish people. We Sephardim always liked to think that in our communities we were self- sufficient, and, while closely attached to the people of Israel, never thought that it was of great importance for us to foster also that smaller unity, the unity of the Sephardi world. There have been many attempts in the past few decades to organise the Sephardim, but these attempts have always been foiled by the lethargy of the individual Sephardi communities and by their refusal to see the importance that such an organisation would have for the Jewish world.

A fresh attempt is being made today to bring together those Jewish communities which have a common tradition and a common way of life, so that we Sephardim may become a real asset to Jewry in the diaspora, and to our brethren in Israel alike. The purpose of such an organisation would be in the first place to raise the standards of Jewish and general education among the Sephardim of the world, an education which would be carried out in the spirit of Sephardi tradition.

For us, education has never meant the mere imparting of knowledge and information, but has meant also the development of the character of the younger generation, so that they may be a credit to us and an example to the world. We have only ourselves to blame if today many of our communities are left without spiritual leaders, so that we have to turn for help to those who do not understand the spirit of Sephardi Judaism.

It is not surprising, therefore, that many of our communities have been led away from the Sephardi camp. That might not seem to many of us to be a great pity, as long as they remained within the camp of Israel. But I strongly believe that in the long run, it will not prove to be an advantage to the strength of Jewish life in general. The effects of history on every one of us are of such a nature that we react best to the exhortations and leadership of those who have been bought up in the same tradition as ourselves, or, at least, who love and understand our traditions.

This lack of spiritual leadership is unfortunately evident today even in the highest places. A Sephardi institution for the provision of teachers, ministers and rabbinic authorities is one of the most pressing needs of the present age. It would be of great value for the development of the rabbinical interpretation of the Torah that worthy Sephardi rabbis should be produced every year, rabbis imbued with the love of Judaism and the understanding of Sephardi tradition.

In the study of the Talmud and other rabbinic literature, the general tendency of Sephardi rabbis has always been to avoid hair-splitting, to study the Law as a whole and try to obtain from it a clear ruling to give guidance in the spirit of the age in which we live. That does not mean breaking the Jewish Law, but re-interpreting it, as it is capable of re-interpretation according to the circumstances and conditions of each successive generation.

We Sephardim, if properly organised, could give a lead to the Jewish world generally. When we come to our smaller unity, that unity of the Sephardi world, I believe that we Sephardim of the British Commonwealth could play a leading part in the foundation of a Sephardi world organisation. One of the reasons is that we are in an advantageous position by virtue of our having been the first community to be established after the re-settlement in the mother country and that, in spite of our numerical inferiority, we hold a position far greater than is commensurate with our numbers.

We can become the best organised Sephardi community in the world. I am sure that this community, in one of the most important parts of the British Commonwealth, a community which has been inspired in the past by Jewish ideals and steeped in Sephardi tradition, will be willing to play together with the rest of the Sephardi communities of the Commonwealth, that part which it is expected to play. In doing so, it will be able to claim that its efforts are not alone directed towards the strengthening of the smaller unity of the Sephardi world, but also towards the strengthening of the House of Israel in the land of Israel and in the diaspora.

RELIGION AND CULTURE

*Address presented to the Jewish cultural circle
of Salisbury, Rhodesia, June 25, 1951.*

To the Jew, culture in general has not meant something which is outside his faith, an addition to his religious beliefs. On the contrary, it has been part and parcel of Jewish teaching and an indispensable means of translating this teaching into reality. Even when the Prophet Isaiah spoke of the future age, in which the highest ideals of humanity would find full expression, he said that on that age would rest "the spirit of the Lord" as well as the spirit of wisdom and understanding, the spirit of knowledge, as well as the fear of the Lord. The ideas of Judaism have never been limited to man's emotions; they survived because they could be expounded by his rational mind.

We have never made the claim that "blessed are those who are ignorant". On the contrary, according to Maimonides, it was only the philosophers - those who were able to combine knowledge with the capacity for thought and the will to lead an ethical life - who would find survival in the world to come. The fear of God could not be exalted to a higher plane unless it was accompanied by a spirit of knowledge, of desire to explore the hidden mysteries of life and to bring into the light the knowledge of nature, even the knowledge of the divine.

The Sephardim have a long and proud history, in which the attainment of worldly culture was considered as of almost equal importance as prominence in the sphere of Jewish religion and letters. In Spain, the Jews developed not only Jewish learning, but they also devoted themselves to science and art.

Spanish Jewry produced men who were able to combine their Judaism with science; men who were able to reconcile Jewish tradition and Jewish law with the new and changing conditions in the world. It was this ability to combine the new with the old and to re-interpret the old in the light of new developments that marked the Sephardi codifiers and commentators on the Bible and the Talmud. It was this attitude that produced the great Sephardi philosophers, Maimonides, Bahia, Halevy, Ibn Gabirol. It was also this attitude that gave rise to the great poets of the Spanish period.

The Sephardi codifiers were influenced by a rational outlook. They were not afraid that by giving reasons and finding out the causes for the laws, they would adversely affect the belief and faith of their people. We need only mention "The Guide of the Perplexed" by Maimonides, which created such a storm in the Jewish world.

The attitude of the Jew towards general culture was also expressed in the attitude which especially the Jews of the Iberian Peninsula adopted towards education. Education to them did not mean only a matter of bringing up their children in the spirit of Judaism and in all its discipline, but it meant also giving them a wider scope, affording them a wider horizon so that they would be ready to take part in all the intellectual activities of the country in which they lived, so that in the sciences and other subjects they might be able to emulate their contemporaries of other faiths.

Although Talmudic teachers realised the usefulness of other subjects, especially of philosophy, yet they somewhat feared them as having perhaps an insidious influence on the development of the Jew. They were afraid that secular knowledge might take away the Jew from his study of the Torah. This fear is evident, not only in earlier rabbinic writings, but also in later rabbinic literature, and, in many cases, persists even up to the present day. We find still that there are people who feel that the study of the Torah - or, rather, the proper study of the Torah - is incompatible with the study of secular subjects on university level.

The spirit of knowledge and understanding, combined with the spirit of God, was also found especially among the heads of the Jewish community in Spain and the rectors of the Jewish academies there.

Professor Neuman, writing about the the personality of the rector of the yeshiva in his history of the Jews in Spain, says:

"He was not only a source of emulation to the students; he was the living embodiment of their highest ideal. It was the fondest hope of a noble disciple to approximate his master in learning and religion. For the rector was no mere schoolman; he was the sage and the scholar. Outside the walls of the academy, in the community at large, he was the custodian of Judaism and a regenerating moral and spiritual force among his people. Despite the antagonisms and defeats which a fearless sage necessarily incurred often in the fight against the abuses of evil men, he was a dominating moral figure in the community and he wielded considerable legal powers. Little wonder then that the scholars of the academy saw in their master the idealisation of learning and the fountain of inspiration for their self- sacrificing studies."

Today, it is the Jewish effort in the land of our ancestors which personifies that great concept of Judaism in which religious sentiment and rational reasoning combine. It was a great religious faith that brought the people to the deserted land of Israel, and inspired them to build a new home for the homeless and the persecuted. It was that faith, the fountainhead of which was the Divine inspiration itself, that gave them strength to persist in their effort and at last to bring its first stage to a successful conclusion. But these pioneers were also men educated in the university centres of Europe, who had obtained knowledge and were capable of thought on the most up-to-date lines, and who were able to combine their zeal and their faith with the methods which were the result of new discoveries and new scientific experiments.

The many problems which face the house of Israel today, in the diaspora and in the land of Israel, will be solved only if this spirit - this bright spirit which refuses to be fettered by fanaticism and narrow-mindedness - permeates our lives as a whole. Our way of thinking, in the religious and in the cultural spheres, must undoubtedly be affected by the establishment of the State of Israel. The historian of the future will be able to judge how far; but we must not refuse to recognise this fact, because by not recognising it we shall cause untold harm to the progress of and the dissemination of the principles of Jewish teaching in general.

We pray that "from Zion may come out the Law and the word of the Lord from Jerusalem." When it does come, it must come in a manner that will be understood by us all, in such a way that we shall be able to reconcile it with present conditions and the developments which have taken place since the destruction of the second Jewish State.

PLANNING FOR THE FUTURE

*Sermon delivered to the Salisbury Hebrew Congregation
Saturday, June 30, 1951.*

In today's Parasha we read the story of the men who were sent by Moses to spy out the land of Canaan. A representative of each tribe was sent out to investigate whether the land which had been promised by the Almighty to His children was good and suitable for the settlement of the people of Israel. They were also entrusted with the task of finding out everything possible about the people who inhabited the land and whether their cities were open or fortified. These men, on their return, gave a most favourable account of the land and its produce, but they thought the people were too strong and mighty to be overcome by the untrained army of the Israelites.

The question which arises is what prompted the messengers to give an account of the conditions in the land which discouraged and demoralised the people of Israel. Their report could not have been true because the truth was seen in a different light by Caleb and Joshua. At the same time they would not have been deliberately perverting the truth.

Could we say perhaps that is was a mistake in judgement that caused them to give such an adverse picture of the land and its inhabitants? They said: "The people we saw in it are men of great stature, and there we saw the Nephilim, the sons of Anak, and we were in our sight as grasshoppers." They took care to qualify their statement by saying that it was entirely subjective. The description was not perhaps in accordance with the exact truth, but it was as they saw it with their inner eye. Philosophers tell us that the things we perceive in our everyday life, their form and shape, are not in fact as we think them to be, but that it is we ourselves, through our own intellectual outlook and perception, who give them different forms and shapes. In the same way did the messengers - the spies - admit that they saw the land and its inhabitants only through their own eyes, which meant that they regarded them in the light of the background which their own qualities and character had formed for them.

This brings us to the conclusion that it was not perhaps an intentional act of evil that made the spies by their report create such confusion and tragedy for their people, but that it was more a question of mistaken attitude.

This attitude can easily be understood if we consider that comparatively only a short time had elapsed since the redemption from Egypt. The people had not had the time - nor were they willing - to acquire an outlook different from that which was shaped by their past in Egypt. In Egypt, as slaves, they had no future; they had lived only in the present, and therefore there was no need to think or strive for the future. They were not even called upon to bring about their redemption by their own efforts, but the Almighty in His mercy Himself wrought the great miracles in Egypt and at the Red Sea which made them a free nation. They thought that in the same way all other obstacles would be removed from their path. When they had to face up to reality, they panicked and, by showing a lack of faith in God, they lost confidence in themselves.

They saw the promised land as a land that "eats up" those who live in it. According to our rabbinic interpretation, they thought the climate was too severe for the children of Israel and could only be withstood by the giants who inhabited the land. They were not ready to form a new outlook, which the different situation and circumstances required. By acting in this way, they not only affected their own future, but also the destinies of the coming generations.

Our rabbis tell us that it was this event which led to the wandering of the children of Israel in the desert for 40 years, and also caused the Almighty to decide not to bring about the conquest of the promised land through divine intervention and miracles, as He had intended. Instead, it had to be conquered by the sheer force of arms of the children of Israel. Had the land come into the possession of the children of Israel through

God's miraculous works, our tradition maintains, then the messianic era would have dawned with the first settlement of our people in the land of Israel in the days of Joshua. But as the land had to be conquered by force of arms it was not worthy of introduction to a new era, an era of universal brotherhood and understanding. The final salvation of the world has still to be achieved.

Thus it was that Dor Hamidbar - the generation of the desert - by considering the situation only from the subjective point of view, caused disaster not only to itself, but changed the course of Israel's history for many generations to come. Hence God's saying about Caleb that he had another spirit with him. He showed faith in God, faith in his people and in himself, when he said: "We should go up at once and possess the land for we are well able to overcome it." He symbolised not the generation brought up in slavery, but the coming generation, the generation inspired with the idea of liberation and freedom. And it was this different spirit with which he was imbued and this different outlook on the world and its conditions that formed his judgement of the land and its inhabitants, that singled him out as the man who should be held up as an example to the rest of the people by God Himself.

Our sages point out that Joshua, although he sided with Caleb, was not so prominently singled out because he was still the pupil of Moses and was directly influenced by his advice. But Caleb stood on his own, and his merit lay in the fact that he was able to think of the future as well as of the present without any outside influence.

This example, which Caleb has presented to us, is the one which must be followed by the leaders of the Jewish people. They must examine the circumstances and conditions of their times not only through an outlook formed by their past experience and consideration of the present, but also having regard to future developments and progress.

The great mistake of Jewry in the British Commonwealth in general, and Anglo-Jewry in particular, has been that we have given very little consideration to our future, especially from the spiritual point of view. We have taken it for granted that our spiritual leaders and those who should guide us in the path of Jewish life should come from the centres of Jewish learning in Europe. We have not taken care to establish new centres and academies for ourselves, which would reflect the needs of Jewry in general and of the Jewry residing in the Commonwealth in particular, academies which would produce spiritual leaders who would understand the needs peculiar to the conditions in which we live and who would strengthen the fundamentals of Judaism throughout this great association of British peoples. It is hardly a credit to us that there is only one college in London, which has to provide ministers, teachers, and even readers, for the communities which need guidance in the Law of God.

We are today paying the price, and a very high price, for this neglect, for having failed to think in terms of the future for British Jewry. But it is not too late. The conditions in which we live make it, thank God, still possible for us to strengthen the basis of Jewish life throughout our communities, to think of our own children as potential leaders, spiritual leaders of our communities, by building academies in England and outside in which the word of the living God will be interpreted and taught.

There is, in short, a great need for the spiritual reorientation of British Jewry throughout the Commonwealth. We cannot go on thinking in terms of the past. Israel will provide the inspiration, but the work must be done by ourselves. We must not think of the Jews in the British commonwealth or, for that matter, of diaspora Jewry in general as incapable of any spiritual effort. On the contrary, given the will and the imagination, British Jewry can prove to be of the greatest support to Israel not merely in the material sense, but in the rejuvenation of Jewish life, in making the principles of the Torah the basis of our everyday life. This task imposes itself on our people living in our ancient land and on all of us living in other parts of the world.

The Torah has sustained us throughout the ages and will sustain us in the future, as long as we are ready to see in it a vital force which can be applied to changing life in changing conditions. Only through the Torah will the State of Israel arise to become an example to all the States of the world, and only by living in the spirit of the Torah will the people of Israel become the leaders of humanity, leading them to a new era when, in the words of the prophet, "many people will say, 'Come ye and let us go up to the mountain of the Lord, to the house of the God of Jacob.' "

SEPHARDIM AND ZIONISM

*Address to the Zionist Society of Salisbury, Rhodesia
delivered on Thursday, June 28, 1951.*

It has often been asked concerning the Sephardim why they have not taken an active part in the Zionist movement, why they have been even antagonistic to it, and, on the other hand, why today in the new State of Israel they have not been able to organise themselves in order to assert their rights and privileges.

Whereas the second question might have some justification, the first one arises out of sheer lack of knowledge of the history of the Sephardi Jews, of the part they played in Zionism, and of the ideas which they contributed towards the movement of the Jewish renascence. The only excuse for it may be that the outspoken antagonistic attitude to Zionism of some Sephardim has been applied to Sephardim as a whole.

If we study Jewish history in Spain, we shall find that although it marks one of the most glorious epochs of Jewish history in the diaspora, it is entirely inspired by the idea of the return to Zion, the idea which was eloquently expressed by all the men of spirit and all the men of letters produced by the Sephardim in that golden age.

Even legend has tried to create a link between the land of Israel and Spain, for tradition has it that the first settlement of the Jews in Spain was formed even before the time of King Solomon, and that King Solomon himself sent one of his rabbis there to visit that settlement. Further, the outstanding family of the Jewish communities in the Iberian Peninsula was that of Abarbanel, who claimed direct lineage from the royal house of David. From the book of Obadiah, it was also derived that the Jews of

Spain were exiles from Jerusalem.

All these traditions were dearly cherished by the Jews of Spain, whose greatest ideal was to return to the land of their ancestors, an ideal which found full expression in the poetry, as well as in the deeds, of Yehuda Halevy, the great poet and philosopher, who lived in Spain in the 11th century. He was prepared to leave the comforts of his native land and forfeit the honour in which he was held by Jew and non- Jew alike in order to make a triumphant return to the land of Jewish past glories. He expressed the credo of the age when, in his immortal poem to Zion, he said: "To where thy God Himself made choice to dwell last abode the children yet shall find."

In his great philosophic work, "Kuzari," Halevy expounded the idea that the land of Israel, unlike any other place in the world, was everlastingly permeated with a spirit of holiness. It was that special spirit of the land which gave birth to prophets and psalmists who were not to be found in any other nation. Halevy also maintained that the house of Israel was the heart of mankind; the land of Israel was the heart of all the world, giving it vitality and strength.

This tradition was continued by other rabbis and philosophers and found realisation in the Sephardi mystics, who established their stronghold in Safed and Tiberias. After Jerusalem was devastated in 1260 by the Mongols, it was the famous Sephardi mystic and philosopher, Nahmanides of Gerona, who arrived in 1267, and found in the city only two Jews. In response to his fervent appeal, a new community was formed in less than a month, with its own synagogue.

Nahmanides may be said to have been the pioneer of the Jewish resettlement in Palestine in the middle Ages, for he attracted many students to the college which he founded in the Holy City. In addition to these students of the Torah, doctors, copyists of Hebrew books, and artisans in different trades came to settle in the ancient land.

When the Jews were driven out of Spain and Portugal, many of them found their way to the land of Israel, and among them were quite a number of Marranos. These exiles were distinguished for their education, scholarship and business enterprise. It was owing to their intellectual superiority that these Sephardim were able to merge the older elements into a single communal organisation, upon which they impressed their own specific character. In fact, it was the Sephardim who comprised the majority of the Jewish population in the Holy Land until almost modern times, when the movement of the return to Israel began to spread among the Ashkenazi communities of Eastern and Central Europe.

Thus, it could be rightly claimed that the Sephardim created the link between those who remained in Israel after the destruction of the Second Temple and the new settlement. It was due to them that the Jews could make the claim that the Land of Israel was never entirely devoid of the children of Israel.

Now when we come to modern Zionism, as represented by Theodore Herzl, we find that Rabbi Yehuda Alkalay, who died in 1878, had suggested many ways and means for the resettlement of the Jews in the land of Israel. These foreshadowed the methods later adopted by the Zionist movement in its system of colonisation. Many historians have called him the precursor of the modern Zionist movement.

It is also worthy of report that when Herzl came to London he found much more support among the Sephardim than among the members of the Ashkenazi community. It was the Sephardi Haham, Dr. Gaster, who gave him unstinted support, whereas Dr. Adler, the Chief Rabbi of the Ashkenazim, maintained an uncompromising opposition to him. The first President of the Zionist Federation after the first World War was Francis Montefiore, who later relinquished this position and became opposed to what he called the new policies of the Zionist movement.

One of the reasons why the Sephardim in England in the main did not give their support to the Zionist Federation lies in the fact that there was never a real English Zionism. All the leaders of that movement were recent comers or sons of immigrants to this country.

Nevertheless, the attitude of the Sephardim in England was more than counter-balanced by the activities of the Sephardi communities in the Balkans, who were staunch supporters of the movement of the Jewish renascence. In fact, the Zionist organisations of the Sephardi communities of the Balkans were considered as the most idealistic and the most advanced in Zionist thought of any of the Zionist organisations of Europe.

It has been claimed by many historians that modern Hebrew literature shaped itself on the example provided by Sephardic authors. They say that it would have been impossible for Ahad Haam, the great Zionist philosopher, to have reached such intellectual achievement if he had not had the works of Maimonides to guide him and help him to find for his thoughts an appropriate form of expression. Bialik, too, the great poet of the Jewish renascence, is inconceivable without Ibn Gabirol, Halevy and Ibn Ezra.

The reason the Sephardim did not play any great part in the political aspect of the Zionist movement lies in the fact that for many centuries they lived in countries where they were allowed, comparatively speaking, freedom of action and movement. Hence, they did not develop that political acumen, which was so evident in their ancestors in Spain.

To those Sephardim who did take a lively interest and an active part in the Zionist movement, this ideal was not merely the means of solving the Jewish problem of statelessness in the Galut, but an ideal handed down from generation to generation, starting from the day when the Jewish people lost their political independence. They did not so much feel the necessity for solving their economic and personal problems, as was the case with Eastern Jewry. Rather, they considered the Zionist movement an indispensable part of Jewish life. Consequently, the political struggle within the Zionist movement was of little interest to them, and as a result there was a lack of political leadership on their part in the movement.

This lack of interest in the political aspect of the Zionist movement has proved to be of some disadvantage to Sephardim in general, especially to those now coming to Israel. Nevertheless, they are finding their feet in the new homeland and are becoming not only politically active, but, are stirring those sections of the Sephardi world who were lukewarm - yes, even antagonistic - to the Zionist idea, stirring them to action and making them aware of their duty towards Israel.

Slowly, the world in general and Sephardim in particular are realising that Israel today, although it has emerged as a direct outcome of the efforts and endeavors of the Zionist movement, is part of Kellal Yisrael, and therefore does not require any partisanship. On the contrary, as Jews have always been united in recognising that the problems of a Jewish community or group in whichever part of the world are also the problems of world Jewry, so today we must realise that Israel is the concern of the Jews of the world. This does not mean interference in any way with the internal political life of the people of Israel. Indeed, the new State has brought the Zionist movement to the crossroads, for this movement has now realised its ideal, namely, the establishment of the State of Israel. This State, therefore, becomes part of the general community and must claim the attention of all Jews, whatever their relationship with the Zionist movement in the past.

Likewise, as we have always claimed to be interested not only in the welfare of any Jewish community in the world, but also in the way that community was fulfilling its duty towards Judaism, so today Israel comes within the same orbit of our interest. It is our hope to see Israel become an example to all the states of the world, just as the Torah expects the people of Israel to be an example to all the peoples of the world.

We must, therefore, regard this as a stage nearer the realisation of that great ideal of the brotherhood of all men. We have every reason to believe that the resurrected State of Israel will bring this great day nearer. The establishment of the new State is, therefore, not only a tribute to the courage of those pioneers who gave all they had for an ideal, not only a tribute to the Jewish people who dreamt their dreams in a world of darkness, but, we pray God, will be also a great asset to this modern world still trying to find its soul.

THE NEED FOR INSPIRED LEADERSHIP

Sermon originally delivered in Judeo-Spanish, to the Sephardic congregation of Elizabethville, Belgian Congo, June, 1951.

In this week's Parasha we read of the famous rebellion of Korah. Korah and his followers were jealous of the power which Moses and his brother Aaron possessed. They considered it unjust that these two should share between themselves the priestly as well as the lay authority, and the rebellion was aimed at breaking this family monopoly of rule over the people of Israel.

Our rabbis represent Korah as saying to Moses: "We all were present at Mount Sinai when the Law was given. We heard the voice of the Almighty and we are all as privileged as you and your brother, Aaron, to share in the rule over God's own chosen people." One might gather from this statement that Korah was merely interested in a democratic principle, that he merely wanted to prevent all the power from being concentrated in the hands of the few.

Let us listen, however, to the words of Moses when he put his case before the Lord. "I have not taken one ass from them neither have I hurt one of them" said he. From these words, the implication is clear that Korah was interested in taking part in the rule of the people only because of the material gain that he could obtain from it.

The thing that puzzles one most in this dramatic and tragic event is the attitude of Moses. We know that in the past, whenever there had been a rebellion, Moses had always prayed for the people and declared himself ready to share their destiny to the full. When there was disquiet among the people because Moses did not return with the two tablets of the Law at the time he was expected to come back, and they made the golden calf and worshipped it, they were saved through the prayers of Moses, although by their transgression they showed that they were not worthy of any consideration from Heaven. The same applied when they rebelled because of the lack of water and of meat, and also when the spies returned bringing a bad report about the people who inhabited the land of Canaan.

Moses intervened on behalf of the people in all these instances; and in his expressions to the Lord he clearly showed that he was ready to be annihilated together with his people, whom he had brought out of Egypt.

In the case of Korah, it is Moses himself who asks God not to accept the offerings of Korah and his followers; and he implies that they should be punished. Is it possible that Moses was more jealous for his own honour and power than he was for the worship of and obedience to the Almighty by the whole people of Israel?

This conclusion, however, seems to be contradicted by the fact that Moses reproached Joshua when he asked him to punish those people who were prophesying in the camp, by saying: "Would that all the people of Israel were prophets." And if Moses had in any way shown jealousy for his own position, then the Torah could not have said about him: "and the man, Moses, was a very humble man."

It seems that Moses saw in the rebellion of Korah, which outwardly appeared to be directed against Aaron and himself, a greater danger than in the disobedience of the people and their past rebellions against the omnipotence of the Almighty. And our rabbis tell us that the danger which Moses foresaw in this rebellion was disunity and anarchy among the people of Israel. Had Korah chosen reasonable and peaceful ways of criticising Moses, there is no doubt that Moses would have been only too ready to listen, providing that the motives for this criticism were unselfish and inspired by a sincere desire for the welfare of the people.

But Moses immediately detected that Korah's actions were not motivated by concern for the people or by an ideal. Our rabbis point out that Korah was able to gather so many followers around him because he promised them that he would help to change some of the laws and ordinances concerning which they had been commanded, and that he would be able to make their lives easier for them. The Midrash says that he ridiculed some of the laws and by this means won much popularity among the people.

These attempts to interfere with the Torah, though serious, would not have prompted Moses to take such a grave view of the whole position if the existence - the very life of the nation - had not been at stake. Criticism and action are justified only as long as they preserve the fundamental values of a nation, of humanity at large, and so long as they do not create anarchy and destroy the unity which is essential for the advance of a nation. In short, changes by constitutional means and criticism within the limits of accepted decency are justifiable and necessary. But when these are undertaken without regard for the safety of the nation and its progress, but for personal aggrandisement and ambition, then it is the duty of the leadership to stand firm, as Moses did. The accusation brought against him of having usurped power was a serious one, but he realised that if he were to show himself weak at this moment, the whole nation would suffer irreparable damage.

There are, indeed, times when leaders of communities, or of nations, must know when to stand firm, in spite of popular feeling and indignation, even if it means forfeiting popularity. There are occasions when leaders are put to this test, and only if they are able to survive it, can they justify their responsible position. So long as they are clear in their conscience that their aims are not for private ambition and are not inspired by selfish reasons, but only by the desire to achieve the best for the community or the nation as a whole, then must they stand firm against attempts to overthrow their leadership, even if these attempts have popular support. Only such leadership can be of any value in times of distress, as well as in times of peace. Only such leadership can ensure that its reputation will survive for the future, as did the name of Moses throughout the ages.

Such inspired leadership is essential today in the Jewish communities throughout the world. Very often, unfortunately, we find people with ability and idealism unwilling or unable to carry out their self-imposed task, because they are afraid of being termed dictators. This common ill in the communities is often the cause of disunity among members of a congregation, or among the congregations of a town, or of a country. It is not a denial of the democratic principle that leaders should rule only by the will of the majority, but, on the contrary, it strengthens the principle that a leader must guide the people and prevent them from falling into chaos and self-destruction.

Today, more than ever, unity is essential for our people; Unity between the State of Israel and the diaspora, thus giving a living example of the inspiring symbol of Kellal Yisrael, of the unity of the house of Israel throughout the world; unity in the State of Israel, and unity in the communities of the diaspora. This can only be achieved by close cooperation and understanding between the leadership and the people who are led. It can only be achieved if leaders and congregations alike are guided by the knowledge that, after all, we are all ruled by one benevolent Ruler, a knowledge which must stir in us the sentiments of modesty and humility which are essential if Israel is to achieve the great task, which he willingly accepted from God Himself; if Israel is to follow in the footsteps of Moses, for the man, Moses, was a humble man.

THE IDEAL OF CHARITY

Sermon delivered at the Lauderdale Road Synagogue, London, on August 16, 1952.

"Thou shalt not harden thy heart, nor shut thy hand from thy needy brother.....and shalt surely lend him sufficient for his needs in that which he wanteth."

Our rabbis, in discussing this passage, say, if your poor brother needs a horse to ride upon, give it to him; if he needs a servant, then you must provide him with one.

This explanation given by our sages may seem rather strange, especially as it deals with the ideal of charity in Judaism. Does it really mean that if a man has been rich and has fallen on evil days, it is our duty to restore to him his former splendour? The idea seems to be that man should not be allowed to suffer unnecessarily because of the change in his circumstances.

The idea of poverty, like most other conceptions in life, is only a relative one. The same standards do not apply in all countries to a person whom we call poor. In some places this epithet is applied only to those who live on the brink of starvation, whereas in others to those who cannot afford all the luxuries that a rich and prosperous land offers to its inhabitants.

Our rabbis of blessed memory were eager to give this passage of the Bible a very wide explanation. They wanted to teach us that it is our duty to give charity not only to those whose poverty is apparent to us because of their physical and spiritual suffering but also to those who might not appear to us at the first glance to be poor. How often does it happen that people we know suffer privation in silence, without our realising the difficulties with which they have to struggle. The reason is that we do not approach our fellow-men until their suffering has gone a little too far for our help to be of any real value.

We are commanded, therefore, to help our brother "in that which he wanteth." It is our duty to find out the way in which our fellow-men live, to find out their problems and difficulties, without expecting them to come to us for assistance, or waiting for their position to deteriorate so much that their poverty becomes apparent to us and a source of embarrassment to them.

It is in connection with today's Parasha that our rabbis also speak of loving-kindness towards our fellow-men, and that loving-kindness can only express itself in our concern, in our real and unselfish concern, for our fellow-creatures. This is the great idea of personal charity, charity which is practiced not only by material help, but by advice, kindness, and above all, friendship.

In our present highly organised society, where also charity is dispensed by organisations and officials, this ideal of personal charity must have a special appeal for us. We must try and help our fellow-men in those spheres in which our help is most needed by them. This might be, to return to the saying of our rabbis, to give a "horse or a servant"; in short, the need of some luxury might be essential for the sustenance of a man's morale, and in such cases the provision of such a luxury is real charity. Such charity can only be exercised if each one of us understands his fellow-men, if we are ready to concern ourselves with the lives of those we call our friends and neighbours, if we allow our eyes to watch their actions without prying into their lives. This is the meaning, in the words of our rabbis, of the passage we quoted, that we should help our needy brother "in that which he wanteth."

My dear Barmitsvah, today when you become a full-fledged member of the Jewish community and responsible for your actions, you should remember that one of your first duties should be always to exercise that great ideal of Zedaka; not common charity, but justice. As our Parasha tells us today, it is not through kindness of heart and noble sentiments alone that we should exercise charity towards our fellow-men, but in the first place because we have been commanded by the Almighty to concern ourselves with the welfare of our fellow-men.

Charity can be practiced in different ways. It does not mean merely giving contributions to different societies which support the poor, the sick and the needy. This is not so difficult to do. But it means, above all, concern for your friend, for your neighbour; finding out whether he needs your help, without waiting for him to come and ask for your assistance; trying to discover whether your friend may need something which, although in your opinion not essential, may mean the question of existence to him. Do not consider yourself a judge as to the needs of your friends. It is not for you to say, after all this or that is not absolutely necessary for him. You do not exactly know his circumstances and the situation in which he finds himself, and you must try and help him "in that which he wanteth." Thus you may not only save him from embarrassment, but you may be able to change the very course of his life and bring happiness where, without your help, there might have been despair. You may bring confidence where otherwise there might be fear.

The ideal of charity can be exercised by kind thought, by kind actions, by advice, by friendship, by understanding. Such charity you can give to rich and poor alike because we ourselves are often in need of advice and guidance, and as we give to those who need our help so do we expect other people to exercise the same kind of understanding and charity towards us.

THE OPENING OF JUDITH LADY MONTEFIORE COLLEGE, RAMSGATE

A Sermon delivered on June 14, 1953.

In the Talmud, we are told that from the New Year to the Day of Atonement one's sustenance for the year is fixed, except his expenditure for the Sabbath and Festivals, and for the instruction of his children in the Law. If he spends less for any of these, then he receives less, and if he spends more, then the Almighty blesses his efforts and he receives more.

This great thought from the Talmud teaches us that while ordinary things can be limited, yet upon matters which are of vital importance no limits must be imposed. The affairs of our everyday life can develop and prosper only within the boundaries fixed by conditions and by our material means; but to matters essential in Jewish life, as is education, no such restrictions are applied.

There is no need to elaborate on the fact that the spreading of the knowledge of the Torah is a Divine injunction, for the realisation of which our Rabbis of blessed memory made every possible effort. We have only to refer to the Talmud where we learn that Rabbi Yehoshua ben Gamla organised the education of the children in the districts, towns and villages of Israel. There is no limit to the efforts and sacrifices that we must make on behalf of Jewish education.

The greatness and originality of the Torah lies in the fact that it has been given through Divine kindness to the people of Israel. The Torah is not only for the few and the experts, but is a heritage to be cultivated and understood by the people as a whole. It is this fundamental principle in Judaism that constitutes the basis of "Talmud Torah", of the teaching of the Torah as a positive command. The Jew does not fulfill his obligations to the Torah merely by obeying its precepts, by living in its spirit or by studying its injunctions; but he must also impart the knowledge of Torah to others and especially to his children. It is this aspect of the Jew's loyalty to the Torah that is expressive of the dynamic and ever active spirit of Judaism: the spirit of Judaism that has sustained us throughout the centuries of exile and has given us strength to face events with calm and equanimity, and confident hope. The teaching of the Torah became, therefore, together with the institutions of the Sabbath and the Festivals, the foundation stone upon which true Jewish life was built. No personal sacrifice was too great to ensure the perpetuation of the immortal message of the Torah which alone could justify the existence and the survival of the Jewish people.

Guided by this idea, Sir Moses Montefiore, the great philanthropist, realised that his work for the defense and the rights of the cause of Israel throughout the world would not be complete unless he made his own contribution towards the spreading of the knowledge of Judaism among his brethren. His original idea was to build a College in Jerusalem, in memory of the late Lady Judith Montefiore. This institution was to consist of ten members for whom dwellings were to be provided. This original plan was gradually changed and the College was eventually built in Ramsgate and named "Ohel Moshe and Yehoodit." The foundation stone of the College was laid by Sir Moses in 1865 on the night of Rosh Hodesh Tammuz, the anniversary of his Wedding Day, the same date on which the Synagogue had been consecrated 33 years earlier. It is, I feel, more than mere coincidence that on Rosh Hodesh Tammuz we are rededicating the College, 88 years after its foundation.

In the words of the biographer, the College was intended as a memorial of the founder's sincere devotion to the Law of God, as revealed on Sinai, and as a token of his love and pure devotion to his departed wife. It was the "distinct wish" of Sir Moses "that the admission as members of the College should be given to all Israelites from whatever part of the globe they may happen to come, provided that their learning and moral and religious character qualify them for the College." It is interesting that the first Collegiates, as well as the first Principal, appointed by Sir Moses, were Ashkenazim. Sir Moses was proud of being a member of the Sephardi Community and heir to its great traditions, but he realised that there was only one House of Israel for the welfare of which Sephardim and Ashkenazim alike have to make a joint effort. It must be a source of great satisfaction, to those on whom the responsibility for the administration of the Montefiore Endowment has fallen, to see the ideals of Sir Moses realised, in the new form that the College has now assumed, through the joint efforts of the Sephardi Community, the World Sephardi Federation and the Jewish Agency. Sir Moses devoted much of his time and energies to helping the big Ashkenazi Communities of Russia and Poland, and today, his endowment has brought together Ashkenazim and Sephardim in order to give succour to that great bastion of traditional Judaism in North Africa, by providing for them spiritual leaders, Rabbis and teachers to guide them in the path of our sacred heritage, the Torah. This Institution is intended primarily for students from North Africa, but it may also exert a spiritual influence on Anglo-Jewish life, especially through its learned Principal and competent staff, who are today undertaking an onerous but sacred task. We pray that their endeavors may contribute towards the realisation of the great vision of Sir Moses of a World Jewry united through the Torah and through the Land of Israel.

We are honoured here today by the presence of His Excellency the Israeli Ambassador. This is a tribute to the memory of Sir Moses and a recognition of the task that the Montefiore College has set out to accomplish. The fact that the Jewish Agency through Rabbi Zwi Gold, the Head of the Department for Torah Education, whom we welcome here today, has been so eager to contribute towards the revival of Ohel Moshe and Yehoodit also reminds us of the part played by Sir Moses in the renaissance of the people in the Land of Israel. The great and sacred traditions bound up with this place inspired the Congress of the World Sephardi Federation to emphasise the importance of the Montefiore College for the Sephardi world in general. The co-operation between the Spanish and Portuguese Community which administers the endowment, the Jewish Agency and the World Sephardi Federation in this field of educational endeavour is of historic importance and its effects will be felt far beyond the confines of the College.

It would be wrong if on this auspicious occasion we were to forget that an effort was make many years ago by my predecessor Dr. Moses Gaster of blessed memory to modernise the College. At last, thanks to the Almighty, his ideas have found realisation.

The work of Sir Moses Montefiore flourished during the reign of Queen Victoria and we pray that the heritage which he handed down to us, this College, may grow in strength and influence during the reign of our Queen Elizabeth II, whose Coronation the people of this island celebrated recently with elation and enthusiasm. In the Talmud Baba Kamma (30a) we read: R. Yehuda says: 'He who wishes to be pious must fulfill the Laws of Nezikin, the Laws applying to damages caused to others.' Rabba says: 'He must obey the Laws of Aboth, the rules expounded in the Ethics of the Fathers, the rules governing our ethical conduct. Others say, however, he must fulfill the injunctions dealt with in the tractate of Berakhot, the tractate dealing with prayers and benedictions to God. The lesson of this passage is that a Jew cannot claim to be pious unless he is complete, unless he has established harmonious relations with his Maker and obeys the civil and ethical Laws of the Torah intended to foster love and understanding. It is our prayer that such students may come out of the Montefiore College which we dedicate today to the task of Talmud Torah.

And finally, let us repeat the prayer of the late Sir Moses Montefiore himself: May God in His Mercy and Goodness grant that the inhabitants of the College may devote themselves to the study of his Holy Laws and may thcy find peace and happiness in their dwellings.

Amen.

MESSAGE TO A BARMITZVAH

*Sermon delivered at the Lauderdale Road Synagogue,
July 24, 1954.*

Our Rabbis and philosophers discuss extensively the reasons and causes which gave rise to different laws in the Torah. They say that the purpose of all the laws is to make our people a kingdom of priests and a holy nation. Each regulation of the Torah has a definite part to play in the fulfillment of this task. Often it may be difficult to define the significance of some laws, but this, say our sages, is due to the limitations of our own knowledge and understanding of the Torah. Among the laws whose reason is difficult to discover are those relating to promises and vows which we read in the Parasha of today. The regulations relating to the making and the annulment of vows appear at first sight strange and unnecessarily complicated. But our Rabbis point out that they have an important task to fulfill in preparing the Jewish people to become a nation endowed with special qualities. These Laws are intended to form and to strengthen the character of the Jew. "That which has gone out of thy lips thou shalt keep and perform" - says the Torah.

Today, when people and nations take their promises lightly, it is of special importance that we should take to heart the regulations of the Torah emphasising the sanctity of promises and vows. It has become today a common saying that a person or a nation will keep a promise only as long as it suits their own convenience. This attitude can be especially observed in international relations. Many of the conflicts which have arisen among the nations are due to the unwillingness of Governments to honour the agreements made by them or their predecessors. This has tended to shake the confidence of the nations in international agreements and to make them suspicious of international undertakings. Because individuals and nations have failed to keep their word, the whole standard of morality has been considerably lowered and the tension in the world increased. The failure to understand the value of a promise or an agreement has had a bad influence in the sphere of international relations and has in addition also affected the relations between man and his neighbour.

In many circles today, the complaint is often heard that the present educational system, while providing the younger generation with a greater amount of knowledge, has failed to build up its character. While in the past it was this aspect which was emphasised in the work of schools and universities, today academic examinations are intended only to test the amount of facts and data that young men and women have had the ability or have shown their willingness to learn and do not seem to be concerned with their personality or character. Education has, therefore, become merely an instrument intended to enable us to earn our living, to raise our economic standard and not to make of us better beings which should be the true aim of education. As a Jewish preacher said "It is the task of education to deal with inborn tendencies in man, to develop them if they are good, to neutralise them if they are evil." Our institutions of learning should be centres where the character of our youth are moulded, places which will produce people not afraid of speaking the truth and ready to perform that which they avow. As the Talmud says: "Let your 'yes' be righteous and your 'no' be righteous. He who exacted retribution from the generation of the flood will exact it of the man who does not stand by his word." Only if we and our sons and daughters learn to stand by our word shall we be able to remove that mistrust which has gripped the world and which has been called last week by the French Prime Minister "a paralysing mistrust, an irresistible tendency to believe nothing, to admit nothing, and very nearly to hope for nothing."

To restore a sense of understanding in the world is a task which should be a challenge and at the same time an inspiration especially to the youth of the world; but this task can be undertaken with a chance of success only if everyone of us learns that a promise is a sacred undertaking which bears the seal of God. By breaking it, we commit a transgression against God, against our own souls and against our fellowmen.

My dear Barmitzvah, today you have made a promise before God and this Congregation of the House of Israel that you would live according to the Laws of the Torah which alone give us the right to call ourselves members of the Jewish Community. Do not take this undertaking lightly - but remember that to a great extent your happiness depends on your readiness to make this promise the basis of your new life which you begin to live today. Perhaps you may still be too young to understand the real significance of this day for you and for that reason you must still rely on your parents to guide you in the spirit of the promise which you made today. Do not forget that your attendance at Synagogue at least every Sabbath is a duty which you must fulfill regularly. Do not think that your work in the Classes has come to an end, it is only beginning now when you will be able to understand more advanced lessons and to grasp the true significance of the teachings of Judaism.

SERMON FOR YOUTH

Sermon delivered at the Lauderdale Road Synagogue, London on November 5, 1955.

At a recent conference on the education of youth, a scholar said that our present system of education is making of our young people men and women who are incapable of feeling the thrill of discovery and success or the pain of disappointment and failure. He said that by over-emphasising the scientific aspect of our present day education our young people are growing up without the understanding of those human qualities which give real joy and meaning to life; people are becoming indifferent to those human relationships which can only be built on understanding and sympathy for our fellowmen. In short, the present-day system of education is making people inclined to take their fellowmen, as well as all events in life, for granted.

This statement must have caused many people to consider the problems which it emphasised and also to ask themselves whether it was correct in the light of their own experiences. One of the first rules in science is that man should not take anything for granted, but that every discovery should be submitted to careful examination and verified under different conditions and from many points of view; yet it seems today that we are becoming accustomed to take everybody and everything for granted. We take for granted kindness and cruelty, generosity as well as meanness. True, we lead today a life too busy to be fruitful, too hectic to be enjoyable. We undertake to do too many things, and in consequence are not able to do justice to them. We have many acquaintances but very few friends.

Today's Parasha begins with the story of Abraham speaking to the Almighty. He sees in the distance three people approaching his tent, and he interrupts his communion with his God in order to run to the three tired men and offer them his hospitality. Our Rabbis point out that Abraham considered the idea of hospitality and kindness to his fellowmen so important as to justify him interrupting his communion with his Maker. The three men, say our Rabbis, might have come in any case and asked Abraham for hospitality and food for they seemed to have travelled a long distance. According to the rules of the desert, it would have been only natural for them to ask for hospitality; but Abraham was eager to show these travellers that he was not merely ready to help them but that they were welcome into his home. Abraham realised that if he was to contribute towards the progress of humanity, he would have to introduce a certain warmth and understanding into human relationships; and he was soon to learn how important these relationships were in the sight of God. For our Rabbis point out that when the Almighty approached him in order to tell him of the intended destruction of the two cities, He emphasised to Abraham that these two cities were to be destroyed because their citizens showed no hospitality to strangers and no kindness to those who needed their help. The Almighty, emphasise our sages, did not destroy these two cities because they had sinned against Him but because they had transgressed against their fellowmen. They had shown no appreciation for human life and no understanding for human feelings; it is this lack of understanding for our fellowmen that is so much pervasive in today's society. It is not, therefore, surprising that there is such a lack of gratitude for generosity and kindness, and even little indignation when our fellowmen have been offended or hurt.

It is also this attitude to human life and human endeavour that has given less and less meaning to the commemoration of the sacrifices of those who fell during the first and second World Wars. Opinions are often expressed that even the two minutes of silence on the day set aside for this ceremony is losing its meaning. Are we really becoming indifferent to the sacrifices of those thousands upon thousands of people who fell on the battlefield during the last two wars? Are we really taking for granted all those sacrifices made by these people in order to preserve for us the fruits of true progress and civilisation? When we stand in silence on this day, we do not merely pay respect to the memory of those who gave their all in order that we should live. But we should think of all those people who were not able to realise their ideals and their plans in life, and who left their children, their mothers and their sweethearts without ever having been able to give expression to their love for them, all those people who wished to create a new and better world but had to give their lives in defense of their island. Indeed it will be a sad day for us all and the future generation when we begin to take these great sacrifices for granted, when we begin to look upon death with equanimity and upon life without pleasure.

Today's Parasha and the Armistice Day itself remind us that all of us, fathers and sons, mothers and daughters, must make a new effort in order to build a life of greater understanding and true human relationship, of more kindness and sympathy for our fellowmen, of more appreciation and sacrifice and of less inclination to take people and things for granted. We must build a new human relationship of greater understanding.

In today's Parasha, we read that when the Almighty intended to destroy the two sinful cities he said "I will go down now, and see whether they have done altogether according to the cry of it, which is come unto Me: and if not, I will know." Our sages point out that the Almighty in His wisdom must have known of all the transgressions of the inhabitants of those two cities; yet He decided to descend from His heavenly abode and make sure that His conclusions were right. By this account, He wanted to show that before judging our fellowmen we should make every effort to understand them. The Almighty came down in order to judge His people and made Himself equal with those whom in His mercy He had created.

This is a lesson which our young people especially should bear in mind today. Their education will be of very little value to them unless it teaches them how to appreciate life, unless it teaches them how to create true human relationships worthy of those who have been created in the image of God.

My dear Barmitzvah, it is this lesson which you should derive from today's Parasha and it is this lesson which you should try and learn throughout your life. Do remember not to take for granted the sacrifices that your parents are making in order to give you the best opportunities in life. Do not take your friends for granted, but try and appreciate them. Above all do not take for granted the blessings that the Almighty has given you. Show gratitude for all you receive. In learning how to be grateful you will also learn how to love and appreciate your fellowmen and how to obey God. Remember that all those opportunities which you have today and many of those things that you can enjoy in freedom in this country have not come to you in an easy way. Thousands upon thousands of young men and women have made the supreme sacrifice so that you may enjoy the true fruits of life, so that you may build a future in keeping with God's commands. May the Almighty bless you and keep you, may He always give you understanding, so that you may be grateful to those from whom you receive, so that you may understand and appreciate the value of kindness, of generosity and of love.

Amen.

THE RELIGIOUS SIGNIFICANCE OF THE STATE OF ISRAEL

Address on the occasion of Israel Independence day,
April 15, 1956.

As we celebrate the 8th Anniversary of Israel's independence, we should ask ourselves what effect Israel has had on our lives as Jews. We should ask ourselves whether we have acquired that deeper understanding of the place that Eretz Yisrael has in the teachings of the Torah and in our history. Today, we still seem to be puzzled as to the way in which we should give expression to the fact that our generation has been privileged to see the re-establishment of the State of Israel. We still seem to fail to understand that our attachment as Jews to the Land of Israel does not derive merely from the historic connection between the Land and the people of Israel, but that this attachment has the very essence of the destiny of our people. Today, when Israel is in danger, let us realise that not only the existence of the State is at stake but also that very concept of life about which the Torah teaches us and which can only be advanced through the Land of Israel becoming a sanctifying influence in our lives.

After the building of the first Temple was concluded, King Solomon offered a moving prayer to the Almighty, as we read in the Bible. He asked that in His mercy He should give to every man according to his ways "whose heart Thou knowest". But when praying for the "stranger who cometh out of every country for Thy name's sake" he said: "Hear Thou in Heaven Thy dwelling place and do according to all that the stranger callest to Thee for." There is a striking difference in the way in which Solomon asks that the desires of these two classes of people should be fulfilled. For the Children of Israel he asks that the Almighty should give them according to their ways, according to what He in His kindness and in His mercy considers is good for the Children of Israel. The strangers, however, should be granted according to their desires. The nations of the world could understand the existence of the Deity only by being granted every wish, by being given what each considered necessary for their existence. The concept as far as the Children of Israel were concerned was quite different. They expected that which the Almighty sent unto them as the only thing that was necessary for their progress and development. While Israel, to fulfill its destiny had to accept the tasks which the Almighty set, the other nations looked to the Deity in order to find fulfillment for their own requests and ambitions.

This distinction has also a bearing on our position today. If the State of Israel exists merely to fulfill our own selfish ambitions, if it is merely of importance to safeguard the existence and the future of the House of Israel throughout the World, then we should have to be afraid. Enemies have surrounded our Holy Land and they are trying to destroy its citizens. But in that new State of Israel, we do not see just the fulfillment of our wishes and even of our prayers, but a manifestation of God's own Will as regards His chosen people. We see in it a sign that the Almighty is in His own way fulfilling the promise which he gave to our ancestors. The new State is a milestone in the fulfillment of that ancient promise and it is only if we look upon the new State from this point of view that we shall realise that it has come here to stay. It is not the work of man, not even the result of those many sacrifices which young Jews and Jewesses made in order to liberate the Land of their ancestors, but above all the work of the Almighty Himself. As such, whatever the schemes of our enemies will be it will continue to exist. But we ourselves, as our sages teach us, must help and co-operate in the work of the Almighty. We must be ready to make sacrifices in order to safeguard the work of our Father who is in Heaven.

It is for that reason that we must allow the influence of the new State to be felt in our everyday life and above all in our religious outlook. I feel that the fact that many of us still fail to understand the significance of the new State is because our spiritual leaders, as well as the Jews in general, have failed to give a realistic expression to the influence that Israel should have on our lives as individuals and as members of the House of Israel.

The Jews have so far failed to emphasise the importance that Israel is having on the development which is guided by the spirit of the Torah. We offer a prayer on Sabbaths for the safety and the future of Israel, but is this sufficient? The time has come when the new State should find expression in our everyday, Sabbath and Festival liturgy.

MATERIAL AND SPIRITUAL PROGRESS

Sermon delivered at the Youth Service of Congregation Shaar Hashamayim, London, September 19, 1959.

What is the aim of our present-day civilisation? Most people would say that it is to achieve greater security for man, higher standards of living and more time for leisure.

All these are definitely praiseworthy because they would make man freer to devote his time and energy to the pursuit of those disciplines which would enhance his moral and spiritual qualities.

But has civilisation succeeded in achieving these aims? On the whole, they have been achieved, but have they produced those beneficial results which earlier generations hoped for, for all mankind?

If we take the countries in which there exists, perhaps, the highest standard of life, we shall find that they are not any longer faced with the problem of overwork, but of leisure time. In spite of opportunities which the citizens of those countries have, it seems that they have not been able to eliminate crime or moral decadence. Indeed, in some of these countries, the deterioration of morals and the increase of crime are evident. This is especially true of juvenile crime.

In olden days, it was argued that there was decadence among the aristocratic classes because they lived on the work of the underprivileged, but today opportunities for a higher standard of life exist for large masses in many countries of the Western world and yet among these classes there has been no effort to raise the ethical standards or to form a nobler moral outlook. Among the young generation today, there is, perhaps, even less sense of responsibility than there was in previous generations although they live in a world in which poverty does not threaten their existence. We find today, especially among younger people, that crimes are not committed because people are in need of bread, but very often because of the very stimulation that crime stirs in man. Are we not right in asking: Has a higher standard of living brought us those benefits for which we hoped and prayed?

We thought that if a man was provided with security, he would be elevated, decent, courageous and possessed of initiative in all the fields of human endeavour. But has man achieved these qualities? Do we find today more moral courage than we did in the days gone by? On the contrary, it seems today that a utilitarian outlook has developed, especially among the younger generation. Today, they do not believe in heroes who are ready to sacrifice their life for an ideal, but in heroes who know how to evade their responsibilities and yet appear great. Heroes who can amass fortunes without making a great effort. Heroes who can live in the present without consideration for the future or respect for the past. Man has become more self-assured from the material point of view; but has this sense of security enabled him to build within himself a stronger spiritual life and a nobler religious outlook?

Now at present we do not think of a revolution in terms of hungry masses trying to secure a piece of bread, but in terms of men greedy for power and ready to sacrifice millions in order to satisfy their lust for vainglory. What, then, has gone wrong with civilisation? Are we not to turn and say that all those ends which we have tried to achieve have been the wrong ends? After all, even our Torah teaches us that man should work for higher standards of living and for more effective security. But it also teaches us that if these aims become an end in themselves, then they cannot produce those benefits for which they are intended.

As we read in today's Parasha, the Children of Israel were told that after they came into the Holy Land they should bring the first fruits of their land to the Lord, "When you come into the land which the Lord your God gives you for an inheritance and possess it and dwell therein"; to possess it, say our Rabbis, means that the land will entirely belong to the Children of Israel; that they will not dwell in fear of the enemy, means that they will achieve a certain degree of security; and to dwell in the land means, continue our sages, to enjoy fully its fruits and the opportunities which it gives to its inhabitants. But the Torah did not allow these things to become the whole goal of Israel's effort. The first fruits, which meant the best fruits, had to be brought to the Lord. The Children of Israel had to be made aware that all their possessions came to them not merely as the result of their work and their effort, but as a blessing from the One who created and guides the world.

The Torah wanted to guard mankind from those pitfalls in which it has fallen today, namely from creating opportunities which offer only material benefits and do not take into consideration man's spiritual needs.

Does this mean, therefore, that a high standard of life, time for leisure and universal security are not the right and the true aims which the generations in the past and our own generation should have endeavoured to achieve? Perhaps, in these very opportunities lies a snare which captivates men's souls. The answer to these questions is found in the Talmud, in Aboda Zara, where the Rabbis say that idolatry is the greatest transgression that man can commit because it denies the very essence of the teachings of the Torah. The Rabbis ask: was not this statement superfluous? And they answer that there are different kinds of idolatry. Very often idolatry does not seem clear to us because it may apply to worshipping things which may not appear to us to constitute a transgression.

A higher standard of life, leisure and security are all praiseworthy aims which we should try to achieve in our life, but they should not be an end in themselves. They should be merely the result of our effort to come nearer to God, to worship Him and to commune with Him.

It may be difficult for a man who lives in security to remember God. It may be difficult for a man who possesses wealth and leisure to think of his Creator, but without such thoughts all his possessions and opportunities become merely achievements which do not endow his life with greater and nobler purposes. And the best way in which we could avoid becoming the victims of such a situation is to remember how to pray to our God, to remember to pray to Him day and night, to save us not only from despair and tragedy, but also from the snares which can exist in material well being and in the sense of security.

THE WORLD SEPHARDI FEDERATION (WSF) AND THE BIBLIOGRAPHICAL EXHIBIT

A lecture delivered to the leadership of the World Sephardi Federation, January 31, 1960.

It must be stressed at the outset that the Sephardi Bibliographical Exhibition was not the result of any political maneuvers on the part of the W.S.F. Our Federation is apolitical and does not in any way interfere with or intervene in spheres which are of political significance. The main task of the Federation is to preserve the Sephardi heritage and to revive it so that it may become an integral part of Jewish culture, religious thought and outlook and for that reason the Federation thought that an exhibition in Madrid may not be merely of interest to both Spaniards and Sephardi Jews. It would give expression to the mutual influences which took place between these two peoples when Jewish Communities were in existence in Spain, but also because the leaders of the W.S.F. and especially it's President, believed that such an Exhibition would give a new impetus to the research in Judeo-Spanish history and culture as well as to new possibilities of the development of such a culture.

Madrid, the capitol of Spain, seemed the obvious choice as the seat of this Exhibition because Spain still contains much unpublished material relating to the period of Jewish history in that country and especially to the golden age that produced a heritage which enriched not only Sephardi but Jewish life in general, more than any other age of the Jewish settlement in the Diaspora. I think it ought to be said that some people did object to Spain because of different reasons. Some of these reasons were based on religious scruples, because the belief still exists that Jewry should not return to Spain and should not in any way respond to any overtures for reconciliation. The belief is deeply rooted that there is a Herem, an ordinance entailing excommunication to the Jews who return to Spain. This belief is so widespread that many people are convinced that there is definitely such an ordinance. Many people have done a great deal of research and so far have not been able to point out the source from which the belief in the Herem springs. Dr. Cecil Roth, writing some time ago in *Judaisme Sephardi,* recounts that he visited many places which were in contact with Spain in ancient times as well as at present and found that the average Jew was quite convinced that there was an order of excommunication in existence, threatening all those who decided even to visit Spain. He enquired from many outstanding Rabbis and scholars as to the origin of this firm belief in the Herem but there was no satisfactory answer. He points out that in 1638 Moses Almosnino's work on Turkish History was published in Madrid by Jacob Cansino "member of a most erudite Moroccan family and an interpreter in the Spanish service who had lived continuously in the Spanish capital for half a dozen years previously". Jacob Sasportas, the first Haham of our Community, was also for a long time the diplomatic representative of the Sultan of Morocco at the Spanish Court. Had there been any such ordinance in existence, it is inconceivable that these people would have found their way into Spain and stayed for a considerable time.

Dr. Roth is of the opinion that the whole idea of the Herem arose from the fact that many Jews who had fled from Spain and settled in various countries, tried for family or business reasons to return to Spain, where once again they had to pretend that they had accepted Christianity and where they had to live as Christians. Many communities, including our own London community, took strong action against these people because they felt that once the Marranos had returned to their Faith they had no right to expose themselves to conditions in which, once again, they had to consider themselves and to be considered as Christians. Such people were, indeed, threatened by the leaders of their communities with excommunication, as is clear from the edition of 1785 of our Ascamot, in which it is stated that any person who has come from Spain or Portugal and has settled in any land in which Judaism is tolerated and afterwards returns to either of these countries, where he is obliged to live as a

Christian, such a person would be excluded from being a member of the congregation. Consequently, according to the opinion of Dr. Roth, "there was in fact no religious objection to the resettlement of Jews in Spain, but there was a very proper and deeprooted objection to members of Spanish and Portuguese communities living in circumstances in which they would have been compelled to disown their faith." The penalties which were connected with the breaking of this order amounted to a Herem and gave rise to the belief that any Jew who returned to Spain would expose himself to the penalty of excommunication.

Attempts by different Spanish governments to bring about a rapprochement between Spain and the Sephardi Jews have been many since the expulsion. They found their finest and strongest expression in the work of Dr. Pulido, who at the beginning of this century appealed to the Sephardi Jews of the world to return to Spain. Dr. Pulido was a senator in Spain. While travelling through the Balkans, he came across many Jews from this part of the world who spoke Ladino, the old Castilian language. Dr. Pulido recounts that in 1903, while he was travelling through the Balkans, he left Belgrade for Orosava by boat, which was running on the Danube between ancient Serbia and Roumania. His wife drew his attention to the fact that just in front of them there were people who were talking a special dialect of Spanish. The surprise and emotions which arose in him when he heard his language being spoken in this part of the world made him enter into conversation with Dr. Bejarano and his wife, well known members of the Sephardi Bucharest community. This was the beginning of the interest of Dr. Pulido in the Sephardim and of all his efforts to reestablish relations between Sephardi Jewry and Spain and to bring about what he called "Judeo-Spanish reconciliation."

Since the time of Pulido, other attempts were made to bring about a closer relationship between the two peoples. In 1915, the Spanish government invited the scholar Abraham Shalom Yahuda to give, in the Academy of Jurisprudence, a series of lectures on Judeo-Spanish civilisation, and Dr. Yahuda was later appointed Professor of the Madrid University in Jewish Civilisation.

In the First World War, Spain did try to help the Sephardi Jews of

Bulgaria and Turkey, as well as those in other lands, by making it possible for them to obtain Spanish nationality when they were in danger. We must admit that even during the last World War, quite a few Jews were saved, especially in Greece, through the intervention of the Spanish authorities. On 19th December, 1924, the Government of General Primo de Rivera offered all the Sephardim the possibility of re-acquiring Spanish nationality provided that they acquired this nationality before 31st December 1930. Not many Sephardim availed themselves of this opportunity, but those who did found it extremely useful, especially if they lived in countries which were later overrun by the Nazi armies.

As far back as 1909, permission was given to build synagogues in Spain. A synagogue in Barcelona, together with a communal hall, has been in existence for some years now, as well as a smaller synagogue in Madrid. Recently, a whole floor in a big block of flats has been acquired as a Communal Centre and as a synagogue by the Madrid Community and this was dedicated only a few months ago. Both Madrid and Barcelona are speedily becoming important centres as far as Jewish activity is concerned, especially in connection with Jewish students who attend the Universities there. These students, in the majority of cases, are natives of Morocco. Especially in Madrid, there is now quite an active Student Society which I addressed during my stay there. This Society is greatly helped by the Jewish Community of Madrid, but in turn it is due to the Society that services are held there both on Friday evenings and on Shabbat mornings. The services are entirely conducted by students without whom sometimes there would not be the necessary quorum for the services. The students meet once a week for discussions and lectures and they are interested in every aspect of Jewish life. There are quite a few Jewish lecturers at the Madrid University and they are very much respected by their other colleagues on the academic staff. It would be wrong to obtain the impression that the only Jewish students in Madrid are of Moroccan origin. There are some Jewish students from America, and Israel, as well as from Turkey and Greece.

Before the last few years, there were quite a few Jews in Spain who tried in every possible way to hide their origin and identify themselves with the Christians of the country. These people, in spite of all the encouragement given by the Spanish Government to the Jewish community, refused to identify themselves with Jewish communal endeavours. It would only be on occasions of death that the community became aware of some of these people belonging to the Jewish people. I was told by many people in Madrid that the reception accorded by the Spanish people as a whole to the Sephardi Exhibition will help Jews who so far have remained far from the Jewish community to make the decision to return to the fold.

The Exhibition was opened on November 18th at 8:00 p. m., in the National Library building. It was arranged under the patronage of the Madrid National Library and with the collaboration of the World Sephardi Federation. Other bodies that collaborated were the Arias Montano Institute, the Faculty of Philosophy of the Madrid University as well as the Royal Academy of the Spanish Language. The Spanish Ministry of Foreign Affairs put at the disposal of the World Sephardi Federation their services, and the Spanish Ambassadors granted the use of the Diplomatic Bag for the transport of the material used. Some months before the exhibition, Mr. Behar, the representative of the World Sephardi Federation in Spain, visited North Africa, Turkey, Portugal, Holland, and Israel, in order to obtain the best material for the Exhibition. All Sephardi Communities and other bodies in these countries were eager to assist the World Sephardi Federation in this endeavour. Most of the material from these parts of the world, including America and England, was sent to Spain through the Diplomatic Bag. The material used was of great value and the insurance for it all ran into thousands of pesetas. The exhibits were divided into the following sections: Documents, books, maps, and other material showing the social, political, economic, Jewish, literary and religious life of the Jews in Spain up to 1492. In the second section, exhibits showed the retention of the Spanish influences in Jewish life in the Balkans, North Africa, England, Holland and America, after the expulsion of 1492.

Of special interest were many periodicals and dailies which were published in the old Castilian language, Ladino, which, according to some scholars, the Jews spoke even before they left Spain. Some scholars say that the special dialect retained by the Sephardim in many communities was not the creation of the time that followed the exile from Spain but that even in Spain itself the Jews had adhered to older forms of language and had retained them. Much material showed the contemporary efforts in different fields of communal, social and literary endeavour of the Spanish Jews throughout the world, as well as documents and books written by Spaniards concerning reconciliation which, as we said, started even before the beginning of this century.

I know that many were impressed by the fact that there were still periodicals published in Ladino, especially in Turkey and in Israel, where there is a daily relay on the wireless in that language and where there are still many people who speak this language and use it for daily purposes. I think it ought to be pointed out here that in Israel the old inhabitants, many of whom came there during the 17th, 18th and 19th centuries, and who were of Sephardi origin, spoke Ladino, and many rabbinic books were written in that language. Indeed, that language was used in many of the yeshivot in the old city of Jerusalem. It is interesting that today we can still find in Israel people whose families have lived in that country for many generations and who still use Ladino as the language spoken within the family. This is of special interest when we bear in mind that the Sephardim took part in the revival of the Hebrew language as much as any other section of the Jewish community. Much of the old Sephardi folklore has been retained in Israel and even among the younger generation there are still people who are able to converse in Ladino and who read the papers published in that language.

The importance that the Spanish people attached to the Exhibition was shown by the fact that its opening was performed by the Minister of Education, Mr. Rubio. Those present included Ramon Pidal, the President of the Academy of the Spanish Language, one of the most prominent Spaniards alive today; the Military and the Civil Governors of Toledo, the representative of the Ministry of Foreign Affairs, Mr. Morales; the representative of the Ministry of Culture, Mr. Goicuechea; the President of the National Library, and many other officials from different Ministries and cultural institutions. To these have to be added prominent professors of the Madrid University as well as quite a few members of the Catholic Clergy. The Jewish community was also well represented and among them were the President of the community, Mr. Blitz, and Mr. Mazin, the vice-President. The Jewish community was very gratified that the World Sephardi Federation has taken such a prominent part in organising the Exhibition and it felt that this Exhibition would help the activities of the community.

I had the honour to be the only speaker not from Spain at the opening of this significant Exhibition. I thanked, on behalf of the Sephardim and of the World Sephardi Federation, the Spanish government for their help in organising this Exhibition. I pointed out some of the Spanish influences which are evident in Jewish culture and I ended by bringing greetings on behalf of the World Sephardi Federation to the Spanish people and the Spanish Government.

I was more than impressed by this opening of the Exhibition. I never thought that such prominent people representing the Spanish Government would attend the ceremony of the opening. I was above all touched by the apparent sincerity of those present in their desire to make this Exhibition a success and to open a new chapter in the Judeo-Spanish relations. It was more than remarkable that all the press was unanimous in welcoming the arranging of the Exhibition and in stating that it meant a new phase in the Judeo-Spanish relations. Even those papers which are closely connected with the Catholic Church like Ya and Aloazar gave very prominent places to the report on the Exhibition and the report was given in a most favourable way. It is not for us to try to find out the political implications of this great welcome to the Exhibition and the prominent way in which the World Sephardi Federation was praised by all the newspapers of Spain. We should be satisfied to take note of the fact that there is a welcome in Spain for the idea of reconciliation and that the Exhibition was acknowledged by all scholars as a true expression of the Judeo-Spanish culture in the past and in the present.

The exhibits were most interesting as one saw books by great philosophers such as Maimonides, Abrabanel, works of art and different fields of literary endeavour. One could not help thinking that the genius of the Jew did find, as far as the Diaspora is concerned, a most fertile soil in Spain. Why? This is a difficult question to answer. There are people who say that the Jews saw in Spain, as far as its climate and its nature are concerned, a country which is very similar to Israel. Perhaps this is to some extent true. But the Jews have lived in many other Mediterranean countries and did not produce a similar golden age. I think the true answer lies in the fact that at least for some time, under the Moslem rulers, the Jews enjoyed freedom and that gave them an opportunity for creative work together with their fellow men of other faiths.

One of the most interesting exhibits, a Sepher Torah that was lent by the Congregation of Bayonne, has a story attached to it that it was brought by the exiles from Spain to Bayonne. As far as I know there is only one other Sepher Torah concerning which there is the same tradition, and which is found in the Great Synagogue of Tetuan. Whether this history is right or not, is not of great importance, but the fact remains that even as far as sacred appurtenances are concerned, the tradition of Spain has survived among the Sephardi communities of the world.

I think that it is only right that at this stage we should pay our tribute to Dr. Richard Barnett, without whose cooperation this Exhibition could not have succeeded. His expert knowledge and his devoted work on behalf of the Exhibition greatly contributed towards its success.

I was very honoured to have been asked to give a lecture in Ladino, on the present position of the Sephardi communities and on their cultural background. In addition, there was a concert of Sephardi music and I was very glad to hear that the town of Toledo has asked for the same concert to be given there, renowned as it is for its Jewish traditions and Jewish connections. It was one of the highlights of our visit to Spain that we were asked by the town of Toledo to visit there and to be their guests. We visited Toledo on a Sunday and although it was a day when all the representatives of the town were busy with a very important canonisation, we were greatly honoured to be received at the gates of Toledo by its Mayor and later on to be entertained by the Civil and the Military Governors of that great city. It seemed rather strange walking through the ruins of the two great synagogues, looking at the inscriptions, imagining the great Jewish past of Toledo and then the expulsion and now after five centuries Jews being honoured in the very town in which oppression and expulsion took place.

Now what are we going to do after the Exhibition, which closed on 18th December? I am very glad to say that Dr. Barnett was present at the closing of the Exhibition and has reported to us that the closing was as solemn as its opening; but what have been the tangible results? Again, this is very difficult to evaluate, I think we can say that the Exhibition has made a very good impression on the people of Spain in general, who perhaps for the first time have realised that there is a Judeo-Spanish culture. There is no doubt that the Exhibition has also given new heart to those Spaniards who always worked for the study of Hebrew and Jewish culture in Spain, like Dr. Pidal, Prof. Castro and Prof. Burgos and others. It has also created the possibility of closer cooperation in the cultural field between the Spanish and the Jews and a tangible result has been the proposal for the creation of Sephardi Academies which would be attached to the Spanish Academy and which would consist of Jews and of Spaniards. It is proposed that it will have its central seat both in Jerusalem and in Madrid and that it will work on the study of the Ladino language and on the history of the Jews in Spain and especially investigate the mutual influences of the Jewish and Spanish cultures. Last, but not least, I think the World Sephardi Federation and its President must be congratulated for the initiative which they took in organising this Exhibition. I think this community, proud of its Sephardi tradition, should take pride in the fact that it was instrumental in establishing the World Sephardi Federation in London, thereby making it possible for it to spread its influence over the Sephardi communities throughout the world. Perhaps here is the place where I should say that if the World Sephardi Federation is to succeed, and is to undertake similar enterprises as the Madrid Exhibition, it must have not only the good will but the tangible support of all the Sephardi communities in England.

ON THE REOPENING OF THE BEVIS MARKS SYNAGOGUE

Sermon delivered on April 14, 1962.

On this day we can truly recite the benediction "Who hast kept us alive, sustained us, and enabled us to reach this time." Whenever we offer our prayers in this Synagogue "Shaar Hashamayim" we experience emotions which by their intensity and by their ennobling effect cannot be compared to the feelings which fill all our being when we worship in other places of worship. For here we feel that we are not alone in our devotions but that generations which began to worship here over 260 years ago become alive before our eyes. Their hopes become our hopes, their doubts and fears become our own, their prayers our prayers. And we are induced to ask ourselves: has their faith, faith in God and man, become our faith? For they lived by their faith. They did not allow unpropitious conditions, seemingly insurmountable obstacles to deter them in their sacred endeavour to build not only a house of Worship in this country, but above all, a community which bears a living testimony of the eternal covenant between God and His people, the House of Israel.

And this our generation of the Spanish and Portuguese Congregation has shown itself aware of its history by renovating this Sanctuary and thereby ensuring that our sons and daughters will be able to direct their prayers to God in this place hallowed by centuries of history and by years of devotion and prayer. Those responsible by their work and by their generosity for this sacred work have not merely strengthened the walls and the foundation of this house of God, but they have given a new opportunity to the young to learn from the example of their ancestors the greatest of all lessons - that man should not live merely for himself and that he should work not only for his own generation but for eternity. This is the only lesson which may give our youth the strength and the vision to look beyond the confines of the present. It is this idea that gives real and true meaning to the selfless efforts of those who made the restoration of this ancient Sanctuary possible.

Let us remember however, that this renovated Snoga imposes a new task upon all of us. A Synagogue does not become a House of God by being renovated either because of its antiquity or because of its traditions. It becomes a House of God through the multitude of worshippers who pray to their Creator within its precincts, through the people who within their hearts echo the words of the Psalmist, "O Lord, I love the habitation of Thy house and the place where Thy glory dwelleth." Indeed all the expense and sacrifice by the Sephardi Community at large will not be justified unless we now make every effort to bring into this Snoga worshippers, old and new, who will make it "The place where Thy glory dwelleth." The Bevis Marks Association has done much to preserve this building and all the ideas and ideals for which it stands; but its efforts must now be directed towards the gathering of a congregation which alone can save this place from neglect and even slow disintegration. For a Synagogue is not destroyed only when its walls have crumbled and when its foundations have been laid waste. Indeed very often a Sanctuary, although in ruins, is still alive because it lives in the hearts of the people. The Temple in Jerusalem has never been devastated. Neither the devouring fire of the enemy nor his lust for destruction could put an end to the House of God in Jerusalem because its idea continued to animate the hearts and the souls of the successive generations of the Jewish people who have never ceased to pray for its restoration.

This is borne out by the Mishnah in Megila that tells us that a Synagogue retains its sanctity even when it lies in ruins and that there is always in connection with it "agmat nefesh" "a sadness of soul" which, as the commentators point out, means that the people do not accept its destruction and pray to the Almighty to afford them the possibility to rebuild it. On the other hand we know that a Synagogue which no longer has worshippers can be sold and the funds used for the building or buying of another Synagogue or school. A Synagogue abandoned by its congregation loses its sanctity, the spirit of the Lord no longer dwells in it. All the skill of the builder cannot preserve a synagogue from dilapidation unless there is the heart of the worshipper that alone can give meaning to a House of Prayer and imbue even an ordinary room with the spirit of God. We, who are proud to belong to the Community of which the most proud possession is this Snoga, must be very careful lest by our own neglect we damage this noble building which the passage of time has failed to do. I am sure that in this neighbourhood there are still Sephardim who can be attracted to worship here. But many of them have for different reasons ceased to be members of this congregation. Some of them have never known the ennobling experience of praying in this sanctuary. We must try to attract people who live in this neighbourhood and this ought to be the first task of the Bevis Marks Association. Once the contact has been created with them it will be the task of the Ministry to maintain it. I earnestly believe that this is the last, and I believe the most glorious opportunity that we have of keeping this Snoga as a House of Worship; for let us remember that unless there will be a congregation in this Synagogue we shall not be able to maintain the interest of the community at large in its welfare. For a Kahal Kadosh is not called upon to maintain a museum building, however noble its past.

Today with happiness and hope we offer our prayers to God in this our ancient sanctuary. We thank Him for His manifold mercies to this our Sephardi Community and for having preserved this House dedicated to His glory through two and a half centuries; for having kept safe in spite of the destruction which time has caused to, and enemy poured upon this noble city.

The prophet tells us as we read in today's Haftarah that at the time when the Almighty will bring full salvation to all His children, He will turn the heart of parents to the children and the hearts of children to their parents. There will be no longer conflict of views and outlooks between different ages. In this Snoga of Bevis Marks, different ages and generations have met for hundreds of years with one single purpose in their minds - to serve the Creator of us all. Today our prayers join with the prayers of our ancestors who built this Snoga and worshiped in it in the past. Parents and children, past and present, have come together to cause the spirit of the Lord to dwell in this House.

ISRAEL INDEPENDENCE DAY ADDRESS

Remarks given at the Marble Arch Synagogue, London, May 8, 1962.

The Independence Day celebrations only have meaning if they symbolise our new attitudes to the different values and expressions in our life as a people and as members of the Jewish Community. These new relationships should be the result of the re-establishment of the State of Israel in our own days and of a conscious desire and effort to act and live according to the inspiration which springs from this event. As the prophet Zekhariah said on the occasion of the return of the captivity of Babylon: "Deliver thyself, O Zion, that dwelleth with the daughter of Babylon." The deliverance by the Lord must be accompanied by the deliverance which must be initiated by ourselves, the deliverance from those influences which are alien to our spirit and our history, and which are the result of millennia of our life in the Diaspora. These influences to some extent, shaped our lives in spite of all the efforts by the successive generations of our people to preserve their loyalties and their outlook on life. The Galut has produced in the Jews two contradictory qualities: the strength not to succumb to the influences of the surroundings in which they lived, and the ability to adjust themselves to the ever changing requirements of these surroundings. These characteristics found expression in all our ways of life; in our communal action, in the education of our children; in consequence, they coloured our views and became part of our social and perhaps even religious attitudes.

It is from these results of Galut that the prophet Zekhariah called upon the people to free themselves after their return from Babylonian captivity; and the same call should be directed to our own generation.

Today we seem to be in danger of forgetting both our past and the tasks which our present circumstances impose upon us. Especially, we are failing to convey to our younger generations the hopes, struggles, frustrations and even martyrdoms which were the lot of our people during the last two thousand years. These reached their climax with the annihilation of six million of our people during the last war, which at the same time ushered in a new era that came into being with the establishment of the State of Israel. We seem to want to save our children the pain of realising the great sacrifices made by their people in the past because we ourselves want to forget them. But in doing so, we are also unable to convey to them the miracle that the God of Israel wrought in our own days, the significance of this miracle for us and the world, and the responsibilities that it imposes upon all of us whether we live in the State of Israel or in the Diaspora.

Immediately after the creation of the State of Israel, fear was expressed that a division may be created between Israel and the Diaspora. Not only has the State of Israel not impeded the unity of the House of Israel but it has given additional strength and real purpose to it. Israel has become the centre of our religious life. Problems which have waited centuries for their solutions are being examined and solved in the spirit of the teachings of the Torah. In the Diaspora, Jews are not becoming indifferent to Jewish values as predicted by some pessimists when the new State was re-established. The reverse has been the case. Israel has stimulated the study of the Jewish past and heritage by both young and old. Indeed we have lived to see the words of the Psalmist fulfilled: "Wilt thou not revive us again; that Thy people may rejoice in Thee".

But with all that, the miracle has not yet become the main inspiration of our actions, the integral part of our existence or the fountainhead of our thought. Miracles are created by Got but they must be sustained by man. We must therefore consciously endeavour to become aware of the existence of Israel in our communal, religious and social life and especially in the methods which we employ to give a Jewish education to our children. This we shall be able to achieve by evaluating our present conditions in the light of our past. It is not in the spirit of vengeance that we must teach our children the true meaning of the Torah's injunction "Zahor" - Remember. They must be taught the past humiliation and fears of their people if they are to understand the improvements that have taken place in the psychological state as well as in the political atmosphere of our people everywhere through the building of the State of Israel. Our Rabbis have taught us that we must recite the Haggadah at the time when bread of affliction and bitter herbs are placed before us. Without the knowledge of the bitterness of slavery, we cannot appreciate or give thanksgiving for the blessing of freedom. Let us therefore not be afraid to remind ourselves and the world of the persecutions which were perpetrated against our people. The changes for good which have taken place in our own situation can only be maintained and further developed if guided by examples of the past - however painful they may be. We must give our children thorough knowledge of our sacred heritage through which they will learn how to live according to God's Will and in keeping with His Divine purpose as it expresses itself in our present day events.

May He who has gathered our martyrs unto Himself, bless and strengthen the State of Israel which He brought into being through His miraculous deed and may He in His mercy teach us how to live and act in the spirit of His miracle.

ISRAEL: DREAM AND REALITY

Sermon delivered at the Great Portland Street Synagogue, London, on Israel Independence Day, April 29, 1963.

On the fifteenth anniversary of the establishment of the State of Israel, we give our thanks to God Almighty for the great miracle which He vouchsafed to our own generation. In His infinite mercy, He demonstrated before the eyes of all the nations of the world, that He still dwells among His people. We are privileged to live in the epoch making days of which the Psalmist spoke when he exclaimed: "When the Lord brought back those that returned to Zion, we were as in a dream."

Some nations, when they achieve their national independence, cease to be dreamers. They become arbiters, not only masters of their own destiny, but, also masters as to the way in which they co-operate with other countries and nations. Their rejoicing very often turns into pride and arrogance, forgetting those who helped them to achieve their aim, and above all, forgetting that there is a God who is the ultimate guide and deliverer. For the Jew, however, as the Psalmist points out, it is different. Even in the hour of his greatest triumph, even when the Almighty redeems the promise which He gave to our Fathers and to our Prophets, the Jew still remains a dreamer. We were like dreamers, as the Psalmist says, when the Almighty redeemed the land and His people. And both the State of Israel and Jewry as a whole, have remained faithful to this great ideal - the ideal of being dreamers. For us, redemption is a constant process in which both the laws of nature and the supernatural Divine miracles are evident and which embraces not only the House of Israel, but all mankind. And it is in pursuing this concept of redemption that the

State and the people of Israel must act in the spirit of the highest religious standards set by the Torah.

In spite of its many preoccupations in the economic and defense fields, the State of Israel was able to extend a helping hand to many new States, in order to make it possible for them to solve the problems which are bound up with the beginning of national independence. Israel has done that without ulterior motives, without asking whether political or economic advantages will ensue from this endeavour. It did not ask for guarantees, or treaties in exchange for this help, because its actions have been inspired by the utterances of our ancient Prophets.

This progressive idea of redemption finds full expression in the words of Micah, who speaks of the latter days - the days which will follow the first stages of redemption - the days when the nations shall go and say "Let us go up to the mountain of the Lord". In those days, no longer swords shall be the decisive factor in international relations, but, the Almighty shall judge between many peoples who will ultimately beat their swords into ploughshares.

Since Israel sees its liberation as part of this wider and all-embracing human salvation, it has been able to assert itself as a political, and above all, as a moral force, in the councils of the leaders and the statesmen of the world.

It is not always practical to be a dreamer, and, especially a dreamer of the kind of which the Torah speaks. For according to Malbim, an outstanding commentator on the Torah, "holemim" in the context of our psalm means people with prophetic dreams - people who see the situations as they will arise, and who implicitly believe that God will act according to His revealed word.

In a world of hard reality, in which calculated interest plays the main part, indeed it is difficult to be such a dreamer. And yet, the State of Israel, by accepting this dream as an integral part of its State programme, has brought credit to itself, as well as to World Jewry. It has performed the mitzvah of Kidush Hashem - the commandment of hallowing the name of the Almighty before the eyes of all the nations, thus laying the foundation of a new concept in international relationships.

We are witnessing the interest of the nations being judged by wrong standards, and righteousness and justice being abandoned in favour of temporary gains. All that is being done in the name of peace. And yet the world seems to have forgotten the lessons which it learned only before and during the last World War that peace cannot be bought by betraying principles which are of Divine origin. Nations and peoples cannot be abandoned and betrayed without evil proving triumphant and destroying the very foundations of civilisation.

Today, while commemorating the establishment of the State of Israel, we have in mind the dangers that beset its path. Once again, the enemies of Israel and the enemies of Jewry, and they are the very same enemies, are conspiring against our people. Today, we ask all the nations of the world: Have you forgotten the millions of people who were annihilated because you had chosen the wrong paths to peace? Have you forgotten the six million Jewish victims who were massacred by a cruel enemy who was allowed to become strong because the nations of the world believed that evil could be appeased?

Let the world realise that there is no division between Israel and the Jewish People throughout the world. If Israel is threatened, then the threat is directed against every Jewish Community; against every Jewish individual in the world.

Indeed, the State of Israel has continued to be a State of prophetic dreamers. We are proud - all of us - of its achievements in the economic, in the cultural and in the moral field of world endeavour. It has well understood its Messianic destiny and it lives and acts in the spirit of this destiny.

Maimonides in his "Hilhot Melahim" says, that the Messianic era will be the time when there will be no hunger or want, when there will be no envy or strife, and when all the world will only have one aim - the achievement of the knowledge of God, Creator of Heaven and Earth. It is our task to help the State of Israel to continue its endeavours in the spirit of the Jewish concept of redemption, as befits the dreamers, the prophetic dreamers of Israel.

Today, we pledge ourselves - as it is our task as the Children of God, - to preserve that miracle that God has vouchsafed to our generation, to preserve it and to defend it from any treachery or aggression. The whole

House sees in the State of Israel the beginning of a new era - that era which the prophets saw in their visions and which they proclaimed by their fiery utterances. We pledge ourselves today that we shall not betray the memory of our six million brothers and sisters. We shall not allow the future generations to say that they have died in vain. And above all, it is the duty of every Jew not to allow the Voice of the Almighty that has spoken to our generation, to be hushed or silenced.

Today, we pray to the Eternal Guardian of Israel to preserve and to guard the State of Israel - the fruit of His own creation - to lead His people to complete redemption and the world to full salvation.

REPORT ON SEPHARDIM OF AMERICA

A lecture delivered at Congregation Shaar Hashamayim, London, 1964.

About three years ago, the Elders were kind enough to grant me three months Sabbatical leave which I would spend in study and research in some Jewish Institute.

I was not able to take my leave as soon as I intended to do, and for that reason, I was given sufficient time to consider different places to which I could go in order to refresh both my knowledge and my outlook - and the outlook of a Rabbi needs refreshing from time to time.

A spiritual leader of the Congregation is today involved in almost all the aspects of communal life, and for that reason, he has very little time to devote to his studies, to research and to keep in touch with new trends in Jewish scholarship and Rabbinical disciplines. And yet, he cannot claim that he is doing justice to his work unless he is able to receive new inspiration and new knowledge from time to time. A Rabbi who is not given the opportunity to devote at least some of his time to meditation and to study, cannot ultimately do justice to his own tasks. Sooner or later, he will necessarily become either narrow in his outlook, or his horizon will become so indefinite and indistinguishable that he will find himself unable to make decisions or give advice. Or, which is even worse, he may not have any views to express and his pronouncements may become cliches and outworn phrases, which he has heard at random from other people holding the same positions as he does, or, which he has read in the distant past when he studied in a Yeshiva or in a College.

For that reason, I was grateful to have had at least a comparatively short time given to me to be able to free myself from communal tasks and duties and to be able to bring under revision my views and even my work. It was impossible for me, even in America, to cut myself off entirely from my work, because almost every week I received communications from my office. Yet, I was able to devote much of my time to lecturing and to research, which, although strenuous and exacting work, proved refreshing for me and afforded me a great amount of spiritual rest.

I was very fortunate indeed to have been given an invitation by the Yeshiva University of New York to become a Visiting Lecturer there for three months in Practical Rabbinics, with special emphasis on Sephardi traditions, Sephardi history, Sephardi outlook and communal relationships. I was invited to give twelve lectures to the post-graduate students, and although I accepted this invitation with a great amount of trepidation because I felt that lecturing to post-graduate students was going to be a new experience for me, yet, I knew that this was an opportunity which I did not dare refuse to accept. And now I know that I was right. Yeshiva University was not only a new experience for me, but I should say - a new inspiration. It proved for me not merely a means of widening my horizons and enriching my knowledge, but, above all, of gaining a new experience both in methods of acquiring and conveying information in communal activities, which are part and parcel of the Yeshiva University.

I feel that I have to say a few words about the past and the present of the Yeshiva University, so that you may have an idea as to the place in which I worked and the atmosphere which permeated my daily tasks and endeavours.

Yeshiva University is a Liberal Arts Institution under Jewish auspices which in 1945 was granted University status and thus, became the first University in America under Jewish sponsorship. This great Institution of Torah and of knowledge and education was established in 1896, when the Rabbi Isaac Elchanan Theological Seminary was founded as the first School in America for advanced Torah Studies. When in 1961 the Yeshiva University celebrated its 75th anniversary, it received congratulations from President John Kennedy, as well as from Governor Nelson Rockefeller and Mayor Robert Wagner, as well as from other leaders, political and cultural, throughout America.

President Kennedy wrote to the authorities of the Yeshiva University: "With the past 75 years as a foundation, the next 75 can only be an era of outstanding achievement for the University and for the nation. The ideal of a Yeshiva University City is appealing and I wish you every success". When President Kennedy speaks of the University City, he has in mind what has been called "the blue print for the sixties" - a thirty million dollar development programme which will enable the Yeshiva University to meet the challenge of the new era and of the new world to Jew and non-Jew alike. The University part of the Yeshiva University is non-denominational and all students who can fulfill the requirements are admitted, whatever their religion may be.

Yeshiva University today has more than five thousand students attending different colleges and post- graduate schools, in which I would say not merely a new type of Jew is being brought up, but, also, in which a new system is being developed in order to give Judaism and Jewish teachings a form which will be in keeping with the demands of our modern atomic age.

Dr. Belkin, the President of Yeshiva University, writing on occasion of the 75th anniversary of this Institution, noted: "A student who pursues his education at Yeshiva University becomes both a better Jew and a better American. He is more deeply rooted in the rich soil of his Faith and he blossoms in the shining light of modern knowledge. He becomes better able to grapple with his peoples' problems and finds himself in a more advantageous position for serving his country."

These are not exaggerated claims. The student at Yeshiva University has the chance of receiving a balanced education, a happy blending of the eternal values of the Torah and contemporary technological and scientific knowledge. One of the University's greatest contributions has been the development of educational facilities for women. Besides the two High Schools for Girls and the Teachers' Institute for Women as well as the Stern College for Women, co-educational programmes are offered also in most Graduate and Professional Schools.

Lecturing in the Theological Seminary of Yeshiva University was an interesting experience, because I had the opportunity of meeting young people from the New World, who were preparing themselves for different professions in life and who were trying to give some of their own enthusiasm to the Jewish Community of America and to their country in the educational enterprise of which they wanted to take an outstanding part.

Of the 120 students to whom I lectured, only about 20-25 were preparing to take the Ministry as their calling. The rest, although studying for the Rabbinic Diploma, were going to be medical men, engineers, teachers, who considered that the knowledge which studying for the Rabbinical Diploma brings, was essential for them as the intelligencia of the Jewish Community in America. This, in my opinion, is a worthy example to be followed by our Community. Among many people, especially the youth of our country, it is thought that only the Rabbi must have sufficient knowledge which would enable him to decide according to Jewish law, or to consider different aspects of Jewish life in the light of Jewish law.

We are failing here to understand the importance of the ordinary Jew and Jewess who can only be inspired by the Jewish ideals if they acquire and possess knowledge of the Jewish teachings. Those hundred students who were studying for the Rabbinic Diploma, although not taking the Ministry as their profession, were going to be a great asset to the Jewish Community of America as a whole. They were going to be leaders of Jewish congregations, and an example to the younger generation, who will necessarily be inspired by the actions and by the lives of these people.

What impressed me greatly about Yeshiva University was that it was not merely an academic institution working in a vacuum. Through the Community Service Division, it keeps in close touch with many Jewish Communities of America. It helps Jewish Communities throughout the country to solve their manifold problems, and especially, it helps young Communities, both with advice and materially, and thereby helps the Yeshiva University to become a true channel for dissemination of the knowledge and the ideas of the Torah throughout the Jewish world of America.

In keeping with this task, the Community Service Division organises many Seminars throughout the country at different times, when young people are on vacation. I had the opportunity of speaking to one of these Seminars during the Winter vacation, and I was amazed to see many young people from the age of fifteen onwards, from different parts of America, coming together in order to learn something about their great heritage. Many of these youths were not from Orthodox homes. Many of them had hardly seen any Jewish ceremonials carried out in their own family circle. They were carefully chosen by Ministers in different communities because they were thought to be good material to become recipients of the true Jewish message. I spoke to some of the young boys and girls whose parents did not keep many, if any, of the Jewish home laws and yet, these young people after having attended two or three of these seminars, have become so enthusiastic about the Jewish Faith and the Jewish Law, that they were able to bring a new spirit into their homes. Even when they failed to do so (and some of them did fail to convince their parents of the necessity to live according to the implications and the commands of the Jewish Law), they still remained staunch in an almost, one could say, hostile atmosphere, to those Jewish ideals which were imparted to them during those few days they spent in these Seminars organised by Yeshiva University.

This Seminar, as all the others, was entirely managed by the Staff of the University, as well as by its Senior Students, who volunteer to give of their little free time, in order to further the great ideals which are bound up with the work of Yeshiva University. For the Staff of Yeshiva University are not merely lecturers - not only research workers - but they consider it their sacred duty to go outside the walls of the University and to influence the Jewish Community and even the nation at large.

Dr. Belkin, the President of Yeshiva University, an outstanding scholar, travels throughout the country, in order to bring to the nation, the message of his great Institution, in order to influence and in order to convince them of the necessity of strengthening this University and widening its scope.

The same is done by Dr. Rackman, the Vice-President of Yeshiva University, who, in addition to this great and responsible task, has his own Community which he has to guide and influence.

On the whole, both the students and the Staff of Yeshiva University work very hard. Their work begins at 8 o'clock in the morning and very often does not end until 7 or 8 o'clock in the evening. The students attend many and varying courses in different subjects, very often with the intention of taking two Degrees, which frequently do not appear to have any connection with each other. Students attend courses for Rabbinics, and at the same time for Mathematics and Science. Today, it has become fashionable for a young American to take not only one, but two, and even three Degrees. Many ladies who have been married for a long time, and who now feel that they may find a little time for study, are returning to their universities, not in order to obtain a degree, or to boast about their University background, but, in order to help either the Jewish Community, or America, in the solution of its manifold problems.

There is in America a thirst for knowledge - a thirst for seeking solutions for world and national problems. There is an active and a sincere endeavour to improve the standards of both living and of ethics in the world in general. There is also a constant effort to persuade people of the importance of religion in human life, and of the part that religion has to play in our every day life. In consequence, the task of such an Institution as Yeshiva University is made easier, because the Government and the people as a whole are co-operating in the advancement of those views which are essentially of Jewish and Torah origin.

It was in this atmosphere of scholarship and practical endeavour that I was able to spend my three months of leave, but, like other lecturers of the University, not only in contact with the students, but also, with the Community at large. I lectured under the auspices of the Yeshiva University to different societies and Congregational assemblies, and in this way, I was once again, brought into close touch with the larger Sephardi Communities.

On my previous visits to America, I was brought in contact with only a small part of the Sephardi Communities, but, this time, I visited nearly all the Sephardi Congregations in New York and lectured to them. In addition I went to other places such as Rochester and also travelled to lecture to the Sephardi Congregation of Montreal. When I addressed one of the largest Toronto Communities, I was also able to address the two

Sephardi Congregations of Toronto and deal with some of their problems.

If it is said that America is a melting pot, then this also applies to the Sephardim. The Sephardim of America comprise the Communities in which the Sephardim were to be found throughout the world. There is the great Syrian Community, divided into the Damascus and Aleppo Communities. Then there is the community from the Balkans, Jews from Rhodes, from Salonika, from North Africa and from Turkey. In addition, there is a considerable Persian and Bukharan Community and last, but not least, there is the great Spanish and Portuguese Congregation, which in Minhag, outlook, and one would almost say history, is very similar to our own Sha'ar Hashamayim.

I have spoken to you very often about Congregation Shearith Israel, the Spanish and Portuguese Synagogue in New York. It was established just about the same time as our own, and is the Mother Congregation of American Jewry, who now number over five million members. It is interesting to note that among many of the characteristics that the Sephardim acquired from the Spanish people, the spirit of pioneering is a prominent one. It is interesting to note that it was the Spanish and Portuguese Jews who brought about the resettlement of our people in this country, and who established the first Jewish Communities in North and South America.

The Spanish and Portuguese Congregation of New York, both by its prestige and work, is the centre of the Sephardi world of America. Its Minhag and its most beautiful Synagogue, have always drawn the attention of the Jewish and non-Jewish world of America, and are a source of pride to all the Sephardim. It goes without saying that it is the best organized Community, which has always tried to live according to its great traditions, and which is now making new efforts in order to influence the other Sephardi Communities of the New World.

The Community, only recently, has given considerable help to a new Congregation in Queens (one of the boroughs making up the City of New York), in order to enable them to build a new Synagogue.

Shearith Israel is the repository of a great tradition and of a remarkable history, and it is interesting to note that throughout the ages it has had Ministers and Hazanim, who have come from our own

Congregation. Its previous Minister was Dr. David de Sola Pool, who is now the emeritus Minister of the Congregation.

A great part of the American Sephardim consist of people who have come from different Balkan Communities. The Community of New Brunswick, New Jersey consists almost entirely of immigrants from Salonika. When I addressed that Congregation, I was able to speak also in Ladino, and the fact that amazed me most was that I was not only understood by those who had originally come from Salonika, but, also, by the second and even third generation who were born in America.

In England, for instance, we find that Ladino has been almost entirely forgotten in the Holland Park Congregation, and it is hardly understood even by the second generation who were born in this country. In America, Ladino and many of the Sephardi customs of the Balkans, have been much better maintained. This is due to the fact that America is largely a country of different nationalities, living in compact communities and adhering to their ancient customs and traditions.

At one function, I was taken aback when a young lady addressed me in such colloquial Ladino, that I have not heard it since I left Yugoslavia; and yet, she was born in the United States. She knew many of the proverbs and it was interesting to note that her Spanish was full of Turkish words.

Seeing the people in New Brunswick, I thought that I was in a corner of Salonika. Among these people, there was not so much nostalgia of the past, as a desire to recreate in their own New World for themselves and for their children, the life that existed in their homeland. This Community has an Ashkenazi Rabbi, who has faithfully learned all the melodies and who is trying his utmost to administer and to lead the Community according to the traditions of Sephardi Jewry. The Synagogue of this Congregation was consecrated only recently. It consists mainly of people who are small traders, whose parents worked hard in order to give their children an opportunity in the new country.

You may just as well ask how was it that this Community found itself in New Jersey. The answer is that when they arrived from Salonika at the beginning of this century, they went to places where there was work for them in the factories, and this was the time when new factories were springing up in that part of New Jersey. They worked in those factories for long hours. They did strenuous manual work in order to build for themselves and for their children a new life.

This is true of almost all the Balkan Sephardim, who are to be found today in Brooklyn, as well as in other parts of New York, such as Long Island and Manhattan.

It was also the opportunity for work that brought about the creation of a Sephardi Community in Rochester in the State of New York. This Community consists almost entirely of Sephardim who came from the small town of Monastir in Southern Serbia. When I heard the names of members of the community, I thought that I was back in my own native country. This Congregation is now almost entirely in the hands of younger people - people who were born in the United States but who invariably can speak the old Ladino language, and who proudly point out that their parents came from the little town in Southern Serbia.

This is not merely a story of success. It is a story of hard work - because I would not say that these people who have come from this small town have met with spectacular financial success. The benefits, the material benefits, which they are reaping today are the result of hard endeavour, of actual physical work - and again, it is greatly due to the sons of Monastir families, that there is today one of the finest Homes for the Aged in New York, which houses members of all Sephardi Congregations. This Home for the Aged, is built in a modern style, with all the modern facilities, and it is run more on the lines of a hotel. One of the most outstanding aspects of this Home for the Aged is that it has also a fully equipped hospital on the premises, so that residents when ill can be treated in the home itself.

To me, it was a special experience to address both the Committee and some of the members of the Home for the Aged. Once again, I was transferred to the atmosphere of the old Sephardi Congregations of the Balkans. Once again, when I spoke Ladino, I was understood. Once again, when I mentioned different proverbs and songs, I knew that I spoke to a people who knew about them and who understood them. And when I went to the Synagogue is New Lots in Brooklyn, it was a house of worship as existed in Salonika, in Monastir, and even in my own home town.

A few Synagogues in that neighborhood are the remnants of the old Synagogues built by the immigrants who came from the Balkans. The ministers and Rabbis who came with their flock still minister to these Congregations. Younger people have moved away - the more prosperous have gone to parts of New York in which the better-to-do live. But the older people, those who have not made such a success in their economic endeavours, remain nearer to the source which is still the well from which they draw. They have serenity and peace of mind in their humble and modest homes in New Lots, a place which was built on the model of their old homes.

But in my opinion, there is a danger to the spiritual life of these people. The Sephardim have always adhered to their own form of service. They have always shown respect for religious leadership, and they never liked to see changes brought about in their own religious life. There might have been reinterpretations as far as their ancient traditions were concerned. There might have been people who abandoned their ancient customs and even the Law of the Torah, but, on the whole, the Sephardi has always maintained, at least officially, standards of religious life which could always identify him with Torah Jewry, its life and its ideals.

Today, however, the ideology of the Conservative is slowly penetrating the Sephardi Congregations in New York. This, in my opinion, is a disaster. This is not a place in which one can talk about the ideology of Conservative Jewry, if a unified ideology exists; but, I feel that whatever the purpose of Conservative Judaism may be, it is strange and alien to the whole spirit of Sephardi Judaism and to the spirit of their historic development.

The Sephardim have always possessed a specific outlook, as far as the religious life of the Jew is concerned. This outlook was strictly in conformity with the Rabbinic decisions of the Sephardi spiritual leaders and with the traditions which became an integral part of Sephardi Jewish life. Many people believe that the Sephardim were always more lenient as far as religious concepts are concerned. This is not true. Very often, the Sephardim adopted stricter decisions that the Ashkenazim.

It is very little understood today that the main codifiers of Jewish law were all of Sephardi origin, like Maimonides, Alfasi and R. Joseph Caro. The way in which the Sephardi lived has never been questioned as to its religious correctness, by even the most extreme Ashkenazi Jew. It was always realised that the Sephardim had their own Rabbinic authorities, whom they faithfully followed - that they also developed a different outlook which they acquired in the course of their communal life, throughout the ages. The Ashkenazim always accepted these standards of their Sephardi brethren and never brought them into doubt as to their correctness from the Halakhic point of view.

I am a strong believer that the Sephardi outlook on religious life and the decisions of the Sephardi Rabbis throughout the ages, may be helpful to Israel in its endeavour to live according to the requirements of the Torah.

I think this is of special importance, especially today when the whole balance of influence of the Sephardim in Jewish life has greatly changed in favour of the Sephardim. Today, more than half of the Sephardi world live in Israel, where they are speedily becoming a majority, and Israel, by common consent, will become the source of main religious influence for world Jewry. Yet, Sephardi ideals are being compromised. The main reason is the lack of spiritual leadership among the Sephardim; also, the lack of a united Sephardi Community as we have it in England.

Many people do not realise that even Shearith Israel, the Spanish & Portuguese Congregation of New York, never had a Haham. They always had Ministers who, by tradition turned for Rabbinical guidance both to Amsterdam and to London, but, mainly to London. Also, the newer Communities which were established in America at the beginning of this century, did not bring with them any of the outstanding Rabbinical authorities, but, only Hazanim and people who could serve only the most basic needs of the Congregation. Unfortunately, the Communities never felt the necessity of establishing a central College or Yeshiva, which would provide them with the necessary Rabbinic and religious leadership. It is not surprising, therefore, that the Conservative have been, to some extent, successful in trying to capture the Sephardi Communities. One is only surprised that they have not been even more successful and that even more extreme ideologies have not taken hold in the Sephardi

Congregations of the New World. This has not happened and is due to the fact that the Sephardi has always had great reverence for his past and for his traditions and he is not very willing to turn away from the path which both his history and his religious authority has laid out for him.

In my opinion, there is still time to turn the Sephardi Communities of America on the road of true Sephardi life. This can only be achieved if they realise their destiny - if they even at this late hour, undertake to establish educational institutions in which young people will be prepared for the spiritual leadership of the Sephardi Congregations. The ordinary Sephardi in America is keen to follow the traditions, to live according to the requirements of Judaism as interpreted by Sephardi Rabbis, but he has very few people who can tell him how to achieve that. In consequence, he is bewildered, he is uncertain of himself and of the views which he feels that he has accepted as part of his life as a Jew. Deeper investigation brings him to express doubts about the correctness of his whole outlook. He knows that the Sephardim have always kept in touch with contemporary life, without in any way breaking the laws of the Torah. But, he does not know how he can achieve this in the frame of contemporary modern life.

This is a problem which does not only face the Sephardim, but also, the Ashkenazim - and not only in America, but throughout the world. But here, we are interested in the Sephardi world and in the way in which we could make the Sephardim, who according to some authorities, amount to nearly a quarter of a million souls in North America, more active in their support of Sephardi enterprises.

As I said before, I had the opportunity of visiting the Sephardi Congregations in Montreal and Toronto. In Montreal there is the ancient Congregation Shearith Israel, which, although now contains hardly any Sephardim, is still considered the premier Congregation in Canada. The President is Captain William Montefiore, but, except for him and a few other members, there are hardly any of the original families left in the Congregation.

It was a great pity indeed that when immigration began to come into Montreal from Iraq and from Egypt, that this ancient Sephardi Congregation did not take advantage of these immigrants and integrate them with their own Congregation. I think the difficulty arose because the Spanish & Portuguese Congregation Shearith Israel did not have the spiritual leadership to deal with this new challenge. Thus, they were not able to undertake the absorption of the new immigrants who possessed a different outlook from their own and also, possessed a Minhag which was somewhat different.

These immigrants from Iraq and from Egypt, as well as from North Africa, for many years now have held their Services in a hall of the Ashkenazi Synagogue called Young Israel. The members of Young Israel, were, indeed, hospitable to these people and allowed them to occupy their premises, not only on ordinary Sabbaths, but, also, on Festivals and even on the High Holy Days. This new Sephardi Congregation, however, has now increased greatly and now has more than a thousand members. For that reason, it had to decide to build a Synagogue of its own and to try and bring about a closer union among all the Sephardim who are outside the Spanish and Portuguese Congregation.

When I was in Montreal some years ago, I addressed this new Congregation and I was very impressed that among them there were people who were very keen to lead the Congregation and to bring about the establishment of a new Sephardi life in Montreal. At the same time, there were many people in the Spanish & Portuguese Congregation who felt that something ought to be done to bring about the union between these two Sephardi Congregations. This idea, however, did not find any realisation and some time ago, it was decided by the leaders of the new Sephardi Congregation, to build a Synagogue of their own. And it was in order to launch the appeal for the building of this new Synagogue that they asked me to come and address their Congregation. I was only too glad to help them and so I travelled to Montreal in order to meet once again the leaders of this new group of Sephardim, to see their problems and to see in which way we from London, could help them. From the very beginning, this Congregation expressed its willingness to come under the auspices of the Office of the Haham and have always turned to us with their problems, as well as for guidance. When I returned to New York, I was very pleasantly surprised to hear that finally the approach has been made by the Spanish & Portuguese Congregation to this new Sephardi Congregation, with a view to amalgamating these two Sephardi groups.

Apparently, the leaders of the Spanish and Portuguese Synagogue felt that it would be a pity to allow this new group of Sephardim who are very active in every way, to create a Congregation of their own. As the Spanish and Portuguese Synagogue has almost all its seats occupied, they offered that this new group could use their hall for all the Festivals, and when suitable, they could join the Spanish and Portuguese Congregation in worship, and the hope was expressed that sooner or later this new Sephardi group, as represented by their leaders, would become an integral part of a larger Sephardi Community in Montreal.

I immediately expressed my view that this would be a very good plan, provided the Sephardi traditions of this new group, were safeguarded. I suggested that some conditions should be put to the leaders of Shearith Israel, and if accepted, that this temporary arrangement should be agreed upon and that every effort should be made in order to create a larger Sephardi Congregation. I was, nevertheless, able to address a large Congregation of Sephardim in Montreal, and although I did not make an appeal for the building of a new Synagogue, I did offer them all our help as far as possible and told them that they should explore the new possibilities, and only if amalgamation proved impossible, because it would damage the Orthodox and the Sephardi character of the new Sephardi group, should they think of building a Synagogue of their own and, thereby, finally deciding to create a new Sephardi Congregation.

From the latest information, however, I gather that the negotiations, so far, have been very successful and that already a group of the new Sephardim, if I may call them so, have joined Shearith Israel. Every hope is expressed that the new arrangement will work out satisfactorily. I have no doubt that such an arrangement will be not only for the benefit of the new Sephardi group, but, also, for Shearith Israel. This is especially of importance when we bear in mind that now Montreal is not the only Sephardi centre in Canada. A new Sephardi centre was created in Toronto some years ago by a group of immigrants who came mainly from North Africa, especially from Morocco. Again, at the invitation of this group, I went to visit the Sephardi Community of Toronto, which, at the time, consisted of two distinct groups. My aim was to bring these two sections together, in order that they should be able to work more constructively.

I was also asked by the general Community in Toronto to address them and this was one of the largest groups that I addressed during my last day there. There were between 350 - 400 people present and I spoke on the importance of Sephardi survival for World Jewry. I found that in Toronto, like in all other places, people were not aware of the Sephardi Communities which existed in many parts of the world, of their problems and also of their potentialities. Thus, it is not generally known that today, the Sephardim constitute a majority in the Land of Israel and that this fact, as well as the new immigration of Sephardim into France, has given the Sephardim a new advantage and made it possible for them to influence the destinies of Jewry in general, especially from the spiritual point of view.

As I said, my main goal was to try to achieve the amalgamation of two Sephardi groups, which existed in Toronto. Both of them were newcomers and their traditions were almost the same. But there were some differences - I would not call them personal, but, I would call them communal, because, one group originated from Tangiers and the other from Casablanca. The antagonism between these two groups became quite sharp, and I had meetings with the leaders of the two Congregations for about two days. At last, I was joined by one of the most prominent Rabbis in Toronto, and we were able to bring about some reconciliation. Rabbi Wurzburger, the Rabbi who showed great interest in the Sephardim in Toronto, undertook to look after their welfare and to see that the suggestions which I laid down could be carried out. On my return to New York, I was 'phoned on two or three occasions by the leaders of these groups and asked to advise them.

At last I am glad to say that they have decided to join forces and to create one Sephardi community in Toronto. This Community now will number over four hundred members and it will be an additional strength to the Sephardim of Canada.

You will notice that I have spoken mainly about the organisation of the Sephardim in Canada. They do not possess any spiritual leadership. They brought with them, as American Jewry did at the beginning of this century, some of their Hazanim, who are helping them with their services. But in the New World and in the new conditions, these people are not proving at all adequate. Ashkenazi Ministers, even if they are available, are not always the most suitable people to lead these Congregations. In addition, the younger people of these Communities, both in America and in Canada, have gone to Ashkenazi Yeshivot. After all, these Yeshivot have their own ancient traditions.

These traditions are not, however, in keeping always with the Sephardi outlook. We know that Sephardi Rabbis very often came to different decisions from their Ashkenazi colleagues. We know that they possessed different outlooks, the result of their different history and of different influences which formed their communal and religious life. To preserve the Sephardi traditions and outlook is not to create a new division between Sephardim and Ashkenazim, but, on the contrary, to preserve a tradition and an attitude which is part and parcel of Jewish life and which can in the long run be only a strengthening element in trying to revive Judaism among the Jewish masses.

I am quite convinced that the spirit of the Sephardi Rabbinate who have always shown courage and willingness to deal with contemporary problems and to face changes which have taken place in the world, will be of great benefit to bring about greater loyalty of the Jewish masses to the Torah. For that reason, I feel that the time has come for the better organized Sephardi Communities, and that especially goes for our Congregations in England and in the Commonwealth, to try and establish a strong Sephardi Rabbinate which could exert its influence on Sephardi Jewry, which would help the Sephardim in Israel to strengthen their religious life and create more Rabbinic authorities with true Sephardi traditions.

Having seen what has happened to many Communities in America, having seen what is happening in France and Canada, I believe that we have no right to show any complacency. We must try to deal with these problems if we are to preserve the Sephardi traditions, not for its own sake, but because it is a duty which we owe to Jewry itself.

REPENTANCE

Sermon delivered at the Lauderdale Road Synagogue, London, September 24, 1965.

In today's Parasha we are told that before his death, Moses called all the Children of Israel and said unto them, "All of you stand today before the Lord your God." The Midrash asks: why was it necessary to say "all of you". That would be quite understood. The emphasis on "all" is, say our sages, because not only the Children of Israel living at that time were present but also the souls to be born in the future. We always must try and understand the meaning of Midrash, and it is interesting in this case to examine the message that the Midrash wanted to convey to us. The lesson which was given by Moses to the Children of Israel at that time was of such importance that all the Children of Israel would have to learn it in different historical periods and in different generations. The message was, first of all, of repentance; and secondly of the eternity of the people of Israel. Moses prophesied that the Children of Israel would turn away from their God and His Law, but that they would also return to it. Repentance was not something which depended on God, but on man himself. This concept of repentance would insure the eternity of the Jewish people, because they would not survive on account of their might or on account of their power, but because of their spiritual values. The Jewish People had to adhere to the tenets of the Torah and the values which were enunciated in order to fulfill its task.

This role which the Jewish People took upon themselves was not of the kind that could be either accepted or neglected. It was part of our very existence, part of our life. Without it, we are not the people of God or even the people of Israel. Our national qualities are not those of other nations. Moses tells the people that they have become a nation, and he tells them so before entering the Promised Land. As a rule, a nation becomes possessed of its national qualities only when it obtains possession of its country. With us, it was different. We became a nation before coming into the Promised Land. It was emphasized that territorial possession was not one of the necessary qualities for our nationhood as is the case with other peoples. Even after the destruction of the Land of Israel, we retained our qualities as a distinct people. Although dispersed throughout the world, we were able to wield an influence out of proportion to our numbers because we adhered in our communities to the concept of those values of discipline, or understanding and of love and fear of God.

In this way, the unity of the Jewish people was created not merely in one period of time, but throughout the ages. This task bound one generation to another up to the generation of Moses when we were promised eternal existence as long as we understood the idea of repentance and of obedience to our Lord. Today perhaps it is right that we should emphasize the Jewish concept of repentance which means not merely to God but to improve relations with our fellow Jew and fellow man; to bring peace where there is strife; to bring comfort where there is pain.

This idea of repentance requires, first of all, return to the study and understanding of our heritage. Our Communities must become training places where a younger and older generation will be prepared for a life of pioneering in the sphere of the spiritual development of the world. In a world where there may be frustration, we must remain full of hope; in a world of pessimism, we must be optimistic. We know that if we are able to influence the course of human history, then there will be a sure return to God and the values which He proclaimed in His Torah. For that reason, it is all too important that we should not destroy our link between generations. There must not be any progressive disintegration in our spirit.

This is one of the greatest problems facing us today when many of us live in countries where we may feel comparatively safe from persecution and even economic oppression. It is perhaps right that we should look back to previous generations and see whether we are now straining the link. We often hear people say, "My parents were very religious. They were very learned. Unfortunately, I had to abandon many of the ideas that they had as regards religion and as regards the Jewish Law." The result is that even children of Rabbis know very little about the Jewish Law and grandchildren are very often even unable to read Hebrew. This is bringing about the full break with the past generations and the neglect of the very task which is the essence of our existence.

In this context return means, first of all, return to the study of our heritage, to the understanding of our Law; without it there cannot be true repentance. In our modern world, we must go back to that contact which we always maintained with previous generations. We need a spring of inspiration. We need a strengthening influence.

Today as we are about to enter the solemn season of penitential days, let us ask ourselves, everyone of us: have we ourselves broken in any way the link with our past? Have we contributed towards the disintegration of the Jewish spirit? Are our children more ignorant of the Law than our parents were? Are our children as faithful to the tenets of the Torah as our parents were? If the answer is negative, then surely the fault lies with us. We must turn and mend our ways by creating possibilities for the spiritual regeneration of our youth.

RAISING OUR RELIGIOUS LEVEL

Sermon delivered at Congregation Shearith Israel, the Spanish and Portuguese Synagogue of New York City, January 7, 1967.

In today's Parashah we are told that the children of Israel refused to pay heed to the message of freedom which Moses brought unto them because of "impatience of spirit and hard work." The literal translation of *kotzer ruah* is "shortness of spirit" or rather "lack of spirit." *Abodah kashah,* "hard work" means, according to the interpretation of our sages, work that brings frustration, which is tiring for the body and which gives no elevation to the soul. Hard work, when undertaken for the sake of achieving a certain aim can prove inspiring, but when such an aim is lacking in our endeavors, they then become a source of demoralization. The children of Israel in Egypt could not understand the meaning of the forthcoming redemption as announced by Moses because they had lost the spirit which had animated the undertakings of their forefathers. They were without courage, without faith, and this situation was aggravated by the fact that they had to do work under cruel conditions and under aimless pressure which did not give them any sense of achievement. The lack of response on the part of the people and their attitude made Moses realize that his people would have to change their outlook if they were to become worthy of divine guidance. It was for that reason that a miraculous redemption became necessary. Through the miracles in Egypt, the children of Israel began to regain their trust in God and the feeling that the Almighty had not abandoned them. This is indicated by the fact that immediately after stating that the children of Israel did not listen to Moses because of impatience of spirit and hard work, the Torah relates the command of the Almighty to Moses: "Go and speak to Pharaoh." Pharoah was destined to become the target of the miraculous manifestations which were to bring about the redemption of the Children of Israel from Egypt.

Our own world is also suffering from lack of spirit and from uninspiring endeavors, which may provide man with his daily bread, but the Torah tells us that man does not live by bread alone. The impatience of spirit is evident today in communal, national and international spheres. It is this impatience of spirit that is giving rise to juvenile delinquency, to widespread crime, and even to world unrest and threat of suicidal conflict. In consequence, any enterprise undertaken becomes a burden rather than the realization of an ideal. Can we, with these unhelpful qualities, hope to deal with the problems which we face in this new age, which in spite of all difficulties offers great opportunities if we know how to grasp them with faith and courage? It is because of impatience of spirit and hard work without real purpose that once again man cannot hear the words of his God and understand the message promising his own redemption.

New ideas, new concepts and new outlooks are required from man if he is to meet the demands of the present age. The Almighty realized that such a change was necessary at a time when the Children of Israel were standing at the threshold of a new era when they were about to become, from a tribe loosely bound by family ties, a fully fledged nation, struggling for its freedom and deciding on its fate. For that reason He appeared to Moses and to his generation under His own personal Name with His attributes of justice and mercy, while to the fathers of the family and of the tribe, to Abraham, Isaac and Jacob, He appeared as God Almighty, the God who inspires man with His might and renews nature with His power. The Children of Israel through Moses were called upon to ponder more deeply upon the concept of deity and to understand its manifestations in the manifold aspects of human life. This change, however, did not come either automatically or mechanically. While the Almighty was ready to reveal Himself more fully to a generation which had to change the very course of human history, He also required a response by this nation in terms of those changes. He, in His mercy, was now asking for individual initiative. The Children of Israel were no longer to achieve their aims merely through the intervention of God, but through their initiative and even independent action. They had to invite this divine intervention and participation in their lives, actions, and in the forming of their destinies.

To Moses, God did not appear as He had done to the first fathers, to Abraham, Isaac and Jacob. To them He appeared on His own initiative because He knew that they were the only worthy people through whom He could reveal Himself to all humanity. To Moses, however, He appeared only after Moses had undergone certain spiritual processes. Our sages represent Moses after he had run away from Pharaoh as meditating in the desert on the destinies of his people, trying to discover the purpose of their suffering in the Egyptian bondage, and also attempting to find out the purpose of human existence. It was only through this mental and spiritual effort that Moses began to understand that behind the history of his people stood the Almighty as the guiding force of all humanity. He also began to understand that God did not have to reveal Himself openly to the eye of man, but that man could seek Him in all the aspects of his spiritual life and physical existence, as well as in the life of every individual human being. Hand in hand with this turning point in the history of the people of Israel, and indeed of all humanity, there came a new recognition of the power as well as of the influence of God, and this recognition was inaugurated by Moses. Moses taught his contemporaries to seek their God and find Him, not only in the annals of history or in the majesty of nature, but above all in the recesses of their own souls. To neglect this search for God would mean to jeopardize man's existence as a civilized being. Today we need to search for new ways leading to the solution of many and perplexing problems facing us as individuals and as members of mankind. But with this search for new ways must go also the search for God. We shall not cause a new era to dawn upon us by defying religious values which alone can give us strength of spirit and true purpose in our everyday undertakings. In creating new values and even in building a new culture, we must not abandon our faith, we must not neglect our prayers. A new civilization can prove effective and bring new hope to man only if it is to be inspired by the spirit of the Eternal Creator.

We read in today's Parashah that Aaron threw his staff which turned into a serpent as the Almighty promised that would happen. Pharaoh's magicians showed themselves capable of performing the same phenomenon, but the staff of Aaron swallowed their staffs. This is interpreted by a rabbi as the basic difference between the Jewish and non-Jewish concepts of civilization. The staff is the symbol of guidance, the symbol of orderly society. Even in times of crisis, as when the two Temples were destroyed, we have been able to seek and find solutions to our difficulties because our influence had grown from the recognition of the Almighty as an ever present force in our lives and in all undertakings. Great crisis, however, in other civilizations brought about their disintegration, as was the case with Greece and Rome. They lacked that spirit with which God through His Torah inspires our thoughts, our endeavors and above all our creative efforts.

The House of Israel must not merely adhere to its concept of civilization, which has stood the test of time, but it must teach it to its neighbors and fellow men if our aim is to make our epoch the dawn of a new era. If parents and children are to resume the control of conditions rather than being governed by them, if fear is to be eliminated from their hearts, this is not merely a challenge which we may accept or reject, but a duty which we dare neglect only at the risk of the knowledge which our generation has accumulated becoming a serpent, destroying everything that is truly alive within ourselves instead of being a staff and a guide to a better and fuller life. This is a duty which imposes itself on every congregation of Israel throughout the world. This is not a new challenge to this ancient congregation which has not only been the founder of the American Jewish community, but which initiated the influence of Judaism on the social and cultural development of this freedom-loving and powerful country of the United States, whose future and hopes are bound up with the destiny of the free world. Once again this congregation and especially the younger generation is called upon to proclaim the message of God as its founders did centuries ago, a message of faith which will fortify those who are of weak spirit and elevate those who labor to no purpose. In fulfilling this today, the congregation must bear in mind the saying of our Rabbis that higher standards apply to matters which concern sanctity. Everything that we do for the congregation or on behalf of the congregation comes within the area of sanctity. It is therefore necessary to establish and approach our task with humility and yet with determination, with piety and yet with resolution. In order to achieve this we must have teachers who will guide the young and inspire the old; who will make an endeavor to resolve the doubts of the young and save them from indifference, and to alleviate the concern of the old and guide them away from depressing fatalism. Let us also remember that our influence will be in keeping with the measure that we are able to revive the ancient traditions and act according to their spirit and demands.

May the young and the old of Shearith Israel in the years to come devote themselves to the sacred task of bringing to the House of Israel and to our faith a new spirit inspired by the past, a new strength fortified by the future, and hope to our neighbors.

With this visit comes to an end the formal arrangement which was made three years ago between the Congregations of Sha'ar Hashamayim in London and Shearith Israel. During this time I was honored to have been given the opportunity to identify myself with the destinies of this ancient Kahal. I am grateful to the Parnas, to the Trustees, and indeed to all the Congregation for their confidence, kindness and, above all, for their friendship. This friendship I value greatly as it transcends any official arrangements. I want to express my gratitude to the Rabbi Emeritus and to my colleagues in the active rabbinate, who have given me their cooperation and their friendship. My prayer shall always be to the Almighty to guide and inspire the children of this ancient and sacred remnant of Israel - Shearith Israel.

REPORT OF THE HAHAM FOR THE YEAR 1970/71

Montefiore College

The Haham continues to take an active part in the work of the College and has been consulted extensively on the proposed future plans of this educational establishment.

World Sephardi Federation

The Haham has taken a great interest in the work of the World Sephardi Federation, giving an address to the European Conference of the Sephardi Federation in Amsterdam in January, 1971 and aiding in the appeal for Israel. He has met many people in connection with this organisation in order to promote the welfare of Sephardim in the world.

The Associated Sephardi Congregations

The Haham has visited Holland Park, Bevis Marks and the Lincoln Institute Synagogues as well as the Manchester Synagogues. He has officiated at a number of weddings and funerals.

The Haham has attended meetings of the committees set up to organise the building of the new complex in Wembley. He has acted in an advisory capacity at all stages of the development of the plans for the new Beth Holim, Montefiore College and synagogue.

General

The Haham continues to be continually consulted on Rabbinic matters, and people avail themselves of the opportunity to speak to him on personal matters. He has kept in touch with a number of Committees who do much work for Israel, such as the J.P.A. and the Torah Department of the Jewish Agency; to name but a few of the bodies that the Haham takes a particular interest in.

The Haham visited Cambridge University where he gave a lecture and has also lectured at Jews' College. During the course of the year the Haham has been to Israel where he was asked to deliver a lecture on the problems of education in the Diaspora to the Jewish Agency Actions Committee. He has been especially invited to attend the Zionist Congress as an individual by the Chairman of the Jewish Agency. He attended a conference in Brussels where he addressed the meeting on Russian Jewry.

During the course of the year Dr. and Mrs. Gaon have entertained 1250 people in their home.

Office

The Haham has had over 700 appointments during the year and on some days had up to 60 telephone calls. He has been helped in the office by his two Rabbinic assistants. Owing to the indisposition of the Haham's secretary, Mr. Morpurgo was called out of retirement to help with the work in the office, and the Haham wishes to thank him for so willingly coming to his aid.

MESSAGE FOR PASSOVER, 1979

Nations are inclined to celebrate their freedom by emphasizing their physical redemption from the subjugation of an enemy. They do not always give importance to the spiritual salvation that comes with national independence.

This attitude is often apparent even among our people. We celebrate the festival of Passover as "Zeman Herutenu", the time of our redemption. This name conveys to many of us merely the idea of the physical redemption of our people from the Egyptian bondage. We do not pay sufficient attention to the words of our sages that not only those who suffered under the Egyptian yoke were saved, but all future generations of our people. The nation, while captive in Egypt, was in danger of being entirely overwhelmed because they were becoming ignorant of the teachings which had been imparted to them by Jacob and his sons. The fact that they had accepted so many of the customs and the ways of life of the Egyptians became evident already in the history of our people and, indeed, throughout the whole period of the First Temple.

Today, we are almost always stirred and united when we become aware of the persecution or oppression of our people in any part of the world. On such occasions, the Jewish communities show with great generosity of spirit and of self-sacrifice, that we are all one people. We do not show much concern for those communities which are being almost annihilated by assimilation and complete alienation from Judaism.

Recently, a convention of Sephardi Rabbis of North and South America, took place in New York under the auspices of the World Sephardi Federation and Yeshiva University. All of us who were present at these meetings were deeply moved by the statements of the Rabbis from South America, that in their communities young Jews and Jewesses are becoming assimilated to such an extent, that in many cases they abandon their heritage of their faith. In some places, ninety percent of the young people are lost to Jewry. Similar situations, it was reported, prevailed also in some communities of North America. There was a desperate plea for more trained teachers and Rabbis in these communities which are threatened with extinction. How many of us ever think of the fact that in many communities, out of one hundred children born, only perhaps ten will remain Jews? Many of us are justly moved to help those of our brethren who are persecuted, but what are we doing in order to produce at least a number of spiritual leaders and teachers who will be able to arrest this tragic process which may prove even more disastrous to our future than the physical enemy.

We Sephardim in this country should make our own contribution to the solution of this great problem. This effort, if it is to be constructive, will require a united Sephardic community which will take its responsibilities for our educational institutions such as Montifiore College seriously. Passover teaches us that the physical redemption from Egypt is significant in the first place because it saved our people from the pagan influences of that land. Today, we must also save our people, not only those who are physically persecuted, but those whose very existence is threatened by assimilation and spiritual alienation.

ISRAEL AND SPAIN

Address to the World Sephardi Federation on the occasion of the establishment of diplomatic relations between Spain and Israel, 1986.

The establishment of diplomatic relations between Spain and Israel is the result of a process and endeavor in which the World Sephardi Federation (WSF) took a considerable part. The World Sephardi Federation's role in this development was encouraged by the Jewish Agency's Department of Foreign Affairs under the leadership of the late Mr. Meir Grossman.

Spain had been very disappointed with Israel's 1950 vote in the United Nations against the admission of Spain. Although the Spanish government and General Franco himself were offended by Israel's attitude, this did not result, as some people feared, in hostile measures against the Jews of Spain.[1] It was thought at the time by some members of the Jewish Agency that the World Sephardi Federation would be the most suitable body to establish the basis for a better understanding between Spain and Israel. In 1958 the Spanish authorities gave permission for the opening of a branch of the WSF in Madrid. Mr. Moses Behar, an Israeli originally from the Argentine, was sent by the WSF to Madrid to be in charge of this new organization. His task was to create closer relations between Spain and world Jewry by emphasizing their common cultural heritage. Mr. Behar worked energetically and soon established contact with the Jewish community in Spain as well as with the Spanish cultural and political leadership. He was greatly assisted in these efforts by Mr. Max Mazin, the president of the Jewish Communities in Spain, which was established in 1956, changed its name to the

Sephardic Federation of Spain, thus becoming a branch of the WSF.

The first and most significant result of the activities of the WSF in Spain was the exhibition of Sephardi culture in the central library of Madrid in 1959. The exhibition was opened by Sr. Jesus Ruvio Garcia Mina, who was then Minister of Culture. I was a witness to a very interesting interlude while walking with Mr. Ruvio and others to the main hall of the library where the opening ceremony was to be held. A man who I understood later was a high official of the Spanish Foreign Ministry approached Mr. Ruvio and told him that the Foreign Minister was anxious that Mr. Ruvio should not say anything that would offend the Arab states who were carefully watching the proceedings. Mr. Ruvio's reply was very determined. He was not ready to accept any messages from the Foreign Minister as he had already cleared his speech with the Generalissimo. In fact, he referred in most valedictory terms to the contribution of the Sephardim to Spanish culture and emphasized the close links between Spain and the Sephardi communities, which were never broken. Mr. Ruvio further stated his hopes that the exhibition would cement the relationship between the two nations, and brought greetings from General Franco. I followed him in the program, and brought greetings from the World Sephardi Federation. I pointed out that the Sephardim considered the exhibition as the first step toward closer understanding, not only between the Sephardim and Spain, but also between Spain and world Jewry which is no longer stateless.

Lectures were delivered on different aspects of Judeo-Spanish relations by prominent Jewish and Spanish scholars during the opening week of the exhibition. They were extremely well attended and the exhibition was visited by many people not only from Madrid, but from the whole of Spain. This exhibition made the Spanish public aware of the part the Jews played in the history of Spain, and was indeed a first step toward closer relations between world Jewry and Spain.

The exhibition of Sephardi culture greatly influenced Spanish public opinion and soon other significant events followed. In 1964 the synagogue of Shemuel Halevi, for a long time used as a church, was made a Sephardi museum by order of General Franco. In the same order, the composition of the executive committee of the museum was stated. It included the president of the Jewish community in Madrid as well as representatives of the WSF. This order in effect provided indirect but official recognition of the Jewish communal organization in Spain and established a relationship between the world Jewish community and the government of Spain.

In March of 1968, the Madrid community laid the cornerstone for the first synagogue to be officially built in Madrid since the expulsion. The scroll which was buried in the foundation of the synagogue was signed by Mr. Mazin, members of the committee, and myself on behalf of the WSF. The Jewish Chronicle, reporting this ceremony, wrote: "For the stone laying, Dr. Gaon composed a special prayer in Hebrew, which he recited. The Spanish translation of this prayer was read by Rabbi B. Garzon, headmaster of the Jewish school of Madrid. The Spanish and Portuguese Congregation of London was represented by Mr. J. O'Hana, who also represented the WSF."

On December 16 of the same year, all Jewry of Spain celebrated the inauguration of the Synagogue in Madrid. The impressive ceremony was attended by many government and civic dignitaries. The chief Rabbi of Argentina and I took part in the procession, as did the recently installed rabbi of Madrid, Baruch Garzon Serfaty. It was one of the most moving moments in my life when I greeted assembled congregation in Judeo-Spanish. Use of this language linked the year 1492, the year of the expulsion from Spain, with 1968, when once again an official Jewish synagogue arose on the soil of Spain. On the 14th of December, two days before the inauguration, this link was emphasized by an order from the Minister of Justice annulling the edict of expulsion of Ferdinand and Isabella. The first to hear this news was Mr. Samuel Toledano, vice president of the Madrid Jewish community, who had gone to the Ministry of Justice to obtain a permit for the opening of the synagogue. Astoundingly, it was to Rabbi Daniel Toledano, the chief rabbi of Spain at the time of the expulsion, that the order of expulsion had been delivered. The day the order was rescinded will always remain indelibly engraved in my mind. All present felt that the intervention of the Almighty in history had once again fully manifested itself. Spain had fully acknowledged the link binding it to its former Jewish citizens.

In the 1960's many Jews from Morocco attempted to leave that country, but the Moroccan government had greatly restricted their movement, making emigration very difficult. They were, however, able to cross from Morocco into Melilla and Ceuta, the Spanish enclaves in North Africa. From there, Spanish boats transferred them to Gibralter and Marseilles, and hence they were flown to Israel. In Gibralter, a special camp was opened to temporarily house these refugees.

These arrangements were made possible through the good will of General Franco. This attitude of Franco was all the more remarkable when one bears in mind that at that time Franco was laying strong claim to Gibralter. As one would expect, the Arab states in general and the Moroccans in particular were pressuring Franco to put an end to this traffic. It was decided, therefore, that a delegation consisting of the WSF and Spanish scholars should see General Franco, on the surface to acquaint him with their plans for the establishment in Madrid of an Institute for Jewish-Spanish Culture but, more importantly, to create an opportunity to thank Spain and the General for the help being given to the Jewish people. The Jewish chronicle of the 8th of July, 1960, reported that General Franco, the head of the Spanish government, had received, the previous Wednesday, a delegation which included Denzil Montefiore, president of the WSF, and Mrs. Montefiore; the Haham Dr. Solomon Gaon; Mr. Max Mazin, president of the Madrid Jewish community; Perez Castro, dean of the Madrid University; and Don Blaz Penar, director of the Institute of Spanish Culture.

At the end of the meeting, all those present felt that General Franco would not give in to Arab pressure, but would continue to facilitate the exodus of the Jews from Morocco.

It is interesting to compare Franco's resistance to Arab pressure in this instance with the extent of Arab influence over the Spanish government in December 1976. At that time "the European branch of the World Jewish Congress that convened in Madrid was due to be greeted by the Deputy Minister of Justice on behalf of the government, and the delegation from the conference was scheduled to be received by the King. The very fact that the conference was taking place aroused the ire of the Arab embassies in Spain. The Spanish authorities bowed to pressure and cancelled their participation in this event."[3]

In the 1960's there was another occasion when Spain was helpful to the Jewish people. During the Six-Day War, the Spanish government was approached by the WSF and other Jewish institutions to intervene on behalf of the Jews in Egypt, many of whom had been placed in concentration camps by then Egyptian President Nasser. These Jews were being maltreated and tortured. The president of the WSF, together with Mr. Michael Marchant and myself, met in London on several occasions with the Spanish Ambassador and his assistants to make them aware of the suffering of Egyptian Jews. We were always met with understanding and sympathy on their part. They made it quite clear to us that they were ready to grant passports, not only to the Sephardim, but also to the Ashkenazim, in order to facilitate their exodus from Egypt. In fact, Spain granted passports to 615 families - more than 1,500 people - thus ending their suffering. Frederico Ysart, in his book, *España y los Judios,* writes: "The Spanish Ambassador in London received letters of thanks from Mr. Denzil Montefiore, the President of the WSF, and from Dr. Solomon Gaon, the Rabbi of the community, on the 27th and 29th of December 1967. Dr. Gaon wrote 'many of us have admired the way in which the Spanish authorities have helped our brethren during the last war, and also, afterwards. We are very conscious of the great assistance which the Spanish government is extending to our people in many parts of the world.'"[4] This action by Spain manifested once again the regard that Spain had for the Jewish nation, and many considered this as a further sign that the Spanish government was about to establish diplomatic relations with Israel.

It was not only the leaders of the intellectual class, like Canteras Burgos and Perez Castro, who identified themselves with Jewry and Israel, but also many prominent members of the Catholic clergy. In 1961 the Amistad Judeo-Christiana (Judeo-Christian Fraternity) was established. The Bishop of Madrid supported the Amistad and approved its constitution, as did the civil authorities. I attended the inaugural meeting of the Amistad and a number of subsequent meetings on behalf of the WSF. In order to foster the study of Judaism, Father Vincent Serrano, a great friend of the Jews and Israel, established the Center for Studies in Judaism which later became the Center for Christian-Jewish

Studies. Seminars on Judaism organized by this institution were mainly intended to help Catholic priests obtain a deeper understanding of Judaism and of the State of Israel. As a consequence, a considerable number of Spanish clergy became active in encouraging closer relations between Spain and Israel.

There were hopes that after Franco's death, King Juan Carlos would be able to influence his government to change its policy toward Israel. These hopes were strengthened when a delegation of the WSF was received by the King on February 27, 1976. This delegation consisted of Mr. Nessim Gaon, president of the WSF, and other representatives of the WSF. His Majesty, the King received us most cordially, and we received a clear impression that he was very anxious to establish relations with Israel as soon as possible. The ministers and members of the Royal household present seemed to share this view.

Years, however, elapsed before Israel and Spain established normal diplomatic relations. This long delay was undoubtedly due to the fact that the Spanish government considered itself dependent on the Arab states which controlled the supply of oil to Spain.[5]

As can be seen from the above, it is clear that the establishment of diplomatic relations between Spain and Israel was not a smooth process, but rather one that was built by perseverance and patience over the course of years, frequently with the help of the World Sephardi Federation. Looking back over the history of this process, it is gratifying to all involved to see the fruits of their labors in the current friendship between the two countries.

NOTES

1. Avni, Haim. *Spain, the Jews, and Franco* (Philadelphia: The Jewish Publication Society of America, 1982), p. 209.
2. *Ibid.,* p. 210.
3. *Ib*id,. p. 210
4. Ysart, Frederico, *España y los Judios en la Segunda Guerra Mundial (*Barcelona: Dopesa, 1973), p. 156.
5. *Spain, the Jews, and Franco,* loc. cit.

THE PRESENT CONDITION OF SEPHARDI LIFE

*An address presented to the convention
of the American Sephardi Federation, Fall, 1990.*

It is difficult to prophesy as to what will happen in the next years because life today is changing swiftly and very often we have no time to consider the essential reasons for those changes.

Recently the Memorial Foundation asked some scholars to write on Jewry and Israel in the 21st century. Four scholars gave their views and although these views were written from different points of view, all seem to agree that the challenges in the new millennium will be severe and will be concerned with Jewish spiritual and even perhaps physical survival. They all considered and emphasized the centrality of Israel in finding solutions for these problems. The following points were emphasized:

1) The survival of our people will take two forms, the communities in the Diaspora and in the State of Israel.
2) Jewish survival will require much effort, and excellent leadership.
3) Each group of Jews must make its contribution to a new Jewish outlook and culture.
4) Jewish education must play an important part in this struggle for survival.

I am not going to speak about the Sephardim in the 21st century but only in the year to come; but I believe that these views have a bearing on Sephardi life and the tasks of the WSF and the local Sephardi federations. We must, first of all, state that our religious outlook was always guided by loyalty and respect for the Torah, even if not all our people were always observant. The Holy Land was always at the center of our religious upbringing and outlook. This attitude must be preserved if we are to play a decisive part in the preservation of our people. Pluralism may be allowed and considered only within these lines. We Sephardim never made a philosophy of breaking the laws of the Torah.

Let us start with the role of leadership. We Sephardim have strongly adhered to the concept of Kehila, community. The community and the family were the basis of our existence. Our communal leaders, rabbinic or lay, always made every effort to maintain integrity in our communal life and sanctity in our family life. Samuel Heilman, one of the four scholars who gave his views about the future of Jewry, says: No one who has observed the extent to which the Jews have entered into the mainstream of society can be oblivious of the fact that one of the signs of this integration has been intermarriage. In America and throughout much of Europe many congregations include families in which one or more members are not Jews. In the USA, about one in four marriages of Jews are with non-Jewish partners. The figures are not significantly different in Europe. According to Prof. Heilman, intermarriage will be part of life in the next century. Attitudes towards it are also likely to change; the future will be one in which intermarriage is a far more acceptable option for Jews. A Jewish family will not necessarily, therefore, be composed only of Jews. There is already evidence of the assimilationist attitude in this regard as demonstrated in the views of Reform and Reconstructionist movements which have recognized the Jewishness of offspring from the marriages where only the father is a Jew. The exclusive character of Jewish life will undeniably diminish in the next generation. For Sephardim who always based our existence and life on purity of the family, this prognostication of Prof. Heilman is, to say the least, frightening. Here our rabbis and teachers have a special task to fulfill. I am not one of those who believes that so-called western values are in every respect superior to those held by non-western people. All of us who had the privilege of knowing and living in Sephardi families, be it in the Balkans, be it in the Far or Middle East, have come to appreciate the family relations where husband and wife lived in terms of mutual equality even if the master of the house was called 'señor'. This is not a call to go back to what some would call primitive times; but we must examine the benefits that society derived from the influence of the family in which there was harmony among its members, the family that was characteristic of Sephardi concept and life.

I think that all those who were present at the meeting of the Sephardi Federation in June must have been impressed by the words of Mr. Hassid who represents the 200,000 Iranian Jews in Israel. He concluded his speech to the assembly with these words: Iranian Jewry is scattered through all the world, we are constantly losing more Jews, because of intermarriage which is assuming dangerous proportions in Europe and in USA. We would like to send emissaries to the Diaspora in order to educate the Jews to come to Israel, we want to educate them to understand Jewish and Zionist values. Hassid and his friends are very concerned about the assimilation that is taking place among Jewry, and above all among Eastern Jewry, the Sephardim, and among them the Iranians. I am mentioning the question of families because this is not a case which concerns only us Sephardim, but also world Jewry. Some years ago the Memorial Foundation realized that there are, in America especially, many people who are not affiliated to communities or to any associations dealing with Judaism. They established what were called programs for Jewish Affiliations. They arranged to send specialists to communities where the affiliation of Jews to Jewish institutions was very weak and where the families showed little loyalty to Judaism. These experts were able to contact different families in these places and persuade them to join in an attempt to revive the Jewish family life and to rejuvenate Judaism among different unaffiliated Jewish people. They have been, on the whole, very successful and I believe that our rabbis, our teachers, our leaders should undertake to do the same thing as the Memorial Foundation did. The Sephardi families in many countries and in America are becoming victims of assimilation and they are in danger of being lost to Jewry and Judaism. I am sure the Memorial Foundation would help any such enterprise by their own experience and by their own guidance.

Today the number of Sephardim in this country is increasing and it is our duty as members of the American Sephardi Federation to make every endeavor to see that the new immigrants as well as the older families which are becoming alienated from Judaism should be brought back to the Jewish community which is today in need of enterprising and visionary people. We must also see to it that the World Sephardi Federation should take some steps in order to ensure the loyalty of the Sephardim to their traditions. There are countries in Europe and in South America where the WSF should undertake serious steps in order to provide both rabbis and teachers who are competent, who are not extreme in their views and who are able to act in the spirit of true Sephardi tradition. I believe that the time has come when the ASF should take the initiative within the WSF in order to see that our movement becomes really popular, and that as many as possible of our people become acquainted with the aims of our federations.

We Sephardim very often have tended to become parochial, thinking only of his or her own community. We must take a wider point of view. The time has come when we have to pull together our resources, our energies and our plans. Younger people have to be attracted to our movement, more meetings have to be held and we must also see how we can influence each other in order to become more effective. We must make a drive for new membership for each branch of the World Sephardi Federation. We cannot just wait for the Jewish Agency to help us in every enterprise; we must go out and obtain means so that we should take the initiative in different fields of action and thereby be of help to world Jewry in the Diaspora and in Israel.

We know that one of the main problems affecting Israel and the Diaspora is the emigration of Russian Jews, mainly to Israel. I do not know how many of us knew that there was a Sephardi community in the south of Russia. The Jews of Georgia, of Bukhara and other places have always been, even during the Communist regime, the fortresses of Judaism. The people in those places continued to go to the synagogue, continued to practice the Jewish law and to learn Hebrew and to study Judaism. Many of these people found their way to Israel and they established communities especially in Jerusalem bearing the names of these famous communities. When we came to try and help Russian Jewry, many of us realized that these people in the South spoke languages other than Russian. For some time I have tried to persuade the Memorial Foundation for Jewish Culture that besides sending books of Jewish content to Russia in Russian, books should also be sent in Georgian and other languages which are spoken by those Sephardic communities. I call them Sephardic because they have a Sephardi Minhag and they have always prayed according to the Sephardi order of prayers. It has now been revealed that many of these communities are in greater danger than people in other parts of Russia because anti-Semitism, especially on the part of the Moslem population, has become very violent.

I told you that those congregations were the bastions of Judaism for many years, but unfortunately, slowly they have been forgetting the Hebrew language, and their loyalty to Judaism has been badly shaken. It is our duty now to strive and think how we can help those communities and in which way we can rehabilitate them in Israel. They will definitely face many difficulties because many people do not regard them even as Russians.

And last but not least, we must think of the Jewish education of our younger people. I told you that the Sephardi communities in Europe and in America are in danger of being almost obliterated because of assimilation. We must always bear in mind that the Sephardim have always had the ability to integrate with the people among whom they lived without assimilating. But today, unfortunately, Sephardim have retained their ability to integrate but not the strength to resist assimilation. The WSF and each of its branches including our own must do all in their power in order to bring Jewish education into the Jewish communities. It is not enough to build synagogues, it is not even enough to see people becoming members of the synagogue; but we must give them a Jewish education and above all the knowledge of Hebrew. Hebrew is bound to become the language that will unite our nation as it was in the past. Hebrew will become the link connecting all the Jews of the world and we have to see to it that this language will become part of the Jewish education of our people.

My friends, the paths which lie before us are not easy. This is only an outline that I am giving you, but I believe that a special committee should be appointed by this conference in order to see that at least some of the essential ideas which will be promulgated at this conference are carried out. It is no good having resolutions which will remain on paper. We should have a committee of younger people and older people who will be able to meet at least once a month, in order to see how the Jewish community here, and among them the Sephardi community, are advancing and in which way we can help our brethren to come back to Judaism.

I began by speaking about the centrality of Israel in Jewish life today and also in the future. The establishment of the State of Israel gave also effect to a special process that began immediately almost after the establishment of the state. This effect is now being felt not only in Israel but also in the Diaspora, especially in the religious communities of the Diaspora. In my opinion the remarkable result of the existence of our State has not been merely the strengthening of the unity of the Jewish people but that the Western religious leadership had the opportunity to come into contact with the Sephardi and Oriental Jewish communities. They must come to realize that the Sephardic creative spirit must be taken into consideration in the new era, in the Halakhic and wider religious and social decisions. It is the duty of the WSF to see to it that Sephardi heritage of Judaism is strengthened and becomes an integral part of Jewish outlook and culture affecting social and religious conduct.

One of the most exciting and I should say elevating events that I witnessed while in Israel was the installation of Rabbi Dr. Marc Angel as the President of the Rabbinical Council of America. In the first place, I was glad to see that such a young Sephardi rabbi was given such a singular honor, and that the Rabbinical Council of America knew how to choose a man of ability and initiative. Above all I was glad to see that for the first time a Sephardi was elected to this position. I believe to a great extent this election was due to the fact that the Jews in the Diaspora like those in Israel began to realize that the Sephardim are not just an ethnic group with interesting customs and colorful attitudes, but that they represent authentic Judaism, that their background is part of the great Jewish religious and cultural heritage. Rabbi Angel is also the first student who graduated from the Sephardi department of Yeshiva University, and who as such received also the semiha of the authorities of the university. I think on this occasion we should pay tribute to the memory of the late Dr. Belkin who had the vision to establish this department and we should express our gratitude to the president of YU, Dr. Norman Lamm, who has made every effort to allow the Sephardi students to be guided according to the traditions of Sephardi Jewry. Torah-U-Madda, Torah and Science, is the guiding spirit inspiring the work and the actions of YU, and this is in keeping with the Sephardi rabbinic traditions. I think that a vote of thanks should go from this meeting to Dr. Norman Lamm and to the faculty of YU for having so generously opened their doors to the Sephardim, enabling them to be educated according to the spirit of their ancestors. Last but not least, our thanks go to Dr. Dobrinsky, known as Haham Bueno, who for the last 25 years has done everything possible in order to maintain the Sephardi spirit within YU. I think that the ASF especially should take more interest and show greater support for the work done by this university. I know that our president has already taken first steps in order to insure that, and I am sure that it will be the duty of the next executive and indeed of all its members to support him in this endeavor.

ACCEPTANCE SPEECH

An address, originally presented in Judeo-Spanish, in Oviedo, Spain, at the ceremony of award of the Prince of Asturias Concord Prize, October 18, 1990.

Our Hahamim (wise men) tell us that we have the obligation of thanking our God and the people that did and do us good, at all times.

In this spirit, I want to glorify the Creator of all the world for giving us this moment when the Principe de Asturias Foundation awards the Prince of Asturias Concord Prize 1990 to the Sephardic communities of the world.

This ceremony shows us that after 500 years, Spain welcomes back the Jews who preserved the language and the traditions of Spain and especially friendship for the old fatherland. Israel was for the Sephardic Jews the Holy Land, and Spain was the second home land. On the door of the cabinet in the living room of my house there were two poems. One of them was the Hatikva, the Hymn of Hope, hope that one day we will return to the Holy Land and bring salvation to the entire world. The Hatikva is today the Anthem of Israel. This poem was translated to Ladino by the well known author of Sarajevo, Mr. Abraham Kapon, who was a collaborator of Mr. Ramon Menendez Pidal. This translation, which is free, talks about the land of Israel, "from where our fathers came, Kings of Israel ruled, where the holy Temple was erected, which was destroyed by the enemy. There is our hope." The other poem is "To You Spain", also written by Kapon, as he says "in the name of the Sephardim, the lovers and preservers of the language of Cervantes".

To you beloved Spain, "mother" we call you, and throughout our lives we will not forget your sweet language. Even though you have expelled us as a stepmother from your womb, we have not stopped loving you as our holy ground, where our ancestors are buried and where the ashes of thousands of tormented and burned still lie. For you we feel fatherly love, glorious country, that is why we send you our glorious salute".

These two poems which could be found in all the houses of the Jews of my small town, expressed the two ideas that guided the life of the Sephardim. The first, Hope, hope that a day will come when we won't be persecuted any more and that we will find salvation in Israel. The second, a strong love for Spain. Although the Sephardim had been expelled from Spain they never felt resentment for Spain and its culture. There are some historians who question why the Jewish refugees of Spain never forgot their old country and never stopped feeling a filial love for Spain. There is only one answer: Of all the Diasporas in which the people of Israel lived dispersed, only in Spain there was a golden era. Unlike in the other Diasporas in Spain, the Jews were not considered as a foreign minority but as an integrated body, well adapted to the Iberic Peninsula. That is why they felt very hurt when they were obliged to leave the land where they had been living for 2,000 years. Only if we consider this fact, we will understand why the Sephardim gave the Judeo-Spanish language (Ladino) such holiness, only second to Hebrew. The most important prayers of the Shabbat, and especially on the second days of the Festivals, were recited in Ladino. Women offered their prayers in Judeo-Spanish not in Hebrew. Many hymns were translated to Ladino and they were sung in melodies of the Romancas of Spain. Fathers and mothers blessed their children in Judeo-Spanish. Until WWII when many Sephardic communities were destroyed by the Nazis, the rabbis in many Sephardic synagogues were allowed to preach only in Ladino, not in the language of the country in which they lived.

The Sephardim wanted to create the atmosphere of Spain in their synagogues, that is why they named them after different provinces and places of the old fatherland. Everywhere in the Balkans, in North Africa there were synagogues that were called synagogue of Aragon, Synagogue of Castilla, Synagogue of Cordova, etc.

Against the intolerance of olden times, we want to ask and offer today for all the people of the earth, for the men and women of good will, a message of tolerance and harmony as the only possible path for the understanding of Humanity.

In the name of the Sephardim I want to give thanks once again to Your Royal Highness, to the excellencies of this foundation, not only for the most prestigious and cultural prize of Spain, but also for the promise that with this prize the doors of the old land will be open for ever to the Sephardic community.

We are full of emotion and hope, as the Israel Ambassador to Spain said, that now that there is a new wave of xenophobia and antisemitism in Europe, Spain takes a different route from this attitude and looks back to its noble past.

I want to finish these words with the old blessing of my fathers. May the Almighty bless Spain, its King and Queen, the Royal family, its governors, and its people.

ESSAYS IN MEMORY
OF HAHAM GAON

TZENIUT: A UNIVERSAL CONCEPT

A lecture by Dr. Norman Lamm
President of Yeshiva University

One of the defining characteristics of the Jewish religious personality is *tzeniut* which may approximately be translated as modesty. Normally, the concept of *tzeniut* is discussed in rather technical terms: how low or how high a hemline, the length of sleeves, the form of dress, the number of square millimeters of skin that may be exposed, and so on. Indeed, these are important issues, but they are aspects or details of *tzeniut*, not its heart. It would be a pity to limit our understanding of *tzeniut* to that which can be measured by a ruler, while ignoring its conceptual matrix. What should concern us is the worldview of Judaism that informs the concept and the practice of *tzeniut*, an exceedingly important Jewish principle and value which touches the fundamentals of our faith. In seeking the broader implications of *tzeniut* and its universal context, we must explore three dimensions of *tzeniut*.

The first of these is the principle of *kedushah,* holiness. The Torah says, "You shall be holy." The Sages of the Talmud comment: *hevu perushim min ha-arayot,* you shall separate yourselves from immorality. The commandment therefore concerns immorality in its strictly sexual significance. The more one distances himself or herself from expressions of illegitimate sensuality, the more one is able to achieve personal sanctity or *kedushah.*

This essay is dedicated to my friend Haham Dr. Solomon Gaon, a man of true modesty who walked humbly with the Lord his God.

How does *tzeniut* relate to *kedushah?* The most fruitful way to begin is by citing an explanation I heard from my illustrious late teacher and mentor, Rabbi Joseph. B. Soloveitchik, *zekher tzaddik li'vrakhah.* The "Rav," as he was known, offers a very trenchant insight: *kedushah* thrives in *he'elem,* in hiddenness, in obscurity, not *be'giluy,* openness. (Indeed, the Torah's euphemism for illicit sexual intercourse is *giluy arayot,* the exposure or baring to public view of nakedness.) These two concepts of hiddenness and openness are most relevant to *kedushah,* which flourishes only in the hidden.

The holiest place in the world for Judaism is the *Kodesh Hakodashim,* the Holy of Holies in the *Beit Hamikdash,* the Temple in Jerusalem. The holiest person during the service in the Temple was the *Kohen Hagadol,* the High Priest. And the holiest day of the year is Yom Kippur. No one may enter the inner sanctum of the Holy of Holies, except the *Kohen Hagadol,* on Yom Kippur. Here we have a converging of three forms of *kedushah:* the *kedushah* of place, the *kedushah* of time, and the *kedushah* of personality - in one place, only once a year, by one person. If *kedushah* is so important, we might have expected masses of Jews crowding the Temple with a great deal of fanfare, marching to the *Kodesh Hakodashim* to participate in this phenomenal concentration of holiness. Yet that is not the case at all -- because *kedushah* does not prosper in the presence of masses. It does not thrive under the gaze of the many, in openness, in revelation, in exposure. Rather, it is the opposite of exposure -- hiddenness -- which is the natural environment of *kedushah.* Holiness grows in the unobtrusive recesses of the soul, not on the stage of one's public persona.

Another example of the Halakha's preference for hiddenness as a prerequisite for holiness is the *Sefer Torah.* The Torah is read on Monday, Thursday, and twice on Shabbat. It is forbidden to touch the inside of the parchment of the Torah scroll, the side on which the writing appears, which is why we use a metal or wooden pointer. Indeed, if one does touch it, his hands are considered "defiled", *tamei yadayim,* and he therefore must wash his hands. The *Sefer Torah* confers impurity upon the hands because otherwise one might become over-familiar with *kedushah;* if that happens, one detracts from the *Sefer Torah's* sanctity. When there is too much exposure, holiness is diminished. Indeed, when the Talmud speaks about not touching the parchment of the *Sefer Torah,* the language it uses is: *ke'she'hu arum,* "when it is naked." At such time, it is, as it were, exposed, naked or: lacking in *tzeniut.*

The Greeks, the Rav says, saw the human body primarily in aesthetic terms. They were obsessed with beauty. But their notion is that beauty does not thrive in hiddenness. Beautiful objects require that they be displayed and admired. Hence, if you accept the body primarily in aesthetic terms, an object of beauty, it demands exposure. This indeed was one of the major elements that occasioned the great collision between Athens and Jerusalem: the Greeks introduced gymnasia into Israel, where sports were engaged in the nude because the body was an object of beauty. But Judaism does not look upon the body primarily in aesthetic terms. That is what, to a large extent, caused the Hasmonean revolution which we celebrate on Hanukkah.

That is not to say that there is no aesthetic in Judaism. When, for instance, the Talmud says that *benot Yisrael yafot hen,* that Jewish women are beautiful, the Talmud was not engaging simply in an off-hand comment. But clearly, in the priority of values *kedushah* takes precedence over aesthetics. The main approach of Judaism toward the human body was not as an aesthetic object but as a religious value, something sacred. But that which is sacred requires covering, distance, the opposite of exposure. Hence, Judaism legislated the laws of *tzeniut,* and demanded covering up, because if indeed the body is sacred and sanctity is more important than beauty, then beauty has to take second place. The laws of tzeniut therefore position Judaism as opposite the Hellenistic tradition.

A few examples may be offered to support the Rav's thesis. In the beginning of Exodus, God calls to Moses out of the burning bush and says, *Moshe, Moshe.* Moses replies, *Hineni.* God continues: "Remove your shoes because the ground you are standing on is hallowed ground." And here God reveals Himself for the first time to the world's greatest prophet: "I am the Lord, the God of your fathers, the God of Abraham, Isaac, and Jacob." How does Moses react? With *tzeniut! Va-yaster Mosheh panav ki yarei me'habit el haElokim.* Moses covers his face because he is afraid to look at God. This fear is not lest God punish or devour him, nor is it the fear of the unknown. It is, more accurately, awe: Moses is overawed. In the presence of *kedushah* the proper response is to close one's eyes and to cover one's face. If *tzeniut* reflects the correct orientation of the human personality to the presence of *kedushah,* then the body, which encloses the human personality, requires similarly that it be covered up.

Another example: The sixth chapter of Isaiah, often referred to as the vision of the "seraphic songs," records the first divine revelation to this great prophet. Isaiah envisions the seraphim, or fiery angels, as they surround the very throne of the Holy One. As they do so, they call out to each other: *kadosh kadosh kadosh,* "Holy, holy, holy is the Lord of Hosts." It is most interesting to note how the prophet describes these angels: each angel has six wings. With two wings the angel covers his face, with two others the angel covers his feet, and with the remaining two he flies. Note: only two of the six are functional - the wings for flying! Four of the six represent *tzeniut,* covering up. Why do they cover up? Because *kadosh kadosh kadosh;* in the presence of *kedushah* there must be covering up. Exposure is abhorrent- - even of angels, beings which have no *yetzer hara,* to whom sexuality is utterly irrelevant. In the presence of *kedushah,* there must always be concealment.

Tzeniut is an indication that a human being possesses a *neshamah,* a soul, and the soul is an aspect of *kedushah. Tzeniut* is therefore an acknowledgement that the human personality, which includes the human body, partakes of *kedushah.* It is not just a fortuitous biological accident devoid of any transcendent meaning or higher moral obligation. Man may be an animal, but man is also an angel because he has the *tzellem Elohim,* the divine spark; he possesses *kedushah.*

The second dimension of *tzeniut* is connected with the experience of *kavod,* usually translated as "glory," "majesty," "honor," or "respect." But "dignity" is a better translation. The word "dignity" itself derives from a Latin root which means value, worthiness. A human being must have a sense of self-respect, an awareness of his own self worth. The source of this human dignity is *Ha-Kadosh Barukh Hu,* with regard to Whom we say *kevod Elohim haster davar* (Proverbs 25:2), the dignity of God lies in hiddenness. Dignity, like *kedushah,* thrives in *haster davar,* in obscurity, in concealment rather than exposure. This holds true for man as well: his concealment is both cause and effect of *kavod*. One who possesses *kavod*, a sense of dignity, will deal with it in a manner compatible with *tzeniut*. Modesty will characterize his conduct and personality as a reflection of that inner sense of worth.

Confronted by a person who is always bragging, always talking about his own achievements, boasting of his attractiveness or intelligence or talent or wealth, we know intuitively that such a person despises himself. He compensates for his poor self-image by proclaiming how great and superior he is, thereby seeking the approbation of others. A person who has self-respect has no need to wear his virtues like a badge and broadcast them to the world. One who lacks this sense of *kavod*, of inner dignity and worth, will expose himself, as if to say, "Look at me. Am I not beautiful? Am I not smart? Do you not like me?" The lack of *kavod* leads to exhibitionism, the opposite of *tzeniut*, whereas a sense of *kavod* will normally result in the practice of modesty or *tzeniut*.

As mentioned earlier, propriety of dress is an aspect of *tzeniut*, but that does not imply that *tzeniut* requires a kind of concerted attempt to look unkempt or unstylish. *Tzeniut* is not the antonym of attractiveness and pleasantness of appearance; it is the opposite of overexposure which, in turn, is a sign of the lack of *kavod*, of self-dignity.

Tzeniut implies *kavod* both with regard to oneself and to others. In its broader sense, the concept of *tzeniut* as *haster davar*, as concealment or hiddenness, bears upon interpersonal relationships. A relevant and significant example is *tzedakah*. The highest expression of this mitzvah occurs when the donor and the recipient do not know each other or of each other. Here, *tzeniut* ensures that *kavod* is extended not only to one's self but, primarily, to the other, in concern for the dignity of another sentient and sensitive human being. To give someone a handout directly is a good thing, but it is not the ideal way, for he is aware of his status as a mendicant. The far nobler way is that of genuine modesty, where in addition to supporting somebody financially in a time of his need, you also support his personality by respecting his *kavod*.

Finally, I propose a third concept, privacy, for which no word exists in classical Hebrew. (The absence of a name does not imply the non-existence of the concept. One can entertain an idea or a value or a precept without consciousness of it as a separate entity and, hence, without a name.) Privacy is a very important concept not only in secular law generally, but also in Halakha where it was very well developed much earlier than in the Western world. (See the chapter on "Privacy in Law and Theology," in my *Faith and Doubt.*) It is part of Judaism's ethics of communication.

In a sense, we might say that the ethics of communication which Judaism prescribes, directly or indirectly, is based upon *imitatio Dei,* the imitation of God or, in the Biblical halakhic vocabulary, "You shall walk in His ways."

In order to define the boundaries of the ethics of communication, we must consider how God communicates with humans, so that we might learn more of how humans ought to communicate with each other. God both reveals and conceals; He communicates, but not everything, not always.

At Mt. Sinai, there took place *giluy Shekhinah,* the revelation of His presence and of His teaching, i.e., Torah. God communicated with Moses and with the emerging nation of Israel gathered about the mountain. It was a communication of self-revelation.

In turn, man communicates with God by "revealing" himself to His Creator. Such is the understanding of prayer by the author of *Tanya* and by Rav Kook, among others.

Hence, in imitation of the Creator, man too must reveal himself to his fellow men as a means of communication. But there is a limitation that is very important: God reveals Himself, but He also conceals Himself. There is a divine sense of privacy which affirms the boundaries of His personality. There are limits beyond which no human may trespass and into which the human intellect may not freely probe. Thus, King Solomon in his Proverbs teaches us, as was mentioned earlier, *kevod Elohim haster davar,* the honor or dignity of God is in concealing matters. And the Talmud (*Hagigah* 13a) quotes Ben Sira who warns us, in what is wondrous to you do not probe; in what is hidden from you do not explore; understand deeply what was permitted to you, but you have no business attending to the hidden things. There is enough unknown in matters available for man's search and research; there are areas, however, that are "off limits" to him. The essence of the Creator is forever concealed from man, and no matter how we will try, we shall never penetrate the inner sanctum of God's essence. He wishes to protect His privacy, as it were.

Similarly, *tzeniut* means respect for the inviolability of the personal privacy of the individual, whether oneself or another, which is another way of saying that *tzeniut* is a respect for the integrity of one's ego, of one's essential self.

Man, in the understanding of Judaism, is fundamentally inscrutable; as much as you know about him, you never know everything about him. Were you really to know everything about him, that would mean that he lacks a core of self and is nothing but a collection of reactions and molecules and organs but not yet a human being. One's humanity, in some sense, is contingent upon his inscrutability, his mystery, his privacy. Man, according to Torah, possesses not only nature, not only his natural self that can be weighed and measured, but also *personae*. The word originally meant a mask, because it symbolizes that aspect of man that is concealed from public view. Beyond that mask is a living, very real human being. This mysterious, vital center of personality transcends the collection of our natural physiological and psychological properties. Not only *is* man a mystery, but he *should be* a mystery. One is obliged to develop a proper sense of self, whereby one is happy with that self even though no one else knows about it, confirms it, or validates it. This does not mean that one ought to be catatonic; a state where one does not communicate with another human being is pathological. In a healthy human being, revelation and communication are balanced in that vital core that remains free and undetermined - the center of personality that has clearly defined boundaries of selfhood. It is this privacy which we confirm when we speak of *tzeniut*. The other aspects of *tzeniut* are but derivative expressions of this core.

The concept of privacy in Halakha is evident in the beginning of the Talmud's tractate *Bava Batra*. The Gemara discusses the question of *hezek re'iyah,* a tort or damage that consists of invading someone's privacy by looking into his property. This visual intrusion into his private domain is regarded as a *hezek* or tort, and is actionable in a halakhic court of law. To take the Gemara's example, assume two partners bought a parcel of land and later decided to divide it. The halakha is that if one partner wants to build a fence to maintain his privacy, even if the other does not, the fence must be built and each pays 50% of the cost. Why? Because privacy is a right; *hezek re'iyah* is a genuine concern.

Now, the partner who does not want the fence must still pay 50% not because he also derives the benefit of privacy, but for quite the opposite reason. The Gemara explains by posing the following case: the partners purchase and then wish to divide a piece of property that is on a slope or diagonal, with one taking the bottom half of the property and the other the top half of the property. They now want to build a fence. But in this case, only one party has to pay the entire amount - and that is the owner of the upper level property. Why? Because the law of *hezek re'iyah* is such that one must pay not in order to gain protection from the visual intrusion of the other party, but rather to prevent oneself from invading another's privacy by spying on him! Therefore, if the two lots are level, each partner has to pay half the expense of the fence to prevent each from spying on the other. But if one is on the upper level and can look into the other's property, especially his roof where the partner who holds the land below assumes he is safe from inquisitive eyes, but the latter can not see the former, the latter does not have to pay at all. Hence, the Halakha requires of one to respect the privacy of his fellow man and - to pay for it. This is the law, and is so codified by the Rambam and in the *Shulhan Arukh*.

Tzeniut is much more than a mitzvah or commandment embodied in the very texture of the Halakha. Consider this: a great deal of Halakha is ethical in nature. *Tzedakah,* the prohibition of gossip, the commandment to bury a corpse if there is no one else to do it, visiting the sick, and so many other laws, both positive and negative, are therefore treated in both the halakhic and Musar (ethical) literature. Are these ethical halakhot only to be considered as mitzvot - or something more than that?

The ethical mitzvot are more than disembodied commands, because they issue from the principle of *imitatio Dei,* the imitation of God. The Mekhilta comments on the verse *zeh Eli ve'anvehu,* "this is my God and I shall glorify Him," that the word *ve'anvehu* is composed of the two words *Ani ve'Hu,* "He and I," that is, God and me. The Rabbis teach that as He is, so I must be: just as He acts morally, so must I. As God is merciful so must I be merciful. So it is with regard to all the "ethical mitzvot" - God not only commands these acts as a matter of law, but He Himself performs them. With the "regular" mitzvot, for instance when God commands us to eat the *korban Pesach,* He Himself does not, of course, eat the Passover lamb. But when God commands us to be kind, gentle, compassionate, considerate, loving, generous - it is because He acts in that manner, and we must not only obey Him but also imitate Him. His actions become the norms. This is what the Rabbis meant when they said that "the Torah begins with *hesed* and ends with *hesed.*" In the beginning of the Torah we read that Adam and Eve were naked. As an act of loving kindness, God prepared clothing for them. Thus, we humans must imitate Him, and we too must provide clothing for the unclothed, the poor. The Torah concludes with the death of Moshe Rabbenu. God performed the act of burying Moses, and because God did it, we do it. The highest realm that humans can reach is the imitation of God's ethical personality.

If we say that *tzeniut* is in imitation of God's ways, that means that God too practices *tzeniut.* But how is it possible to say of God that He is modest? If we take *tzeniut* in the conventional context, that it implies clothing that covers certain parts of the body, etc., it is an absurd irrelevancy. However, we can speak of God as having a sense of privacy.

In the philosophic and Kabbalistic traditions, one aspect of God is His knowability, His accessibility to our intellectual curiosity, His readiness to allow us to seek Him out, His relatedness to us. To know God is, after all, a great mitzvah. In Isaiah's famous vision of the Messianic era, the culmination of the redemption will be *umale'ah haaretz deiah et Hashem,* that the earth will be filled with knowledge of God as the waters cover the sea.

But at the same time that God is knowable by man, both Jewish philosophy and Kabbalah teach that in His essence God is absolutely unknowable. He is infinitely remote from man's inquisitive mind, totally impervious to man's unquenchable desire to know. That is why, in the Kabbalah, the essence of God is called the *Ein Sof,* the Infinite. However,

R. Hayyim of Volozhin says that the real, inner meaning of the term *Ein Sof,* or endless, refers to our search for understanding of Him: that there is no end to our efforts to know His essence; we must fail. It is His nature to remain mysterious, infinitely remote. This vast inscrutability of God is the inner boundary of His privacy. He resists man's desire to know Him, and limits his longing theological curiosity. This is the concept of the privacy of God.

Of course, Judaism wants us to understand. It wants us to understand nature, all knowledge of the world and of man. It wants us to know Torah and to know God. To know Him is one of the loftiest ambitions and most heroic achievements of *homo religiosus,* religious man.

But both philosophers and mystics have taught that only certain aspects of God are accessible to man's intellect. Thus, what God *does* can be pondered; His "actional attributes" are such that we may attempt to describe and understand them, and we are bidden to imitate them. But when it comes to the divine Essence, to what He *is,* His inner self, we can only know what He is not - His "negative attributes." We are strictly limited in our ability to apprehend Divinity: encouraged to know what we may, discouraged from the futile task of going beyond our ken. Just as man, if he were totally knowable, would be less than human, so God, if He were totally knowable, would be less than divine. God is, as it were, a very private Individual. Just as He reveals Himself, He conceals Himself.

The prophet Micah spoke words which remain one of the great formulations of man's duty on earth: "It has been told to you, O man, what is good and what the Lord requires of you, but to do justly and to love mercy and to walk humbly with your God." The last of these three items, "to walk humbly" or modestly, is, in the Hebrew, *hatzneia lekhet. Hatzneia* is from the same root as *tzeniut*. To live a life of *tzeniut* is a matter of imitating God - -"to walk humbly with your God." As He is merciful, I must be merciful; as He is gracious, I must be gracious; and therefore, as He practices *tzeniut,* privacy, so must I practice *tzeniut* and I must be modest and establish my own privacy and refrain from encroaching upon the privacy of my fellow humans. We must imitate the Almighty and learn from Him how to relate to others and to ourselves.

Man cannot flourish in a meaningful way without revelation. Just as God reveals Himself, so man cannot flourish without self-revelation or communication. And he must supplement that with its opposite: *tzeniut* or privacy, keeping the center of his personality mysterious and unknown, unexposed, unbreached.

IV

Tzeniut in its larger sense reflects the faith in the human potential for sanctity, *kedushah*. It reflects a respect for one's self and for others - for their *kavod*, their dignity. It is also a halakhic and ethical expression of the inalienable and inviolable privacy of man, based upon imitation of God. *Tzeniut* is also, therefore, a statement about God: that He is *kadosh kadosh kadosh*, He is holy, and that *melo kol haaretz kevodo*, the entire world is filled with His *kavod*, His majesty or dignity. Finally, *tzeniut* is a characteristic of God: He is private and, therefore, the acme of religious and moral development takes place when, in our own lives - - in every prosaic aspect of dress, of speech, of mannerism - - we reflect the highest and ultimate demand of the Holy One as it came to us through the prophet Micah *ve'hatzneia lekhet im Elohekha,* to walk with *tzeniut* - - with and in imitation of the Lord our God.

ELLEH TOLEDOT:

A STUDY OF THE GENEALOGIES IN THE BOOK OF GENESIS

by Rabbi Hayyim Angel
Congregation Shearith Israel and Yeshiva University

Having spent most of my childhood Shabbatot in Congregation Shearith Israel with the Haham, and having had the privilege of speaking to him on many occasions, I consider Haham Gaon one of the great influences on my life. Besides his remarkable warmth, scholarship, and dedication to the Jewish community, he was able to strike a unique balance between strength and gentleness in leadership. I miss the Haham, and hope that all those whom he inspired continue to follow his noble path in Jewish communal leadership.

I

INTRODUCTION

The book of Genesis is among the most popular biblical texts. The dramatic narratives of the creation, the flood, and the lives of our Matriarchs and Patriarchs contain profound lessons relevant to all generations.

Yet, among the inspirational narratives in Genesis, we find a considerable amount of material that appears to be of lesser interest, such as the lists of names chronicling the lineage of Cain, Seth, Noah's sons, Ishmael, and Esau. For the most part, these sections receive little attention from teachers and students. On the surface, they do not seem to merit a place in the Torah.

But, of course, these passages *are* in the Torah, leading careful readers of the Bible to ask why it was deemed important to include them. And in fact, several Midrashim and later commentators elucidate these genealogies in a brilliant manner, pointing out their significance. In this paper, we will consider the texts in light of these commentaries.

II
4:14-6:3
THE GENERATIONS OF CAIN AND SETH

The Torah begins with the creation of the world, the story of the Garden of Eden, and the rivalry between Cain and Abel. After Cain murders Abel, God decrees that farming (Cain's original occupation) would become unbearable for him; Cain is condemned to spend the rest of his days as a lonely wanderer.

After hearing the decree of his punishment, Cain leaves Eden, has a son Enoch, and builds a city in honor of his son. The Torah then lists the line of Cain's descendants through Lemekh,[1] at which point it records several details:

> Cain knew his wife. She conceived and gave birth to Enoch. [Cain] was building a city, and he named the city Enoch, after his son. Enoch had a son Irad. Irad had a son Mechuyael. Mechuyael had a son Methushael. Methushael had a son Lemekh.
>
> Lemekh married two women. The first one's name was Adah, and the second one's name was Tzillah. Adah gave birth to Yaval. He was the ancestor of all those who live in tents and keep herds. His brother's name was Yuval. He was the ancestor of all who play the harp and flute. Tzillah also had a son, Tuval Cain, a maker of all copper and iron implements. Tuval Cain's sister was Naamah.
>
> Lemekh said to his wives, "Adah and Tzillah, hear my voice; wives of Lemekh, listen to my speech. I have killed a man by wounding [him], and a child by bruising [him]. If Cain shall be revenged seven times, then for Lemekh it shall be seventy-seven times" (4:17-24).[2]

Two points emerge from the Torah's interest in Lemekh and his children. First, Lemekh's children were responsible for significant technological and cultural developments. Yaval domesticated several species of animals; Yuval was a pioneer in music; and Tuval Cain, in his metallurgic expertise, presumably was instrumental in the development of both farming implements and metal weapons.

Moreover, the account of Lemekh speaking to his two wives[3] deserves attention. According to various interpretations of his statement, one may deduce either that Lemekh had killed one or more people (possibly Cain),[4] that he was denying God's Providence (Rashi), or that he was threatening his wives with death if they would not listen to his every wish (Radak). In any case, Lemekh's harsh declaration displays a notable absence of fear of Divine retribution. His model was the original Cain: Cain received Divine protection (see 4:15) and had lived seven generations, despite having intentionally murdered his brother. Lemekh reasoned that he would live even longer, and not be punished for his wrongdoing. Such a godless attitude represents a pattern that was emerging; people were sinking into a state of immorality for which God would decree their death.

This attitude, however, appears to have originated with Lemekh's ancestor, Cain. When Cain heard the decree of his punishment, he decided that a direct relationship with God carried with it too much responsibility. Therefore he stated "and I am to be hidden from Your face" (4:14). By severing the connection with his Creator, Cain paved the way for his descendant Lemekh to be unafraid and unashamed of murder. Following those Midrashim which assert that Lemekh killed Cain, this connection would become ironic--Cain was indirectly responsible for his own demise.

After tracing Cain's lineage, the Torah relates that Adam and Eve had another son, one who brought some hope to the world from a spiritual point of view:

> Adam knew his wife again, and she gave birth to a son. She named him Seth--"Because God has granted me other offspring in place of Abel, whom Cain had killed." A son was also born to Seth, and [Seth] named him Enosh. It was then initiated to pray with God's Name (4:25-26).

As the reader absorbs the fact that Lemekh represents a godless and immoral society, Seth's family begins to pray directly to God.[5] This contrast allows the reader to perceive a fascinating aspect of the development of humanity: the conflict between pursuing a relationship with God and not doing so existed since the dawn of history.[6]

Chapter 5 proceeds to trace the genealogy from Adam until Noah:

> This is the book of the Chronicles of Adam. On the day that God created man, He made him in the likeness of God. He created them male and female. He blessed them and named them Man *(Adam)* on the day that they were created. Adam lived 130 years, and he had a son in his likeness and form. He named him Seth. Adam lived 800 years after he had Seth, and he had sons and daughters. All the days that Adam lived were 930 years, and he died (5:1-5).

As the Torah enumerates Seth's descendants, it neglects any mention of Cain or Abel in the genealogy of humankind. Radak and Abarbanel explain that since Cain and Abel produced no offspring who lived beyond the Flood, the Torah excludes them from the history of humanity.

Moreover, the Torah states that Adam was created in the likeness of God, and that Seth was born in Adam's likeness. This statement implies that Cain was *not* in the image of God, and some Midrashim understand this to be the case.[7] Such a contrast between Seth and Cain encourages the reader to identify the distinguishing characteristics of each family line.

> Seth lived 105 years, and he had a son Enosh. Seth lived 807 years after he had Ensoh, and he had sons and daughters. All of Seth's days were 912 years, and he died (5:6-8).
>
> Enosh lived 90 years, and he had a son Kenan (v. 9) . . . .
>
> Kenan lived 70 years, and he had a son Mahalalel (v. 12) . . . .
>
> Mahalalel lived 65 years, and he had a son Yered (v. 15) . . . .
>
> Yered lived 162 years, and he had a son Enoch (v. 18) . . . .
>
> Enoch lived 65 years, and he had a son Methuselah (v. 21) . . . .
>
> Methuselah lived 187 years, and he had a son Lemekh (v. 25) . . . .
>
> Lemekh lived 182 years, and he had a son. He named him Noah . . . (vv. 28-29).

In its description of Seth's family, the Torah adds considerably more detail than it had for Cain's progeny. It specifies the age of each person when he had the son who would be a direct progenitor of Noah, how many years that individual lived after having that son, and then the total number of years that person lived.

While this chapter and the list of Cain's descendants seem uneventful, M.D. Cassuto[8] writes at great length about them. Most fascinating is the parallel he detects between the actual names on the two lists. Noting that the Hebrew word *enosh* is synonymous with *adam*--both meaning "humankind," Cassuto sets up the following generational chart of names:

CAIN'S FAMILY	SETH'S FAMILY
1. Adam	1. Enosh
2. Cain	2. Kenan
3. Enoch	3. Mahalalel
4. Irad	4. Yered
5. Mechuyael	5. Enoch
6. Methushael	6. Methuselah
7. Lemekh	7. Lemekh

One immediately recognizes that, with only minor variations, the lists are identical (note that the third and fifth members of the two lists are simply inversed)! According to Cassuto, the Torah is subtly informing us that while both families hailed from Adam and Eve, and both genealogies contained people with the same or similar names (suggesting a close relationship between the two groups), they still turned out remarkably different. Following Cassuto's observation, we will now consider how the contrasts between the two lists shed light on the broader picture found in the narratives surrounding these genealogies.

THE FAMILY PHILOSOPHIES

Cain said, "My sin is too great to bear! Behold, today You have banished me from the face of the earth, and I am to be hidden from Your face. I am to be restless and isolated in the world, and whoever finds me will kill me" (4:13-14).

> Adam knew his wife again, and she gave birth to a son. She named him Seth--"Because God has granted me other offspring in place of Abel, whom Cain had killed." A son was also born to Seth, and [Seth] named him Enosh. It was then initiated to pray with God's Name (4:25-26).

The representative philosophies of the two family lines were diametrically opposed to each other: while Seth's family prayed to the Creator, Cain had proclaimed to God "I am to be hidden from Your face" (4:14). Seth's family advocated a way of life involving a direct relationship with God. Cain's chose a life devoid of religion, and sank to the depths of immorality as reflected by Lemekh--Cain's only descendant with a biblical voice.

LEMEKH

> Lemekh said to his wives, "Adah and Tzillah, hear my voice; wives of Lemekh, listen to my speech. I have killed a man by wounding [him], and a child by bruising [him]. If Cain shall be revenged seven times, then for Lemekh it shall be seventy-seven times" (4:23-24).

> Lemekh lived 182 years, and he had a son. He named him Noah, saying, "This one will bring us relief from our work *(mi-ma'asenu)* and the anguish of our hands, from the soil that God has cursed" (5:28-29).

Cassuto notes that the two Lemekhs contrast with one another. Cain's Lemekh represents a godless existence, denying Divine retribution for murders he either had committed or planned to commit. Cain's Lemekh reflects the moral decrepitude of his time.

In contrast, Seth's Lemekh casts a ray of hope into the world. At the birth of his son Noah, he proclaims that "This one will bring us relief from our actions and the anguish of our hands, from the soil that God has cursed" (5:29). Rashbam explains that Noah was the first child born after the death of Adam; Lemekh thought that the original curse on the land brought about by Adam's eating from the Tree of Knowledge (see 3:17) would become invalidated once the sinner who caused it was no longer living. Thus, Noah would herald a new age in agriculture.

Cassuto broadens this interpretation, understanding Lemekh's naming of Noah in the context of Lemekh's realization that the world was morally deteriorating. Lemekh hoped that Noah would bring a righteous dimension to the world. The results were hardly surprising: Cain's Lemekh was a murderer, helping to cause the flood; Seth's Lemekh, in his unusual piety, produced Noah, the only one righteous enough to survive that same flood.

ENOCH

> Cain knew his wife. She conceived and gave birth to Enoch. [Cain] was building a city, and he named the city Enoch, after his son (4:17).

> Enoch lived 65 years, and he had a son Methuselah. Enoch walked with God for 300 years after he had Methuselah, and he had sons and daughters. All of Enoch's days were 365 years. Enoch walked with God, and he was no more, because God had taken him (5:21-24).

In addition to the contrasts Cassuto finds between the family philosophies and the two Lemekhs, another distinction arises from the two family lists, relating to the Enochs. Cain, who had been punished with a life of wandering, constructs a city for his son, Enoch. Rashi (v. 16) writes that Cain thought he could outsmart God, going beyond the limited area he thought to be under God's jurisdiction. The *Me`am Lo`ez* points out that by building a city, Cain was rebelling against God, trying to replace his prescribed nomadic existence with the stability of a comfortable city. While Enoch himself was not responsible for these actions, the tainted city permanently bore his name.

In contrast, the Enoch who descended from Seth was of an entirely different fabric. He "walked with God" (5:23). This powerful contrast between the two Enochs--both identified with their respective family philosophies--further reflects the differences between Cain's hiding from God, and Seth's calling out to God.

THE CAUSE OF THE FLOOD: HINTS FROM
THE LISTS OF NAMES

At the time of the two Lemekhs, the world was divided into two groups: the godless, immoral Cain group; and the God-fearing descendants of Seth. But at the beginning of chapter six, we learn of a change in the status quo:

> Man began to increase on the face of the earth, and daughters were born to them. The sons of God *(benei E-lokim)* saw that the daughters of man were good, and they took themselves wives from whomever they chose. God said, "My spirit will not continue to judge man forever, since he is nothing but flesh" (6:1-3).

Who were these "sons of God"? Some Midrashim aver that these were fallen angels, who were marrying humans.[9] Alternatively, Rashi asserts that the nobles and judges (also honorably called *"elohim"* in the Bible)[10] were exploiting the masses, taking their daughters by force.

Ibn Ezra, however, suggests the possibility that the *benei E-lokim* were those people who had followed a Godly existence, namely, the descendants of Seth. In contrast, the earthy Cainites are called *benot ha-adam*. Based on this interpretation, the beginning of chapter six pinpoints the true source of the moral corruption of humanity: when Seth's descendants intermarried with Cain's descendants, the godless immorality of Cain came to dominate the entire society, rather than only half of it.

It is noteworthy that Cain's descendants were able to overpower the religious progeny of Seth. It would appear that Seth's descendants, while good, were not particularly strong in their faith. Several Midrashim indicate that Seth's righteous descendant Enoch died "early" because he was religiously unstable.[11] Although he followed God, he was prone to reverting to wickedness. If Enoch (who receives special attention for his close relationship with God) had such a weak religious backbone, it is reasonable to assume that the others would have fallen prey to Cainite influences as well. At this tragic point in history, God saw that the physical lusts of *all* people were uncontrollable, and decided to start a new world stemming from the only individual whose faith was strong enough to withstand the intermarriages with Cainites--Noah.

Rather than interrupting the story of the development of humanity, the genealogies of chapters 4 and 5 in fact provide the underlying story of the cause of the flood! The details gleaned from the two lists convey a deeper understanding of how humanity moved into a life of depravity and lewdness--eventually leading to destruction.

III

10:1-11:32

THE GENERATIONS OF NOAH'S CHILDREN

After explaining how humanity became corrupt, the Torah relates the story of Noah and the flood. The world is destroyed, with only Noah and his immediate family surviving from among all people. After the flood, Noah plants a vineyard, becomes drunk, and then fades from prominence. The Torah (chapter 10) then lists seventy descendants of Shem, Ham, and Yefeth.

> These are the chronicles of Noah's sons, Shem, Ham, and Yefeth. Children were born to them after the flood. The sons of Yefeth were Gomer, Magog, Yavan, Tuval, Meshekh, and Tiras. . . From these isolated nations branched out into their lands. Each had its own language for its families in its nations (10:1-2, 5).
>
> The sons of Ham were Cush, Mitzraim, Put, and Canaan...Canaan fathered Sidon (his firstborn) and Heth, as well as the Jebusites, the Amorites, the Girgashites, the Hivites, the Arkites, the Sinites, the Arvadites, the Tzemarites, and the Chamathites. Later the families of the Canaanites became scattered (vv. 6, 15-18). . . .
>
> Sons were also born to Shem. He was the ancestor of the Hebrews, [and] the brother of Yefeth, the eldest (v. 21). . . .
>
> Such were the families of Noah's sons, according to their chronicles in their nations. From these, the nations spread over the earth after the flood (v. 32).

Ramban (v. 5) asks why the Torah found it necessary to record the founders of the world's seventy nations,[12] most of whom have little bearing on the rest of biblical history. He answers that this chapter was included in the Torah so that we can determine the origins of Abraham and the seven Canaanite nations (vv. 15-18). While this response explains a small portion of chapter 10, other reasons must be found to explain why the *entire* passage is included. To understand fuller implications of this passage, we will consider the next list of names, in chapter 11.

After the story of the Tower of Babel (11:1-9), the Torah lists the generations of Shem's family, leading to the birth of Abraham. The structure of this chapter is similar to that of chapter 5, which had related the generations from Adam to Noah:

> These are the chronicles of Shem: Shem was 100 years old when he had a son Arpachshad, two years after the flood. Shem lived 500 years after he had Arpachshad, and he had sons and daughters (11:10-11).
> Arpachshad was 35 years old when he had a son Shelach (v. 12)....
> Shelach was 30 years old when he had a son Eber (v. 14)....
> Eber was 34 years old when he had a son Peleg (v. 16)....
> Peleg was 30 years old when he had a son Reu (v. 18)....
> Reu was 32 years olds when he had a son Serug (v. 20)....
> Serug was 30 years old when he had a son Nachor (v. 22)....
> Nachor was 29 years old when he had a son Terach (v. 24)....

While the genealogies in chapters 5 and 11 are similar, there are notable distinctions between the two lists. First, Seth's family lineage includes some details about the family and its members (they pray to God; Enoch is righteous; Lemekh names Noah to bring hope to humanity). This is not the case in Shem's family. Until we arrive at Terach (Abraham's father), the Torah provides no details. This distinction appears to belittle the collective contribution of Shem's descendants. They bestowed nothing of lasting value to the world.

Additionally, in Seth's lineage, the Torah specifies that each person died. In Shem's lineage, this seemingly obvious fact is omitted. Prompted by this inconsistency, Seforno (11:11) notes that all of Seth's main descendants (i.e., those listed in chapter 5) died before the flood. Perhaps they were so righteous that God felt they did not deserve such an extreme punishment as did the rest of humankind. Therefore the Torah emphasizes that they died, i.e., before the flood.

In contrast, when Abraham was born, Noah was still alive. In fact, *all* of Shem's descendants listed in chapter 11 were alive at least until Abraham had discovered God.[13] Seforno asserts that the Torah deliberately omits mentioning the deaths of Shem's descendants to highlight Abraham's greatness. God wanted everyone alive--even the righteous Noah--to witness a truly superior individual.

Through this interpretation of Seforno, a structure of the entire book of Genesis begins to emerge. The first eleven chapters of Genesis present the universal history of the world, whereas chapter 12 (the story of Abraham) marks the commencement of a new era--the foundations of the Israelite nation. The Torah also enables the reader to contrast the characteristics of the two most righteous people until that point in history: Noah and Abraham.

Noah was the most righteous person in his time (6:9), and was chosen to rebuild society. Yet, Noah does not pray on behalf of humanity, but instead builds an Ark to save only himself and his family. Following the flood, Noah becomes drunk; he does not appear to have raised society to a higher level. Since the list of Shem's descendants has no detail, the text subtly indicates that the world was no better than it had been before the flood. The Noah experiment was a failure. Although Noah was personally righteous, he did not help others come closer to God. As a result, he held no influence over future generations.

Abraham, in contrast, helped others both spiritually and physically. He is portrayed midrashically as having attracted many adherents to monotheism.[14] Additionally, he prays on behalf of the wicked cities of Sodom and Gomorrah, hoping God will have mercy on them (18:23-33)--a notable contrast to Noah's lack of prayer for the world.[15] Moreover, when Abraham hears that Lot had been captured, he immediately risks his own life and defeats the four armies (14:11-16).

Abraham's concern for others distinguishes him from Noah's descendants. This upgrade in righteousness is reflected in the list of Shem's descendants. After going from Shem until Terach without distinguishing any descendant, the Torah continues:

> These are the chronicles of Terach. Terach fathered Abram, Nachor and Haran. Haran had a son Lot. Haran died during the lifetime of his father Terach, in the land of his birth, Ur Casdim. Abram and Nachor married. The name of Abram's wife was Sarai. The name of Nachor's wife was Milcah, the daughter of Haran (who was the father of Milcah and Yiscah). Sarai was sterile; she had no children. Terach took his son Abram, his grandson Lot (Haran's son), and his daughter-in-law Sarai (Abram's wife). With them, he left Ur Casdim, heading toward the land of Canaan. They came as far as Charan and settled there. All of Terach's

days were 205 years, and Terach died in Charan (11:27-32).

Besides the unusually lengthy description of Terach's progeny, the Torah marks him off by stressing "these are the chronicles of Terach." Thus, the Torah indicates that the birth of Abraham represents a clean break from Noah's descendants. Abraham would herald a new spiritual era in the world--one concerned with the well-being of all humanity.

Abraham's nation develops through Isaac and Jacob. When the children of Israel go to Egypt, the Torah (46:8-27) enumerates their families: they have exactly seventy family members, as did Noah's family in chapter 10. In light of this parallel, it may be suggested that the book of Genesis is structured around the contrast between Noah and Abraham. The seventy nations of the world are paralleled by the seventy Israelite families.

The Gemara (Sukkah 55b) asks why seventy sacrifices were brought throughout the Sukkot festival (see Num. 29:12-34). It answers that the offerings were for the atonement of the seventy nations of the world! The Jewish people, represented by their own seventy families, continued to pray for the seventy nations of the world--Noah's descendants. By prescribing the seventy Sukkot sacrifices, God reminded the Israelites of their ongoing responsibility to emulate Abraham, caring about the spiritual welfare of all people.

IV

25:12-18

THE GENERATIONS OF ISHMAEL

The Torah recounts the many trials and tribulations of Abraham. In chapter 16, Sarah who is barren, offers her handmaid Hagar to Abraham as a concubine. Abraham accepts, and Hagar becomes pregnant. Hagar begins to despise Sarah, who then harasses her so that Hagar takes refuge in the desert.

While in the wilderness, an angel appears to Hagar, promising that she will bear a son to Abraham. Hagar returns to Abraham and gives birth to Ishmael.

Ishmael appears only two more times in Genesis: he mocks Isaac, bringing about his own banishment from Abraham's household (21:8-21); and when Abraham dies, Ishmael returns to assist Isaac in the burial of their father (25:9).

After Abraham is buried, the Torah lists Ishmael's descendants:

> These are the chronicles of Ishmael son of Abraham, whom Hagar the Egyptian, Sarah's slave, bore to Abraham. . . There were twelve princes for their nations. . . [His descendants] lived in the area from Havilah to Shur all the way to Assyria. They overran all their brethren (25:12-18).

Immediately following the short list of Ishmael's descendants, the Torah proceeds with a lengthy account of the story of Isaac and his sons, carefully chronicling the conflict between Jacob and Esau. As we have seen when contrasting Cain's descendants with Seth's descendants, the longer account accompanies the more important of the two.

VI

36:1-43

THE GENERATIONS OF ESAU

The Torah chronicles the story of Jacob and Esau, Jacob's encounter with Laban, his subsequent reunion with Esau, and his return to Canaan. At this point in the narrative, the Torah devotes chapter 36 to the descendants of Esau. Verses 1-19 trace Esau's own children and family leaders; verses 20-30 record the tribal heads of the Hori, the original inhabitants of Seir; verses 31-43 record the eight Edomite kings who ruled before the nation of Israel had its first king.

Again, Midrashim and commentators explain why the Torah includes this list. Several Midrashim and later commentaries point out that some of the marriages recorded in this chapter were incestuous; this chapter demonstrates how immoral Esau's family had become.[16] Seforno (v. 31) notes that none of the kings of Edom were native members of Esau's family; Esau had produced nobody worthy of leading his family. Ramban adds that there were no dynasties among these kings, showing their political instability and unworthiness.

In a different vein, Radak asserts that this passage was written in

Isaac's honor. Since Isaac was righteous, the Torah wanted to show that even his wicked son Esau produced a prestigious family. Alternatively, Rambam (*Guide* III:50) writes that this passage has halakhic ramifications: later, the Torah commands the Israelites to eliminate Amalek (Deut. 25:17-19), but at the same time forbids them from harassing the other families of Edom (Deut. 2:2-8). The lineage presented here specifies the exact family lines so that the Israelites would know whom they should spare.

Rashi, following the Talmud (Sanhedrin 99b), writes that this chapter was written to criticize our forefathers for not having accepted Timna as a convert. Timna was part of the original Hori nation which had inhabited Seir before Esau conquered it (v. 22). According to the Talmud, Timna approached Abraham, Isaac, and Jacob, trying to join their impressive family. However, they rejected her. Undeterred, she became a concubine of Eliphaz, one of Esau's sons (v. 12). Because our forefathers did not accept her, she had a son Amalek, who became the biblical archenemy of the Israelites.[17]

Rashi (37:1) also explains the contrast between the lackluster account of Esau's descendants followed immediately by a lengthy account of Jacob's family history (similar to the contrast between Ishmael and Isaac):

> After [the Torah] wrote for you the dwelling places of Esau and his generations briefly, for they were not distinguished or significant to explain how they settled or the order of their wars, or how they drove out the Horite, [the Torah] explains to you the dwelling places of Jacob and his generations fully, all the changes in their fortunes; since they were significant before the Omnipresent to relate at length regarding them.
>
> And similarly you find regarding the ten generations from Adam to Noah, so and so begat so and so. But when it came to Noah, [the text] dealt at length with him. And so similarly regarding the ten generations from Noah to Abraham, [the text] was brief with them, but when it reached Abraham, [the text] dealt at length with him.
>
> It may be compared to a pearl which fell into the sand; one searches in the sand and sifts it in a sieve until he finds the pearl; and after he has found it he throws away the pebbles from his hand and retains the pearl.[18]

According to Rashi, though the Torah records Esau's generations, their significance is eclipsed by the longer record of the family that would achieve lasting greatness--that of Jacob.

Beyond these reasons why Esau's lineage is recorded in such detail, this passage casts light on a broader issue that epitomizes the relationship between Jacob and Esau throughout the Bible. To understand this matter more fully, we must consider another biblical list: the Israelite wanderings through the desert at the end of the book of Numbers.

> These are the journeys of the Israelites, who had left Egypt in organized groups under the leadership of Moses and Aaron. Moses recorded their stops along the way at God's command. These were their stops along the way: [The Israelites] left Ra'mses on the 15th of the first month. On the day after the Passover [sacrifice] the Israelites left triumphantly before the eyes of the Egyptians. Egypt was still burying all their first-born, who had been killed by God, and God had destroyed their idols.
>
> The Israelites left Ra'mses and camped in Sukkoth.
>
> They left Sukkoth, and camped in Etham at the edge of the desert (Num. 33:1-6) . . . .

As with the lists of genealogies in Genesis, the commentators explain why this detailed passage is included in the Torah. The *Sefat Emet* (*Mas'ei* 5653) provides a broader reason for the inclusion of this passage, stating that it elucidates a deeper relationship between Jacob and Esau. Jacob, even when he initially suffers, will eventually succeed. In contrast, Esau's gains are illusory--he appears to succeed, but in the end he fails. Stated differently, a lifestyle modeled after Esau involves quick-fix solutions and short-term gains, but it ends in emptiness. One who emulates Jacob will act slowly and deliberately--often making painful sacrifices--and will achieve long-term, permanent gain.

This interpretation has wide-ranging ramifications on the contrast between Jacob and Esau, starting from their very births. Esau was born fully developed, a hairy baby (25:25); for this reason, he was called Esau, meaning "complete, made" (Rashi, Rashbam). In contrast, Jacob tagged along (25:26), clinging to his older brother's heel. Jacob's inauspicious birth would symbolize his existence; he would spend much of his life trying to catch up with Esau.

Esau immediately wins the love and respect of his father Isaac

(25:28); Jacob must wait many years before being appreciated by his father (27:33). Jacob employs foresight in acquiring the birthright from his brother: Esau wanted food *now,* while Jacob happily invests a bowl of lentils to gain the lasting benefits of the birthright (25:29-34).

While Esau hastily marries Canaanite women, causing grief to both his parents (26:34-35), Jacob travels and then patiently works for fourteen years to marry within the family--winning him blessings of his parents (28:1-7; 29:20-30).

When returning to Canaan after his prolonged stay at Laban's house, Jacob is the father of eleven sons and one daughter. In contrast, Esau already is a chieftain over at least 400 men (32:7). Moreover, Esau receives his inheritance of Seir almost immediately (Deut. 2:4-5, 22) and becomes head of a large tribe. In contrast, Jacob and his sons descend to Egypt, enduring some 250 years of exile--most of that time enslaved or wandering in the desert--before emerging to claim their inheritance.

Similarly, the genealogy of Esau in Genesis 36 contrasts with the chronicle of the Isarelite travels in Numbers 33. Esau's nation began with a quick start and foundation of a monarchy. They would already be under the regime of their eighth king by the time the fledgling Israelite nation was traversing the desert--slowly and painfully developing into a nation. But after the quick beginnings of the Edomite monarchy, their gains were negated by King David's conquest of Edom (see II Sam. 8:14). Eight Israelite kings reigned before Edom regained its independence (see Gen. Rabbah 83).

VI

CONCLUSION

ELLEH TOLEDOT:

A SPIRITUAL HISTORY OF THE WORLD

In reviewing the lists of names in Genesis, we find that they provide a spiritual history of the world, bringing together the narratives that surround them. The phrase *elleh toledot* (these are the chronicles of) appears ten times in various forms in Genesis.

1. The Chronicles of Heaven and Earth (2:4)

The first record of chronicles in Genesis does not refer to a genealogy of humans; rather, it recapitulates the creation account. Unlike chapter 1, which presents the creation in its proper chronological order, chapter 2 rearranges the creation so that all revolves around the creation of human beings.

> These are the chronicles of heaven and earth when they were created, on the day God completed earth and heaven. All the wild shrubs did not yet exist on the earth, and all the wild plants had not yet sprouted. This was because God had not brought rain on the earth, and there was no man to work the ground. A mist rose up from the earth, and it watered the entire surface of the ground. God formed man out of dust of the ground, and breathed into his nostrils a breath of life. Man thus became a living creature . . . (2:4-7).

By emphasizing man's role in creation, the Torah indicates that of all species created during the six days of creation, man was the most significant--the chosen species.

2. The Chronicles of Adam (5:1)

As we have seen, Chapters 4 and 5 explain that the world was divided into two halves: those who pursued a relationship with God, and those who consciously avoided a connection with their Creator. By considering only the Godly descendants of Seth in the Chronicles of Adam, the Torah indicates that a Godly life produces righteousness, whereas a godless life will result in the immorality of Lemekh. When the two groups intermarried, the entire human race was doomed. Only the righteous Noah, a descendant of Seth, would survive them. Thus, Seth's family was chosen to continue the human race.

3. The Chronicles of Noah (6:9)

After listing the generations of Seth in short form, the Torah writes expansively about the righteous Noah. As Rashi (Gen. 37:1) states, this structure of the text contrasts the stronger righteousness of Noah with the mediocrity of his predecessors. Noah was chosen from Seth's progeny to survive the flood and rebuild the world.

4-5. The Chronicles of Noah's Sons (10:1; 11:10)
6. The Chronicles of Terach (11:27)

The lists of Noah's descendants in chapters 10 and 11, when studied together with Jacob's seventy family members in chapter 46, indicate that there are two types of righteousness: one where the righteous individual does little for his compatriots, and the other where the individual actively pursues and encourages a moral and religious life for other people. While some of Noah's descendants may have lived good, moral lives, they were not instrumental in building a better society than the one before the flood.

Abraham's descendants, divided into seventy families, represent a new way of living--a life emulating Abraham's outgoing righteousness. While both Noah and Abraham founded permanent nations in the world, Abraham achieved a greater relationship with God, and a higher level of morality than did Noah. The fact that the Torah presents Terach and family as a new list of chronicles further reflects this powerful contrast between Noah and Abraham.

The relationship between Noah's descendants and Abraham's descendants is visible even in the laws of sacrifices. The Jewish people offered seventy sacrifices each Sukkot for the seventy nations of the world, symbolizing Abraham's concern for all people.

7-8. The Chronicles of Ishmael and Isaac (25:12; 25:19)
9-10. The Chronicles of Esau and Jacob (36:1; 37:1)

The Torah's distinction in the lengths of chronicles clearly indicates the Torah's preference for Isaac and Jacob. Their descendants would face hardship and suffering, but in the end they would attain lasting good.

Since these are the last chronicles in Genesis, the reader understands that there will be no more selection processes in the founding of the Jewish nation. Jacob's twelve sons would become spiritual heirs to their father. Their family philosophy was most apt for their descendants' eventual receiving of the Torah, which entails a lifestyle involving short-term sacrifice to attain a permanent, long-term good.

To conclude, then, we have seen that the genealogies help the careful reader understand the deeper significance in the development of humanity. The ten lists of "chronicles" found in Genesis serve to cement the narratives together, providing a more comprehensive understanding of the book of Genesis and the Bible.

NOTES

1. Ramban (v. 17), following those Midrashim which state that Lemekh killed Cain (see discussion below), writes that the Torah records the seven generations of Cain's descendants to teach God's compassion--that He waited seven generations before punishing Cain; and also to demonstrate that people are accountable for their actions--from the fact that Cain eventually paid with his own life for murdering his brother.

2. All English translations of Torah texts in this paper are taken from Aryeh Kaplan's *The Living Torah*. New York: Moznaim Publishing Co., 1981.

3. Gen. Rabbah 23 indicates that in those days, every man married two women. One was reserved for bearing children, the other for conjugal relations. Usually, the husband ignored his child bearing wife after she had her children, and treated the other wife like a prostitute. In contrast, Radak (v. 19) believes that the Torah mentions that Lemekh had two wives, precisely because he was the first man to treat women in such a degrading manner. According to either interpretation, the Torah is offering a hint at the moral decline of humanity at that point in history.

4. See, for example, Tanhuma *Bereshith* 11 and *Lekh Lekha* 7, which state that Lemekh had killed his ancestor Cain.

5. Interestingly, many Midrashim understand this verse to mean that people began to tend toward idolatrous practices. See, for example, Tanhuma Yashan *Naso* 24; Midrash Psalms 74; Pesikta Rabbati 5.

    But Ibn Ezra, explaining the plain sense of the text, finds this verse quite complimentary of Enosh and his contemporaries--that in fact they pursued a direct relationship with their Creator.

    Seforno, taking a middle position, explains that while righteous people began praying to God, the Torah records this fact because a majority of the world was lapsing into paganism and idolatry. See also Shabbat 118b; Gen. Rabbah 23:7.

6. It is curious that all technological developments were brought about by the godless descendants of Cain. "Secular scientists" appear to have existed even then.
7. See Tanhuma *Yitro* 10; Pirkei D'Rabbi Eliezer 22.
8. In *Perush al Sefer Bereshith*. Ninth edition. Jerusalem: Magnes Press, 1987, pp. 154-204. Originally published in 1944 under the title *Me-Adam Ad Noah*.
9. See Pirkei D'Rabbi Eliezer 1:22; Shir ha-Shirim Rabbah 2:15; Midrash quoted in *Torah Shelemah* 16.
10. See, for example, Ex. 21:6; 22:7,8.
11. See Gen. Rabbah 25:1; Midrash quoted in *Torah Shelemah* 62. Rashi here also accepts this negative perception of Enoch.
12. The idea that the world is divided into 70 nations (originating from chapter 10 of Genesis) is well documented in rabbinic literature. See, for example, Sukkah 55b; Gen. Rabbah 66:4; Shir ha-Shirim Rabbah 1:3; Lam. Rabbah 1:23.
13. According to various midrashic opinions, Abraham was either three, 48 (Gen. Rabbah 30:8 and many others), or 50 years old (Pesikta Rabbati 21) when he discovered God. Rambam asserts that he was 40 (*Yad, Avodat Kokhavim,* 1:3). Since Noah died when Abraham was 58 years old, the latter had discovered God by all accounts.
14. See Sanhedrin 99b; Gen. Rabbah 84:4; Num. Rabbah 14:11; Shir ha-Shirim Rabbah 1:3.
15. Ibn Ezra, noting Abraham's seemingly superfluous request that the righteous people of Sodom be "in the city" *(be-tokh ha-ir),* points out that Abraham was not referring to righteous people who removed themselves from their wicked surroundings. Rather, Abraham was pleading specifically on behalf of those righteous people who lived among the people, those trying to influence them to do better. Thus, Abraham was interested in his own, higher form of righteousness while pleading on behalf of the wicked cities.
16. See Tanhuma *Vayeshev;* Gen. Rabbah 82; Rashi; Abarbanel.
17. See Ex. 17:8-16; Deut. 25:17-19; I Sam. 15, 30; and the entire Book of Esther--Haman was descended from King Agag--an Amalekite.
18. Translation from *The Pentateuch and Rashi's Commentary: A Linear Translation into English*. Rabbi Abraham ben Isaiah and Rabbi Benjamin Sharfman. Genesis. Brooklyn, N.Y.: S.S.&R. Publishing Co. Inc., 1949.

RABBI ISRAEL MOSHE HAZZAN ON MUSIC

by Professor Edwin Seroussi
Bar-Ilan University, Ramat Gan

INTRODUCTION

The uses, functions and content of the music in the synagogue have been a subject of concern for our sages since at least the times of the Geonim in Babylonia (9th century), from whose times the first documents on this subject are extant.[1] Since the medieval period and up to modern times, Sephardi rabbis were attentive to this issue, responding to frequent queries by their flock on this matter. Many rabbinical consultations on music rest on two premises: first, on the idea that the music of the synagogal services is an open system, i.e., new music can be potentially adopted following the individual decision of the cantor; second, that as a consequence of this open system, there is a constant tension between the advocates of a developed musical approach to the public performance of the liturgy and their opponents, for whom expanded musicality obscured the content of the liturgical text and the concealed intentions embedded in its smooth flow.

A Sephardi personality whose opinions on music were widely mentioned in the musicological literature is Rabbi Israel Moshe ben Eliezer Hazzan (Izmir, Turkey, 1807 - Beirut, Lebanon, 1863), one of the most remarkable Sephardi intellectuals of the nineteenth century.[2] He lived during a period of upheaval, when traditional Sephardi Judaism started to confront modern European culture in the Ottoman Empire and

North Africa.[3] To summarize Rabbi Hazzan's position as rabbinical authority, we may quote Prof. Jose Faur's evaluation:

> His contemporaries recognized him as a leading scholar in rabbinic literature, jurisprudence, philosophy and theology. They applied to him the dictum, "From Moses to Moses there arose none like Moses", meaning that from the days of Moses ben Maimon until the days of Moses Hazzan no one had measured like either one of them. Rabbi Hazzan advocated religious humanism as a viable alternative to the negative effects of rational secularism. He also pointed out the dangers that the political ideology of the Enlightenment posed to the European establishment in general and to the Jews in particular. His views were widely known in Sephardic circles: from Morocco, Portugal and Holland in the West to Syria, the Holy Land and Egypt in the East. Rabbi Hazzan was one of the earliest and most articulate spokesmen on behalf of Jewish national autonomy, advocating the revival of Hebrew language and the establishment of a National Fund to purchase land for a Jewish home in Israel.[4]

At a very early age R. Hazzan moved with his father to Jerusalem where he was educated in the most prestigious rabbinical academies of the city and obtained his ordination as rabbi. He then embarked on an unusual international career for his time, traveling around the Jewish world as an emissary from Jerusalem and serving as chief rabbi in the communities of Rome, Corfu and Alexandria (Egypt). During a mission to London in 1844, he was active in the struggle against the incipient Reform movement.[5]

Rabbi Hazzan was apparently an accomplished *paytan* before he left the Land of Israel. In the Sephardi sphere this means that he was both a singer and a composer of religious poetry. Hazzan's background in the music of the Middle East provides the background for his interest in the musical customs of the Jews in Western Europe. During his ceremony of installation in Rome on August 21, 1847, Rabbi Hazzan heard the novelty of the choral music characteristic of the Italian synagogues at that time.[6] A choir of forty youngsters performed at this ceremony and the afternoon prayer (minha) which followed at the Scuola Catalana singing Psalm 16 and *Va-ani zot beriti* (Isaiah 59:21).[7] Choirs were also an established institution in the Italianized synagogues of Corfu and Alexandria where

Rabbi Hazzan served too.[8]

Rabbi Hazzan's opinions on music were expressed in one of his most important works, the responsa *Kerah shel Romi* (Livorno, 1876). Some of his views were known to the earliest researchers of Jewish music such as Eduard Birnbaum[9] and Francis L. Cohen.[10] Moshe Geshuri was the first, and thus far only, author to present a relatively encompassing appreciation of Hazzan's opinions on music. According to Geshuri, R. Hazzan "investigated the problems of Jewish music more than any other Sephardi scholar."[11] Later on, Yehuda Ratzhabi, in a study on the use of secular melodies in the synagogue, quoted extensively from Hazzan, citing him as an example of a lenient approach to this subject.[12] Finally, Amnon Shiloah quoted one passage on music by Hazzan which we shall discuss in detail later in this article.[13]

Despite this widespread interest, Rabbi Hazzan's opinions on music were never presented in their entirety nor were they analyzed in their historical, social and cultural context. These are the purposes of the present study.

EXCERPTS ON MUSIC IN *KERAH SHEL ROMI*

Passage I (Folio 1A)

The Bah (Bayit Hadash) was asked concerning the practice in synagogues of using music which is sung in the houses of worship (of non-Jews).[14] It is only forbidden regarding melodies which are unique to the non-Jews, since then (these melodies) are practices of idolatry, analogous to their altar which is completely forbidden (for us to use) . . . But if the music is not unique (to non-Jewish worship) then it seems to me that there is no prohibition, since we certainly do not learn from them the non-Jewish way of worship.

. . . Concerning the ruling of the Bah on the matter of music, since it is at hand, we shall say something about it. With all due respect to him, the matter of music, even music unique to non-Jewish worship, is not analogous to (the laws pertaining to) an altar.

Passage II (Folio 2a)

And if this tune *(Qol)* which the non-Jews sing in their houses of worship is one of submissiveness that penetrates the heart according to the art of music and according to what one was accustomed; and lacking it, the hearts and minds of the congregation will not be in a proper mood -- can it be believed that because fools went astray and established this music in their houses of worship, that we should also forbid something our nature demands? This is one of the five senses which gives pleasure to the body. Why should there be a difference between (the sense of hearing) and the sense of taste and the sense of smell? (It is permitted in the Torah) for Jews to taste sacrifices and smell the incense (even though non-Jews taste offerings and smell incense in their houses of worship). Isn't this because a person cannot overrule his natural spirit, common to all humans? The same law and the same reason applies to the sense of hearing and music, which relates equally to all people. . . . Can the Italian Jew, for example, overturn his natural (feelings) acquired in his homeland? (He is obviously influenced by the music he hears every day in the theatres, circuses and streets.)

According to the reasoning of the Bah, why isn't it forbidden to say Habdalah on a cup of wine next to the *tebah* (reader's desk), since also in the churches they make a blessing over their wine? Thus, the conclusion is as we have stated. In a matter which is natural and needed to all people, each according to its own laws and faiths, it is not relevant to make a prohibition. Otherwise, people could not live in peace (since there would be so many prohibitions).

And I have a great proof that everything that has a good reason -- whether because of pleasure or honor or because nature demands it by virtue of the customs of the various lands -- even if that thing is unique to the religious service of some churches of whatever national background, not only is this thing permissible to Jews and there is no prohibition of following in the ways of non-Jews; but quite to the contrary, it is a mitzvah to follow in their ways to beautify our synagogues with all types of beauty and honor which are equally (appreciated) by all human beings of that land -- even if this practice is unique to the (non-Jewish) places of worship.

Passage III (Fol. 4a)

There is a great difference between the Moslems and the Christians in this matter. The Christians never considered our prayer and our rituals to be heretical and shameful, as the Radbaz wrote about the Moslem (attitude towards Jewish worship).[15] On the contrary (the Christians) praise and glorify our recognition of God's oneness. Since we are valued respectfully in their eyes, the Radbaz would admit that we should improve our religious services and especially our synagogues so that they (Christians) will not scoff us saying: a beautiful Torah in an ugly vessel. This is because (the Christians) know the value of our Torah and mitzvot and prayer, which have been translated into the languages of their lands, as is known. Returning to the words of the Bah, let us say that if the Bah had studied the details carefully and had distinguished between music -- which has its own reason -- and an altar (which is purely for their worship and is considered as) a practice (law) without a reason -- he would not have written as he did. . . .

And I call into witness heaven and earth that when I was in the great city of sages and scholars, Izmir, I saw among the illustrious sages those who were great singers according to the art of music. At their head was the illustrious Rabbi Abraham Ha-Cohen Arias. For the musical form for the High Holy Days, which requires great submissiveness which is called among them *hizun*, they used to go to the Christian churches on their holy days, (and would stand) behind the wall (so that they could hear the church music) in order to learn from the (the Christians) the submissive tone which deeply moves the heart. From those melodies, they arranged wondrous *kadishim* and *kedushot*. And this is a great proof to all I have said and explained above; and this is enough. And I have found another support (for my position) in the responsa of the Gaonim *Qobetz Gadol*, number 152. . . who conclude that. . . it is forbidden for a hazan of a synagogue to sing in a language other than Hebrew; but as far as the melody itself is concerned when singing the Hebrew words, it does not matter (whether they derive from non-Jewish sources).

Passage IV (Folio 4b)

Whence have we Jews inherited the melodies and pleasant chants of the Psalms of David, which are heard in our holy cities? Don't we have a clear verse which says: "How can we sing the song of the Lord on foreign soil?" The fact is that (the ancient melodies) were forgotten. (It is said that we only have one original melody left and that is to "LeDavid Barukh Hashem Tzuri" (Psalm 144). (This melody survived) for three reasons: first, it is a fast tune, and overpowers like an actual song of battle. Second, it is amazing that Jews of all places, whether in Asia, Africa or Europe, all sing this particular Psalm in the same manner, which is not the case with any other prayers and services. In Moslem lands, the melody of our prayers is like that of the Moslems; in Europe, (our prayers are sung to melodies like the) melodies of the Christians. Yet, when it comes to this psalm (144) all are identical. I, who travelled all over these continents, did research in this matter. I found it to be true and evident that this melody remained to us as an inheritance from our ancestors -- but none others. Wherever the Israelites were exiled, the Jews learned the melodies of those lands. In Israel and all Arabia, the melody of our prayers, *kadishim* and *kedushot* are all based on Arabic music. In Turkey, our music is Turkish; in Christian lands, our music follows the Christian patterns. And who can deny that which is experienced? Shall we say that all Jews erred in this matter? Rather, they certainly were concerned that only Hebrew be used (in their synagogues for prayers) but as far as the melody is concerned, what can we do (except borrow the music of the lands in which we live) since our original holy melodies no longer remain for us?

Passage V (Folio 4b)

To tell the truth, I have been troubled all my life in that I have seen a number of pious and righteous people who would not listen to nor allow singing in the land of Israel in Arabic, even on excursions. (They would not sing) unless the poet set the song to Hebrew words. . . (but the law is that the prohibition of singing certain songs is dependent) on the content and not on the language (of the song. i.e. songs with improper and indecent themes should not be sung in any language; songs with proper content may be sung in any language, not only in Hebrew.)[16]

COMMENTARY

Rabbi Hazzan expressed his views on two issues related to music: 1) The relation between Jewish and non-Jewish music, and 2) The antiquity and origins of synagogal music.

THE RELATION BETWEEN JEWISH AND NON-JEWISH MUSIC

The main argument in favor of using non-Jewish music (Passages I-III and V) is developed a propos a question regarding the use of clocks in the synagogue. The core of the argument rests on Hazzan's opposition to the ruling on synagogal music by Rabbi Joel Sirkis, the Bayyit Hadash, who forbids music used in Christian rituals, even if the text is changed into Hebrew. One can clearly observe here the difference between the Sephardi and the Ashkenazi approach to the surrounding non-Jewish culture. The bitter confrontation with the Christian Church in Europe created among the Ashkenazi Jews a strong feeling against the use of any cultural asset that epitomized Christianity, even if tangentially. Sirkis, following the previous Ashkenazi lineage of ruling on this matter, did not allow any music that was specifically associated with Christian rituals even if the words were changed to Hebrew, the holy tongue.

Hazzan opposed Sirkis' view on the basis of the essence of pure music (i.e. music without words), that of a symbol which is universally perceived by all human beings through the sense of hearing. Music can not be compared, as the B"H argued, to an altar *(matzevah)*. The altar is a tangible, visible symbol of *avodah zarah* and was already prohibited by the sages.

Each human being is naturally born into a specific musical culture, and this inherited musical culture cannot be forbidden or avoided. On the other hand, language is a specific symbol of each people and should be controlled. This is the rationale for the substitution of Arabic or Turkish words by Hebrew sacred texts in the religious songs of the Sephardi and Oriental Jews since the time of the Ge'onim. Hazzan himself was engaged in this task during his youth in Eretz Israel, as he testifies (Passage V).

Rabbi Hazzan's opinion on music is therefore not an apologetic argument in support of the general similarity which he found between music in Italian synagogues and that of Christian churches. It is a vindication of the Sephardi view on music as opposed to the Orthodox Ashkenazi position on this matter. This argument should be particularly understood in its historical context, i.e. in reference to the struggle against the Reform movement in which Rabbi Hazzan played an active role. He perceived no danger to traditional Jewish identity and values in the use of any music of the gentile culture into which a Jew is born, provided that a sacred Hebrew text is fixed to it. He ruled in favor of music to strengthen and enhance the aesthetic image of the Jewish services in the eyes of modern Jews and non-Jews. One has to bear in mind that the lack of decorum in the traditional Jewish synagogue was an important issue in the agenda of the Reformers.

Hazzan's argument is also based on his own experience of youth in Turkey. The reference to the "Christian churches" in his native city of Izmir may be slightly misleading to the uninformed reader. He is referring to the Greek Orthodox church of this city whose "Christian" music is a branch of the classic Ottoman music tradition, a heritage shared by Muslims (particularly the Sufi sects, such as the Mevlevi), Christians (Greeks and Armenians) and Jews in the Ottoman Empire since the late sixteenth century.[17] Moreover, we are in a position today to throw light on the work of the great Izmirli *paytan* and composer Rabbi Abraham Hacohen Arias who is mentioned by Rabbi Hazzan. Some of Arias' compositions for the synagogue, based on his own poems or on those by his predecessors (e.g. Rabbi Israel Najara), are extant in musical notation. These notations were prepared by the distinguished cantor from Izmir, Isaac Algazi (1889-1950). The pieces by Arias were most probably transmitted to Algazi by his masters, e.g. his father Salomon "Bulbuli" Algazi and Shem Tov Chikiar, both of whom lived close to the times of Rabbi Arias.[18] Arias composed in the old style of Ottoman music, a style which was prevalent in the Greek Orthodox Churches of Izmir too. In fact, this close musical interaction between the three religious faiths of the Ottoman Empire provided the background for the wide musical horizons of Hazzan and nurtured his tolerant views on music.[19]

THE ANTIQUITY AND ORIGINALITY OF SYNAGOGAL MUSIC

On the basis of his remarkable cosmopolitan experience and his views that: a) a close interaction existed between Jewish and non Jewish music throughout history, and b) that synagogal music is an open musical system, Hazzan draws the conclusion that there cannot be an "original" Jewish music (Passage IV). Hazzan's views contrast with those of the later nationalist scholars, especially A.Z. Idelsohn, who advocated the existence of a fundamental musical heritage common to all Jews. Rabbi Hazzan argued that the original music from the Temple times was lost because the exiled from Zion did not continue to sing it in foreign lands, as it is written: "How can we sing a song of the Lord on alien soil?" (Psalm 137:4). He concluded, on the basis of his empirical observations, that the melodies of each Jewish community differed from one another. He found only one melody which should be of great antiquity because according to his experience it is sung with the "same" melody in every community. This is the melody of *Le-David barukh*, Psalm 144 chanted at the opening of the *arbith* (evening) service at the conclusion of the Sabbath.[20] This view of Hazzan can be supported by factual evidence. The melodies to which this Psalm is sung to this day in Ashkenazi and Sephardi communities indeed employ similar motifs.

The uniqueness of the liturgical music repertory of each community is a fact of life which should be taken into consideration when a Jewish congregation selects its staff. In his pamphlet *Divrei Emet Ve-shalom* which deals with the relations between the Portuguese and Ashkenazi communities of Amsterdam, he says:

> "We... therefore ought to select a leader in our religious affairs from the midst of us, whose office it is to be acquainted with the language, customs, and sacred melodies, political history, and to adhere closely to all the observances in the ceremonial worship and liturgy of the congregation over which he is to preside."[21]

CONCLUSION

The open-minded opinions on music of Rabbi Hazzan should not be misinterpreted as an overall liberal overture in favour of radical changes in matters of ritual and custom. When asked by a contemporary Italian colleague whether shaving on *hol ha-mo'ed* can be permitted on the basis of a comparison with his lenient ruling on music, Hazzan flatly rejected the idea and replied:

> Our dear friend! The stature of my ruling on music as of my ruling on shaving [on *hol ha-mo'ed*] is literally as the height of two high mountains. First, music itself was never forbidden in the Talmud and not by any

poseq among the great teachers. Only the Rabbi B"H (one of the greatest zealots, as it is known) wanted to compare [music] to their laws [of the gentiles] as the altar *[matzevah]* and he forbade it. And I stretched my imagination with evidences, and [music] was anyway permitted. But here the prohibition of shaving is already a famous ruling *[gezerah]* in the Talmud...[22]

His distinction between visual symbols as opposed to the pure sonic symbols (e.g. music without words, the sound of the clock bells) reflects a modern approach which recalls the views on music by some nineteenth-century philosophers. We cannot assume, however, that Rabbi Hazzan was acquainted with the reflections on music by Kant, Schopenhauer or Hanslik. His approach to music stemmed from a rather independent process of thinking which was rooted in the rulings of his Sephardi predecessors (some of whom are mentioned by him, e.g. Maimonides, Salomon ben Simeon Duran, David Ben Abi Zimra) as well as on the particular fate of Jewish musical culture in the world of Islam in general, and the Ottoman Empire in particular.

NOTES

1   For a selection of texts on this subject see, Israel Adler, *Hebrew Writings Concerning Music in Manuscripts and Printed Books from Geonic Times up to 1800* [HWCM], Munchen, Henle, 1975 (RISM B IX2). For succint overviews see, *idem, La pratique musicale savante dans quelques communautés juives en Europe aux XVIIe et XVIIIe siècles*, Paris, 1966, vol. I, pp. 10-22; Edwin Seroussi, "A Hassidic Exemplum in Judeo-Spanish Homily of the Early Nineteenth-Century: A New Source on 'Secular' Music in Synagogal Singing," *Jerusalem Studies of Jewish Folklore*, vol. 11-12 (1990), pp. 121-138.

2   Hazzan's opinions on music were succintly discussed by José Faur, "Sephardim in the Nineteenth Century: New Directions and Old Values", *Proceedings of the American Academy for Jewish Research* 44 (1977), pp. 29-52, esp. pp. 49-51. I am thankful to Prof. Faur for his insightful observations on a preliminary version of this article.

3   See, Marc D. Angel, *Voices in Exile: A Study in Sephardic Intellectual History*, Hoboken 1991, chapter 10, esp. pp. 157-8.

4   José Faur, *Rabbi Yisrael Moshe Hazzan: The Man and His Works*, Haifa: Raphael Arbel Academic Publishers, 5739/1978, English summary, p. 17. Faur's monograph

was reprinted together with the published writings by Hazzan (Jerusalem, 1990/1). See also: Abraham Galante, *Les juifs d'Izmir* (1937), 74ff; Moshe D. Gaon, *Yehudei ha-mizrah be-Eretz Yisrael,* vol. 2 (Jerusalem, 1938), pp. 251ff; Abraham Ya'ari, *Sheluhei Eretz Yisrael,* 2nd. ed. (Jerusalem 1977), pp. 176ff, 729-732; *Encyclopaedia Judaica* 7, col. 1552; *Jewish Encyclopedia* 6 (1904), p. 288.

5   See his *Kin'at Tziyon,* Amsterdam 1846. This subject is discussed by A.R. Malachi, *"Milhemet ha-yishuv ba-reforma"* ["The War of the Yishuv against the Reform"], in: Sh. Darakh, *Perakim be-toldot ha-yishuv ha-yashan* [Studies in the History of the Old Yishuv], Tel-Aviv 1971, pp. 338ff.

6   News concerning the music of modern synagogues reached the East and the reactions were disapproving. The most detailed document on this issue is a responsum by Rabbi Hayyim Palache of Izmir on the use of instrumental music (particularly the organ) and the employment of gentile musicians in the modernized synagogues of Paris. See, Hayyim Palache, *Lev Hayyim,* vol. 2 (Izmir 1868/9), responsum no. 9. See also Faur, "Sephardim in the Nineteenth Century", p. 50, n. 79.

7   The ceremony is described in: *Il Possesso dell'eccelentissimo Sig. Mose Israel Hazzan de Gerusalemme Rabbino Maggiore dell'universita Israelitica di Roma.* Roma 1847, esp. pp. [1], 17-19. See also, Roberto Bonfil, *"Tmurot be-minhageihem ha-datyyim shel yehudei Roma bi-tqufat kehunato shel Rabbi Israel Moshe Hazzan (5607-5612)"* ["Changes in the Religious Customs of the Jews of Rome during the Tenure of Rabbi Israel Moshe Hazzan (1847-1852)"], *Scritti in Memoria di Enzo Sereni: Saggi sull'Ebraismo Romano a cura di Daniel Carpi,* Attilio Milano, Umberto Nahon. Jerusalem 1970, pp. 228-251.

8   A detailed description of the ceremony of installation at the Italian synagogue in Corfu is also available: "un coro di eletti giovani, sopo intuonati i versi 56-57-58-59 del Salmo 118 fece risuonar l'aere di un Cantico in verse Ebraici, che il Professore Sr. Leon Giusto....appositamente scrisse colla Traduzione in versi Italiani". At the end of this ceremony the choir sang Isaiah 59:21 and Psalm 72.

9   Eduard Birnbaum, in *"Briefe aus Koenigsberg" Juedische Kantor* 5 (1883), no. 43 (30 November), p. 348.

10 Francis L. Cohen, *"Le-David Barukh", Jewish Encylopedia* 7 (1904), pp. 659-661, esp. p. 660.

11 Moshe Geshuri, *"Iyunim musikaliim le-ha-rav ha-sfaradi Israel Moshe Hazzan"* ["Musical studies of the Sephardi Rabbi Israel Moshe Hazzan"], *Sinai* 19, no. 2 (November 1955), pp. 118-125.

12 Yehuda Ratzhabi, *"Ha-niggun ha-zar ba-shir u-ba-fiyyut"* ["The Foreign Melody in

the Song and the Piyyut"], *Tazlil* 6 (1967), pp. 8-13, esp. pp. 10-11.

13   A. Shiloah, *Jewish Musical Traditions*, Delaware 1995, pp. 82-83. See also, idem, "The Music of the Jewish Communities in Greece and Turkey and Its Relation to Byzantine Music," *Musica Antiqua* VII (Acta Scientifica, Bydgoszcz, 1985), pp. 247-256.

14   Rabbi Hazzan refers here to Rabbi Joel Sirkis (Lublin, 1561- Cracow, 1640), called the Bayyit Hadash, in his *She'elot u-teshuvot* (Frankfurt de Main 1696-7, end of siman 127). According to Adler: "[Sirkis] sees no objection to the introduction of new musical compositions into the synagogue even if they originate in the church, but only on condition that the 'specific' chants of the church are avoided... 'for it is not from the Christians that we borrow...these chants, but from the science of music'". See Adler, *La pratique musicale* (above n. 1), unpublished English translation of chapter 1, p. 9.

15   "It has become widespread among the Arabs that the Jewish service has no decorum and that the Jews spit, cough and talk during their prayers". This quotation, part of an old taqqana (ordinance) by Maimonides on the repetition of the Amidah, was translated from Arabic to Hebrew by Rabbi David Ben Abi Zimra (RaDBa"Z, 1479-1573) in his own responsum on that issue. See, Israel M. Goldman, *The Life and Times of Rabbi David Ibn Abi Zimra*. New York, 1970, p. 107.

16   Faur (1977) assumed that a piyyut with the acrostic "Israel Hazzan" found in Ms. Jerusalem, Mossad Ha-rav Kook no. 110, fol. 31a, may be of the authorship of Rabbi Israel Moshe Hazzan. This assumption cannot be supported because this manuscript clearly belongs to the eighteenth-century Ottoman-Hebrew tradition. It is noticeable, however, that around the 1840s, there was a renaissance in the writing of piyyutim in Jerusalem under the influence of immigrant paytanim from Aleppo. Manuscripts from this period show that the Jerusalemite paytanim indeed employed Arabic melodies for their new songs. See, Edwin Seroussi, "On the Beginnings of the Singing of Bakkashot in 19th Century Jerusalem," *Pe'amim* 56 (1993), pp. 106-124. (In Hebrew)

17   For a general overview of classic Ottoman music among the Turks see, Karl Signell, *Makam: Modal Practice in Turkish Art Music,* Seattle 1977; for the Ottoman Jewish scene, see Edwin Seroussi, "The Turkish Makam in the Musical Culture of the Ottoman Jews: Sources and Examples," *Israel Studies in Musicology* 5 (1990), pp. 43-59. Shiloah *(Jewish Musical Traditions,* p. 83 and note 23) assumed that Hazzan is referring to the neo-Byzantine style that crystallized in the Greek Church after the 1830s.

18   On Jewish musicians of Izmir see, Abraham Galante, "*Les juifs dans la musique*

Turque," in *Turcs et juifs,* pp. 101-109, reprinted in Galante's *Histoire des juifs de Turquie,* vol. VIII, Istanbul 1985, pp. 66-73; *idem, Histoire des juifs d'Anatolie,* 1er. Volume: *Les juifs d'Izmir* (Smyrne), Istanbul 1935, pp. 163-167; on Chikiar see, Shabetay Dinar, "*Shemtov Chiquiar, maestro compositor de musica oriental,*" *Voz Sefaradi* (Mexico City), II (1967), 40-42. Piyyutim by Arias were published in *Siftey Renanot* (Izmir, 1862/3), a collection of responsa by his son, Rabbi Hayyim Yossef. Other songs appear in *Noten Zemirot Ve-hallel Ve-zimra* (Saloniki, 1879). Two musical compositions by Arias were published by Isaac Algazi in his edition of the *Fasil Makam Huseyni* (Istanbul, 1925). These compositions are: "Peshref Usul Devri Quebir" on a text by Israel Najara and "Beste Usul Hafif". Other transcriptions by Algazi of works by Arias are in my possession and will be published in my upcoming book *Ottoman Hebrew Music and Sacred Poetry.* Compositions by Arias could still be found in the memory of members of the "Maftirim" choir of Izmir. One piyyut by Arias was recorded in the city of Petah Tiqvah by Susana Weich Shahak and myself from Mr. Binyamin Chikiar who immigrated from Izmir to Israel in 1947.

19 This trend continued in the twentieth century. Cantor Moshe Vital, originally from Magnesia and later active in Izmir, Rhodes and Jerusalem, used to attend in his youth (ca. 1920) the dervishes' gatherings on Friday afternoons to learn melodies for the synagogue, as did other Jewish cantors in Turkey. See, Moshe Vital, "Lecture at the first convention of hazzanim and conductors in Palestine, Jerusalem," *Die Shul und die Chasanim Welt* (June 1938), p. 3. (In Hebrew)

20 See Birnbaum, 348; F.L. Cohen, VII, pp. 659-661; A.Z. Idelsohn, *Hebraisch-Orientalische Melodienschatz,* Wien-Berlin-Jerusalem, vol. 2 (1922), Gesange der Persischer Juden, p. 2, note 2 and pp. 75-76.

21 Moshe Israel Hassan, *Words of Peace and Truth: A Reply.* London [1845] printed by Samuel Meldola, p. 5.

22 *Kerah shel romi,* fol. 18b.

THE ATTACHMENT OF MOROCCAN JEWRY TO THE LAND OF ISRAEL ACCORDING TO RABBINIC LITERATURE

by Dr. Henry Toledano
Hofstra University

INTRODUCTION

The love of Moroccan Jews for Eretz Yisrael and their deep attachment to it permeated all aspects of Moroccan Jewish life including prayers, poetry, customs and rituals, humor and folklore. This centrality of the Land of Israel in Moroccan Jewish life found expression in a number of specific and concrete manifestations, the most striking of which are:

1. The generosity and readiness with which they extended financial assistance to the old yishuv in Eretz Yisrael through the institution of *shelihut* as well as other forms of fund raising.
2. The Messianic-Nationalistic motif in the Moroccan *piyyutim* and the important role these *piyyutim* played in spreading and intensifying Zionist or Messianic fervor among Moroccan Jews, due in great measure to their popular aspect.[1]
3. Customs unique to Moroccan Jews that were based from their inception on the attachment to and love of Eretz Yisrael.[2]
4. Actual aliyah to Eretz Yisrael which dates back to the earliest days of the yishuv, an aliyah which really never stopped.[3]

In examining the ties between Moroccan Jewry and Eretz Yisrael, we have at our disposal a number of diverse sources which bear on one aspect or another of this relationship.[4] One of the most important sources for the study of the centrality of Eretz Yisrael in Moroccan Jewish life is Moroccan rabbinic literature in its diverse modes of expression and literary genres, including biblical and talmudic exegesis, mystical literature, responsa and interpretative legal literature (i.e., commentaries on the *Shulhan Arukh, takkanot,* (enactments or ordinances) *piyyutim* (religious poetry), *derashot* (homiletics and sermons), and historiography and personal correspondence.[5]

Of these, the *piyyutim, takkanot* and responsa bear directly on Moroccan Jewry's attachment to Eretz Yisrael.

For this article, we will focus our attention on several examples of responsa literature which have a direct bearing upon several aspects of the relationship between Moroccan Jewry and Eretz Yisrael. Specifically, the texts I propose to examine are: first, a responsum by Rabbi Raphael Ankawa dating from 1902, which bears directly on the *shelihut* activity in Morocco, the generous response of Moroccan Jewry to the needs of the old yishuv, and the general attitude of this Jewry to Eretz Yisrael.

Next, I will consider a number of responsa by Moroccan Jurists--decisors (Poskim) from different periods (1732-1868) all dealing with various aspects of emigration to Eretz Yisrael. I will first translate and/or summarize pertinent passages of these texts, and then draw the appropriate conclusions based on the contents of the texts.

Before proceeding with the analysis of these texts it is worthwhile to point out why the information culled from these legal sources is most reliable. Certainly the authors of these texts were not historians; their aim was not to narrate, record, or even interpret historical events. Accordingly, they had no interest in promoting any particular thesis or theory. Their primary concern was to provide religious and spiritual guidance and decide legal issues brought before them in accordance with halakhah. But in doing so they obviously had to use their judgement in lending more weight to one opinion over another and in deciding which rule to apply to a particular situation. And it is in this process that their in-built bias in favor of Eretz Yisrael is quite evident. Furthermore, their decisions reflected not only their own personal attitudes, but those of the people as well; for these rabbis (in all their decisions and enactments) were always sensitive to the contemporary needs and moods of the people. Indeed one of the unique characteristics of rabbinic leaders in Morocco was their readiness and willingness to meet the needs of their times and their communities imaginatively, boldly, and decisively.[6]

It is also important to point out that while the number of responsa discussed in this article is limited, nonetheless they are typical and representative of the thinking of Moroccan rabbis and Moroccan Jewish public. It will be shown later that the information derived from these responsa regarding *shelihut* activity in Morocco and Moroccan aliyah during the eighteenth and nineteenth centuries is amply corroborated by numerous other sources, rabbinic and non-rabbinic.

I

RESPONSUM BY R. RAPHAEL ANKAWA:

TRANSLATION AND SUMMARY

The first text to be examined is a responsum dating from 1902 by Rabbi Raphael Ankawa.[7] The subject of R. Ankawa's responsum is a dispute between the rabbis of Tiberias and those of Jerusalem over the allocation of one half of the estate of a certain wealthy woman from Mogador, who in her will bequeathed one half of her estate to the needy of her native city and the other half to those of Jerusalem. The problem arose when R. Eliyahu Yiloz, an emissary from Tiberias who was involved in defending and upholding the will of the deceased lady against the claim of the surviving husband, claimed a share of the estate for Tiberias. R. Yiloz collected the signatures of a number of people who testified that most of the women in Mogador (or elsewhere in Morocco) used the name Jerusalem to designate all of Eretz Yisrael. Accordingly, R. Yiloz argued that the half of the estate left by the deceased to Jerusalem ought to be divided equally among the four holy cities, Jerusalem, Hebron, Safed, and Tiberias. He, of course, claimed the share of Tiberias. Naturally, the rabbis of Jerusalem opposed R. Yiloz's contention and appealed to R. Ankawa to intervene in the matter. The issue R. Ankawa was asked to rule on is whether by Jerusalem the deceased intended only Jerusalem or all of Eretz Yisrael.

R. Ankawa begins by stating that ideally he should not get involved in this matter, for the great scholars of Eretz Yisrael can certainly deal with the issue which concerns them more competently; there are kings and officers among them from whom learning and Torah go forth.

But since he was asked, he feels obliged to render his opinion. He rules that the deceased, in leaving one half of her estate to Jerusalem, must have intended only that specific city. He offers four arguments to support his decision: the first and last arguments are based on purely legal halakhic principles, but the second and third arguments bear directly on our subject.

SUMMARY OF ARGUMENT 1

In drafting contracts, the rule is that precise and specific wording must be used; accordingly, the terms of a contract are to be strictly construed, and we may not assume that whoever drafted the contract, used its terms in a general or figurative sense. A will is a contract. Therefore, even if the deceased was one of those who used the name Jerusalem to designate all of Eretz Yisrael, the scribes who wrote the will knew the rule, and must have ascertained that she meant Jerusalem specifically before writing it in the will.

SUMMARY OF ARGUMENT 2

If we construe Jerusalem as cited in the will to mean all of Israel, i.e., the four holy cities, then each of them would get only one fourth of the half of the estate, that is one eighth of the estate. It is inconceivable that any Jew would give a city in the Diaspora, though it be one's own native city, preferential treatment over any holy city in Eretz Yisrael, let alone over Jerusalem which would be the case if Mogador received one half of the estate and the four holy cities of Israel received only one eighth each.

SUMMARY OF ARGUMENT 3

It is apparent that the woman in question was the daughter of the great philanthropist *(Rodef Tsedakot)*, R. Ya'akov Iysh whose home was always open to solicitors from Jerusalem, whether they were community emissaries or private solicitors collecting funds for themselves, all of whom were received most hospitably in his home. Therefore, since solicitors from Jerusalem were found frequently in her father's house, it is reasonable to assume that she was more likely to favor Jerusalem *(da'tah keroba lyrushalayim)*.

This is similar to R. Joseph Caro's ruling in Yoreh De'ah, (Chapter 258:4) which states: if a man orders that 200 zuzim or a Torah scroll be given to a synagogue (without specifying which synagogue), we give the money or the Torah scroll to the synagogue in which the man used to pray in his city. Therefore, here too, since the deceased was accustomed to see solicitors from Jerusalem in her father's house regularly, she must have intended Jerusalem specifically.

SUMMARY OF ARGUMENT 4

Even if we assume that we really cannot know what the woman intended by Jerusalem, we still must rule in favor of Jerusalem. The reason for this is that Jerusalem will be entitled to a share of the estate regardless of what the woman intended (the only question is whether it is entitled to half of the estate or to only one eighth of it), whereas the other cities would not be entitled to anything in the event that the deceased intended Jerusalem specifically. Therefore, Jerusalem's claim to a share of the estate is a sure claim *(vaday)* while that of the other holy cities is in doubt *(safek)*. We fall back then on the well-known halakhic principle that the party having a sure claim has the presumption in its favor *(ein safek motzi midei vaday)* and the party that has a sure claim gets all. And adds R. Ankawa, this rule is agreed upon unanimously by all the authorities as is clear from the *Tur* and the *Shulhan Arukh*. Therefore, here too, the right of the other holy cities is in doubt and cannot take away the right of Jerusalem which is a sure right.

ANALYSIS OF SECOND ARGUMENT

Judging by the extensive discussion R. Ankawa devotes to the second argument, it is clear that it must have been the overriding consideration in his decision. Therefore, in order to fully appreciate the forcefulness of his decision, let us examine his second argument more closely.

He begins thus:

> The second argument is based on reason and logic. For even if we assume the deceased to have been one of those women who designated by Jerusalem all of Eretz Yisrael, still in this instance, she must have meant only the specific Jerusalem which is holier than the other cities. And the reason for this assumption is that since the deceased willed half her estate to the poor and the scholars of Mogador, and the other half to Jerusalem, she could have only meant to the specific Jerusalem, and not to all the holy cities; for if you argue that she meant all the holy cities of Eretz Yisrael, is it conceivable *(hayitakhen dabar ze leha'alot al hada'at)* that she should bequeath half of her estate to Mogador and the other half to be divided among the four holy cities (in which case each of the holy cities receives only one eighth while Mogador gets one half!). And if only *(halvay!)* she had willed one fifth of the estate to Mogador, and the other four fifths to Jerusalem, I could argue that perhaps she meant by Jerusalem all the four holy cities, for in that case, Mogador would receive no more than any of the four holy cities (which would get one fifth each). But now that she left a full half of the estate to Mogador, heaven forbid that we advance an argument that makes this woman faithless in her will *(Sota Betsavatah)* in preferring a maidservant over her mistress,[8] that is making a city in the Diaspora, Mogador worthier than cities in Eretz Yisrael, worthier even than Jerusalem.

Because the second argument is based on reason, R. Ankawa seems to ensure that all possible objections to it are refuted. Accordingly, he raises a number of possible objections to his line of reasoning and proceeds to dismiss them one by one.

OBJECTION NUMBER 1

One may argue that by Jerusalem she might have intended all the holy cities in Israel and if as a result Mogador received more than any of the cities in Eretz Yisrael, this was in accordance with the principle that the poor of one's own city come before those of any other city, *(aniyei irkha va'aniyei ir aheret aniyei irkha kodmin).*

R. Ankawa's answer to this objection is that, first, there is a difference of opinion among the legal authorities as to whether or not this principle applies when the other city is one in Eretz Yisrael. Second, if she intended to give preference to Mogador, in accordance with this principle, she should have left the entire estate to Mogador; that she did not do so indicates that she was not acting on the basis of *aniyei irkha kodmin.*

OBJECTION NUMBER 2

One might argue that by Jerusalem she meant all of Eretz Yisrael, and that she was acting on the basis of the *aniyei irkha* principle. The reason she did not leave her entire estate to Mogador is that she felt that one half of the estate could provide adequately for the poor and scholars of Mogador, and therefore she willed the other half to Eretz Yisrael (however it might be allocated among the holy cities). To this objection, R. Ankawa's answer is that the terms of the will show that only the fruits (profits earned) of the estate were to be used for the needs of Mogador. Surely, argues R. Ankawa, the usefruct of half the estate will in no way cover all the needs of the poor and the scholars of Mogador. Therefore, he argues, it is clear that she did not intend to satisfy all the needs of the poor and the scholars of Mogador; nor did she act on the basis of the *aniyei irkha* principle, since she did not leave the entire estate to Mogador; rather she thought both Mogador and Jerusalem equally merited her generosity.

Rabbi Ankawa argues further that the deceased did not act on the basis of *aniye irkha* principle, because in her will she aimed to help the poor and the scholars who busy themselves with the study of Torah (in both cities). And certainly, she could not have given preferential treatment to Mogador over Jerusalem from which shall go forth Torah, and it is more appropriate and fitting that one give preference to (the scholars) of Jerusalem for from Zion shall go forth pure and clear Torah.[9]

Having disposed of all objections, R. Ankawa concludes his second argument thus:

> Therefore, we need not bother and get involved in the controversy of whether or not the poor of one's own city rate preference over the poor of Eretz Yisrael. We can continue to raise other arguments, but since our reasoning is self-evident *(pashut me-atsmo)*, we need not prolong our discussion by adducing other proofs--for this matter is really simple enough. And now we go back to our original argument, namely, since the deceased left half her estate to the poor of Mogador, is it conceivable to assume that she meant the other half of the estate to be divided between the four holy cities in which case the priest's wife would be revered less than the innkeeper *(lo tihye kohenet kefundakit)*. Therefore, it is clear that by naming Jerusalem she intended only one city in Eretz Yisrael, in which case Mogador would be equal to one of the holy cities (i.e., Jerusalem) each receiving one half of the estate.

It is interesting to note the striking imagery R. Ankawa uses to contrast Mogador with cities in Eretz Yisrael: maidservant versus her mistress, and innkeeper versus priest's wife.

Finally R. Ankawa introduces another possibility; perhaps the deceased intended to leave half her estate to only one city in Eretz Yisrael, but that she might have believed that all the holy cities were called Jerusalem, in which case a new problem arises, namely, which of the four cities is entitled to the bequest? R. Ankawa would exercise judicial discretion and assume that the real Jerusalem, which is holier than the other three cities, was intended. In support of his reasoning, he quotes the Talmud (Ket. 85b) and the *Shulhan Arukh (Hoshen Mishpat,* chapter 253:29): If a person says I give my possessions to Tobiah and there are two people named Tobiah (in that city) of whom one is a scholar *(talmid hakham),* he gets preference. So, here too, argues R. Ankawa, we accord preference to the city that is holier than the others. And clearly, Jerusalem is holier because of the sanctity of those who dwell in it, and because of the fact that Jerusalem has a greater Jewish population (than the other three). Therefore, the deceased clearly intended Jerusalem, the glorious city.

DISCUSSION

From this responsum we learn a number of things about the relationship between Moroccan Jewry and Eretz Yisrael.

First of all, the very fact that a woman in Mogador willed half her estate to Jerusalem, (whatever she meant by Jerusalem) testifies to the centrality of Eretz Yisrael in the life of Moroccan Jewry. She is not the only person to have done so. In fact, wills and trusts drawn up by Moroccan Jews in favor of Jews living in Eretz Yisrael constituted a regular source of income for the Jewish settlement there. A number of responsa indicate that Moroccan Jews often left a share of their estate (and in some cases even all of it) to the Jews living in Jerusalem and the other holy cities. Sometimes, they established trusts whose income was earmarked for helping the needy and the scholars of one of the four holy cities.[10]

Second, the fact that an emissary from Tiberias happened to be in Mogador at the time, as well as the fact that the woman is presumed to have frequently seen emissaries and other solicitors from Jerusalem in her father's house (argument 3), all this reflects the fact (attested by other sources) that emissaries from Tiberias and Jerusalem (and in earlier times, from Hebron and Safed as well) visited Morocco with some frequency. Morocco was considered a central region of *shelihut* activity.[11]

Third, the controversy between the rabbis of Tiberias and those of Jerusalem with regard to which city is entitled to what share of the Mogador woman's estate is not new. We know of similar controversies in the past, the most well-known being the three-way controversy between the rabbis of Tiberias and Jerusalem, and those of Meknes over the allocations of funds raised in Meknes for the two cities in Israel. R. Ya'akov Ben Yekutiel Berdugo (1783-1843), the great decisor of Meknes in his time, sided with the rabbis of Jerusalem thereby bringing upon himself the ire of the rabbis of Tiberias. Rabbi Ya'akov Moshe Toledano published in his *Otzar Hagenazim,* the three-way correspondence in this controversy (nine letters in all).[12] Again, the very dispute shows the importance of Morocco as a source of income for Eretz Yisrael.

But perhaps the most telling point of this responsum is that, in ruling for Jerusalem, R. Ankawa bases one of his arguments (perhaps the most decisive one) on the premise that no Jew could conceivably give more generously to a city in the Diaspora--though it be his or her own city--than to any of the holy cities in Eretz Yisrael, let alone more than to Jerusalem. Furthermore, R. Ankawa argues that the deceased could not have given preference to Mogador since her aim was to aid and promote the study of Torah (in either city), and it is more likely and more appropriate that one give preference to the Torah of Jerusalem, for from Zion shall go forth pure and clear Torah. This expresses a clear bias, namely, that the Torah and scholars of Eretz Yisrael are superior and worthier of support than others. Finally, R. Ankawa asserts several times in the course of his discussion, that Jerusalem is holier than the other holy cities *(shehi yoter kedosha mehaberoteha).* This obviously reflects the attitude of Moroccan Jews for whom the magic name Jerusalem came to designate all of Eretz Yisrael.

Finally, it is worth noting that Rabbi Ankawa's responsum is truly a model of a Sephardic *pesak halakhah* in terms of its lucid and elegant style, its well defined structure, its straightforward presentation of the issues involved, its logical and orderly development of the arguments (halakhic and non-halakhic), and its focus on the issue at hand and avoidance of tangential discussions and digressions. It is a fine example of the very desirable features of a *pesak* outlined in a recent essay on the subject by Rabbi Shalom Messas, the Chief Sephardic Rabbi of Jerusalem and a very important contemporary halakhic authority.[13]

II

RESPONSA ON ALIYAH--SUMMARY AND TRANSLATION

The other texts to be examined concern emigration to Eretz Yisrael. They include a number of responsa and several entries in commentaries on the *Shulhan Arukh.* These texts emanate from different cities in Morocco and different periods and were authored by eminent jurists-decisors *(poskim),* all recognized as undisputed legal authorities of

their times. These texts deal with various issues revolving around emigration to Eretz Yisrael. For example:
1. Can a man compel his wife against her will to accompany him to Eretz Yisrael?
2. In the event that she refuses to join the husband and he divorces her, must he pay the ketubah, or does she forfeit her right to it?
3. When following a divorce the mother retains custody of minor children, can a father intending to make aliyah take the children with him?
4. When a man makes a vow to go up to Eretz Yisrael and is then unable to do so, may his vow be annulled retroactively as is the case in ordinary vows?

The central issue in deciding all the above and related questions is whether or not residence in Eretz Yisrael is a continuous obligation incumbent upon the individual Jew for all generations. Assuming that it is an obligation, can it be overridden by the fear of danger involved in travel (*sakanat derakhim*)--whatever the nature of the danger?

In order to follow the sometimes entangled arguments and discussion in the sources, it seems useful to review briefly the halakhic background of this question.

The Mishnah in Ketuboth states: All may be compelled to go up to the Land of Israel but none may be compelled to leave it.

If he (the husband) desires to go up (to the Land of Israel) and his wife refuses to go up, she is to be compelled to go up; and if she still does not consent, she may be divorced without payment of the ketubah (the marriage settlement). Conversely, if she (the wife) desires to go up to the Land of Israel and the husband refuses to go up, he may be compelled to go up, and if he does not consent, he is forced to divorce and pay the ketubah. (Ket. 110b)

So far the talmudic rule is clear and succinct. The matter is complicated however by a statement of the Tosafot, who state that this rule was not in force in their day for two reasons:
1. the danger of travel;
2. the opinion of Rabbi Haim Ben Hananel ha-Cohen who maintains

that residence in Eretz Yisrael was not obligatory in his day. His reason is that residence in Eretz Yisrael entails the obligation to fulfill numerous commandments which depend on the land, and which during the many centuries of exile have fallen into disuse, a fact which renders their careful observance very unlikely.

The statement of the Tosafot is somewhat problematic and is capable of two interpretations.

1. The Tosafot are offering two separate arguments why the talmudic rule is not valid in their time: a. the danger of travel, and b. Rabbi Cohen's opinion;
2. Both reasons offered by the Tosafot are those of Rabbi Cohen and are interdependent, i.e., we worry about the danger in travel because residence in Eretz Yisrael is no longer a mitzvah. This is significant because if both reasons are those of R. Cohen, since R. Cohen's opinion is disregarded by normative halakhah, we fall back on the mishnaic rule that it is an obligation. If, on the other hand, the Tosafot's statement represents two distinct arguments, then even if we disregard R. Cohen's opinion, we still have to consider the danger of travel argument. The Mordechi attributes both arguments of the Tosafot to R. Cohen and so do two of our decisors (R. Sha'ul Abitbol and R. Raphael Moseh Elbaz) who accordingly dismiss the danger of travel argument as well.

The next important halakhic source is R. Joseph Caro's code (*Eben Ha'ezer* 75:4) which essentially repeats the talmudic rule that either spouse may compel the other to go to Eretz Yisrael. Yet, in the very next paragraph (75:5) he adds: Some maintain that the mishnaic rule that all may be compelled to go up the Land of Israel is in force only when it is possible (to travel to Eretz Yisrael) without [exposing oneself] to danger, therefore from the extreme West (Morocco) to No-amon (Alexandria) we do not compel [the spouse] to go, and from No-amon upward we compel [the spouse to go] either by land, or by sea during the dry season, if there are no highway robbers (or pirates).

The second opinion cited by R. Caro is that of Rashbash (Rabbi Shelomo Ben Shimon Duran) who maintains that residence in Eretz Yisrael is an obligation, but concedes that nowadays because of the danger of travel, it is binding only on those who live in the proximity of Eretz Yisrael (as from Alexandria upward) and not on those who live at great distances from Eretz Yisrael (as from Morocco to Alexandria) (*Teshuvot Rashbash*, no. 2). R. Caro's statements in paragraphs 75:4 and 75:5 seem to contradict each other and again two of our decisors deal with this seeming contradiction and reconcile it. See examples F and G below.

Following are several examples of the responsa on the subject.

EXAMPLE A

Rabbi Ya'akov Aben Tsur (1673-1752), who was a judge in Fez and Meknes, rules that a man may not compel his wife to go with him to Eretz Yisrael and that if he decides to go alone, he must pay her the ketubah in full. But the reason for his decision is not that he does not consider residence in Eretz Yisrael in his time to be an obligation; on the contrary, throughout his responsum, he takes it for granted that it is obligatory in accordance with the mishnaic rule all may be compelled to go up to Eretz Yisrael. The reason for his decision is that in this instance the ketubah contained an oath made by the husband not to take his wife from her city to another without her consent.

And, argues Rabbi Aben Tsur, while an oath not to perform a mitzvah is not binding, where the oath is formulated in general terms, it is binding even with regard to the (non-performance) of the commandment. Thus, [while one may not take an oath not to eat matzah on Passover], if a person takes an oath not to eat matzah throughout the year, since the oath is binding with regard to the rest of the year, it is also binding with regard to Passover. Therefore, concludes R. Aben Tsur, here too, since the oath was made with regard to any other city, and since it is binding with regard to other cities in the Diaspora where there is no mitzvah involved, it is binding also with regard to Eretz Israel.

CONCLUSION

Theoretically, at least, one may argue that had the oath in the ketubah stipulated specifically that the husband may not take the wife to Eretz Yisrael, R. Aben Tsur would have ruled against the wife in accordance with the rule an oath is not binding with regard to [the non-performance of] a mitzvah. (*Yoreh De'ah*, 239:4).[14]

EXAMPLE B

The next Moroccan rabbi to deal with the issue of aliyah to Eretz Yisrael is Rabbi Yoseph Toledano (d. 1788), a rabbinic scholar of Meknes.[15] He discusses residence in Eretz Yisrael in connection with the rule that if a person makes a vow to go up to Eretz Yisrael (and is then unable to go), the vow may be annulled retroactively, just as in the case of ordinary vows, (*Yoreh De'ah,* 228:36). The problem is that in a preceding paragraph in the same chapter (228:28), R. Caro rules that if one makes a vow with regard to a commandment, it may not be annulled retroactively. The apparent conclusion seems to be that he does not regard residence in Eretz Yisrael in his time as an obligation. Indeed, a number of authorities quoted by R. Toledano arrive at this conclusion. R. Toledano also contemplates this possibility but dismisses it on two grounds:

1. Everyone agrees that charity *(tzedakah)* is a great mitzvah even in our time, yet R. Caro rules that one who makes a vow to give charity (and is then unable to do so), his vow may be annulled retroactively *(idem,* paragraph 42); clearly, this is a mitzvah that can be annulled.

2. If R. Caro does not consider residence in the Eretz Yisrael to be a mitzvah, how is one to explain two of his rulings:
   a. A husband may compel his wife to go (with him) to Eretz Yisrael (*Eben Ha'ezer*, chapt. 75:4);
   b. If a resident of Eretz Yisrael sells his slave to someone residing in the Diaspora, the slave is to be freed by the new master who loses his money (*Yoreh De'ah,* chapt. 267:82).

R. Toledano therefore asserts that R. Caro considers residence in Eretz Yisrael to be a great mitzvah even in our time and offers another explanation why a vow to go on aliyah may be annulled retroactively.[16]

Quoting numerous authorities who support his position, R. Toledano expresses impatience with Mahrikash (R. Ya'akov Kastro, a contemporary of R. Caro), and others who assume incorrectly that R. Caro does not consider residence in Eretz Yisrael in our time a mitzvah. Thus he states, "I heard but can not understand how it is possible to attribute to R. Caro the opinion that it is not a mitzvah to go to Eretz Israel." He then quotes numerous rabbinic sources which extol the merit of residence in Eretz Yisrael including the rabbinic statement that whoever (is able to but) does not go up from the Diaspora to reside in the Land of Israel is considered as refusing to accept upon himself the yoke of Heaven. Therefore, R. Toledano states: "He who has the wherewithal to go up (to Eretz Yisrael) and does not go (preferring to remain) in secure quarters, has no remedy for his affliction."

Then, on a more personal and emotional note, R. Toledano adds:

"And God (only) knows that were it possible for me to go, even alone, I would travel day and night with neither rest nor repose until I reach the land of tranquility and inheritance. Grant my wish, O, God, (while I am) in this world, for the sake of Thy Great and Holy Name. Amen."

CONCLUSION

The whole tenor of R. Toledano's discussion conveys the impression that he is engaged in a passionate campaign to prove that residence in Eretz Yisrael is a great mitzvah and that R. Caro must hold such a view. R. Toledano simply does not seem to be able to conceive it being otherwise.

EXAMPLE C

The next Moroccan rabbi-jurist to take up the issue of residence in Eretz Yisrael is Rabbi Sha'ul Yeshu'ah Abitbol of Sefrou (1739-1808).[17]

He rules that a man may compel his wife to go with him to Eretz Yisrael, and if she refuses to do so, she forfeits her right to the ketubah. R. Abitbol bases his decision on the talmudic rule in Ketuboth (110b) and that of *Eben Ha'ezer* (75:4) to the same effect. Interestingly, R. Abitbol quotes also R. Yehudah Halevi's Kuzari (which he calls *kol yehudah* -

book II, sec. 22), a passage where Halevi reaffirms the talmudic rule and in general extols the merit of residence in Eretz Yisrael. To my knowledge, R. Abitbol is the only decisor who refers to Halevi's Kuzari in this legal context.

As far as the wife's alleged excuse of the fear of danger en route to Eretz Yisrael, R. Abitbol dismisses it outright. If every woman were allowed to invoke this excuse, then the mishnaic rule that all may be compelled to go to Eretz Yisrael would have no practical application. After all, says R. Abitbol sarcastically, the mishnaic rule was not meant to apply only to miracle workers who could leap miraculously over great distances in one instant, but to all ordinary Jews who travel by normal routes which invariably involve some risk.

R. Abitbol goes on to explain that it is a principle that when the performance of a commandment is at stake, we do not concern ourselves with the possibility of danger, for one who is engaged in the performance of a mitzvah will know no evil, and no harm befalls those engaged in the fulfillment of a mitzvah. Surely, the mitzvah of residing in Eretz Yisrael will protect those engaged in its fulfillment from all risks of danger, since the very going there constitutes (part of the process) of fulfilling the obligation.

R. Abitbol concedes that his opinion is in disagreement with the Tosafot and with Rabbi Haim Cohen who maintain that the talmudic rule is not in force in our days.[18]

R. Abitbol proceeds to introduce a subtle distinction between sure danger and the mere possibility of danger. He concedes that where there is reason to believe that the performance of a commandment will expose one to certain danger, we do not rely on divine protection. He quotes a number of sources to support this point. R. Abitbol adds that this is indeed the opinion of the Rashbash quoted by R. Caro (*Eben Ha'ezer*, 751:5) and that Rashbash's rule that from Morocco to Alexandria we do not compel a spouse to go to Eretz Yisrael against his or her will applies only when there is sure danger.[19]

Finally, after a long and exhaustive discussion of the sources and the issues involved, R. Abitbol introduces a bit of local realia by offering another reason why, in the case under discussion, the husband may compel his wife to go with him to Eretz Yisrael. Nowadays, he argues, staying in Sefrou involves more danger than going out of the city, and even without the issue of Eretz Yisrael, Sefrou is a good place to leave. He describes the many miseries to which the city and its inhabitants are exposed: attacks at the hand of rebellious bands, forays of Berber tribes, famine, inflated prices, and scarcity of money.

CONCLUSION

Essentially, R. Abitbol maintained that notwithstanding the possibility of danger en route to Eretz Yisrael, the mishnaic rule is in force even in our time, and a man may compel his wife to accompany him on aliyah. No harm befalls those engaged in the performance of a mitzvah, and certainly the mitzvah of residence in Eretz Yisrael will protect those engaged in its fulfillment beginning with the preparation of the trip. R. Abitbol concedes however, that where there is reason to believe that the performance of a mitzvah will expose one to sure danger we do not rely on the protection of the mitzvah.

EXAMPLE D

Another Moroccan rabbi to deal with this issue is Rabbi Petachya Berdugo[20] (1764-1820), who was a judge in Meknes.

In a responsum dealing with the question of whether a man may compel his wife to accompany him to Eretz Yisrael, R. Berdugo rules that the husband may not do so for two reasons:

1. Moroccan Jews follow Rashbash's opinion adopted by R. Caro (*Eben Ha'ezer*, chapt. 75:5) that when great distances are involved (as from Morocco to Alexandria) there is a greater likelihood of danger en route to Israel and therefore we may not compel one spouse to accompany the other on aliyah.
2. In the case under discussion the husband made an oath not to take his wife to a different country without her consent. There is a difference of opinion as to whether he may compel her to go with him to Eretz Yisrael. Since the matter is under dispute, the wife may claim that the established rule is in her favor and since the

husband cannot prove otherwise he may not compel her.

EXAMPLE E

Another rabbi from Meknes, Rabbi Raphel Berdugo (1742-1822) deals with aliyah in connection with the laws governing the sale of a Torah scroll.[21]

Commenting on R. Caro's rule that one may not sell a Torah scroll except in order to fulfill the commandment of studying the Torah, R. Berdugo reports that people have been permitting the sale of a Torah scroll in order to defray the cost of the trip to Eretz Yisrael, for aliyah is the equivalent of studying Torah.

EXAMPLE F

The next Moroccan decisor to deal with the issue of aliyah is Rabbi Ya'akov Ben Yekutiel Berdugo (1783-1843), also a judge in Meknes.[22]

R. Berdugo deals with a case of a divorced couple where the mother had custody of their two three-year-old daughters whom the father wanted to take with him to Eretz Yisrael. R. Berdugo rules for the husband.

R. Berdugo's first argument is that the rule stated by Maimonides and R. Caro that the mother has the right to custody of her minor children was conferred by our sages on the presumption that (under normal circumstances) the children are happier in the company of their mother *(debetzavta de imam niha leho)*. Quoting R. Shemuel de Medina (a contemporary of R. Caro), R. Berdugo argues that this rule was enacted to serve the interest and welfare of the children and not that of the mother. Therefore it only applies when both parents are in the same city, in which case their being with their mother does not result in any loss of the father's rights. Nor is the father deprived of the opportunity to show them love and tenderness and to educate them. But if the parents are not in the same city, the father has the right to take the children with him.

But R. Berdugo's most forceful arguments in support of his decision are based on considerations of the aliyah. Thus, he argues, when the father wants to go to Eretz Yisrael, it would be inconceivable to deny him the right to take his children with him. If the mother can keep the children, she would thereby prevent him from fulfilling the commandment of residence in Eretz Yisrael. When aliyah is involved, surely the interest of the children and their welfare will be far better served by their going with their father to Eretz Yisrael. For it is a great merit for them to go to the Holy Land and strike roots in a secure place and in the company of their father who will bring them up, educate them, and eventually find them a spouse, like an eagle who rouses his nestlings, gliding down to his young.

Finally, R. Berdugo argues, even if the mother's right to custody were a right of the mother (which is not the case), when aliyah is at stake, she loses that right, just as she loses the right to stay in her native city, since her husband may compel her to go with him to Eretz Yisrael against her will.

In a subsequent responsum, R. Berdugo touches upon the fundamental question of whether or not a husband may compel his wife to accompany him on aliyah. He rules that the husband may do so. R. Berdugo explains that in years past, they used to rule that a husband may not compel his wife to go up with him to Eretz Yisrael because of two considerations:

A. R. Caro's rule in 75:5 that from Morocco to Alexandria we do not compel because of the likelihood of danger;
B. The custom of inserting in the ketubah contract a promise by the husband not to take her to a different country without her consent.

But nowadays, adds R. Berdugo, we see that everybody says that it is possible to go to Eretz Yisrael from anywhere without being exposed to excessive danger. At the same time, they have stopped the practice of including in the ketubah such an oath so that that reason is no longer valid either.

CONCLUSION

R. Berdugo not only believes that residence in Eretz Yisrael is an obligation, but maintains that it overrides the mother's right to custody of her minor children. The merit of residing in Eretz Yisrael serves the children's welfare far better than their staying with their mother.

EXAMPLE G

Another Moroccan decisor who deals with the issue of aliyah in connection with the right to custody of minor children is Rabbi Raphael Moshe Elbaz (1823-1896), a judge and jurist of Sefrou.[23]

In three related responsa, he deals with the case of a widow who wanted to take her 11-year-old son and seven-year-old daughter with her and her parents to Eretz Yisrael. Her husband's family tried to prevent her from doing so, maintaining that the children might be exposed to danger.

In his decisions as well as in his discussion of the halakhic principles involved, R. Elbaz echoes the opinions of R. Sha'ul Abitbol and R. Ya'akov Ben Yekuti'el Berdugo (discussed above), follows closely their arguments and even uses their very phraseology. Essentially, the decisive factor in his decision is the interest and the welfare of the children which he (like R. Berdugo), feels are better served by their going with their mother to Eretz Yisrael. In a subsequent responsum, he concedes that where the mother remarries, the children's welfare would be better served by staying with their father's relatives, because of the assumed tendency of widows who remarry to neglect the children of their former husband. In a third responsum, R. Elbaz reconsiders the matter concluding that even when the mother remarries, separating the children from their mother will be harmful to them. Therefore, their welfare dictates that their mother be allowed to take them with her.[24]

CONCLUSION

Like R. Abitbol, he too believes that the residence in Eretz Yisrael is incumbent on all Jews even in our time, and we need not concern ourselves about the possible danger of travel. The mitzvah of residence in Eretz Yisrael will protect those engaged in its fulfillment, from the minute they begin preparing for the trip. Likewise, R. Elbaz quotes approvingly R. Abitbol's distinction between sure danger and the mere chance of danger, and concedes that where there is sure danger we do not rely on the protection of the mitzvah. He too cites several sources to support this distinction.

DISCUSSION

Although given the time span covered by these texts (17th-19th centuries), they represent but a few cases of aliyah, one must bear in mind that the above legal texts are not abstract or academic discussions. Rather, they represent actual cases that the decisors had to rule on. Naturally, not every case of aliyah involved rabbinic adjudication. Moreover, a number of other responsa (not examined in this article) deal with individuals who sold their homes and liquidated their businesses in order to go to Eretz Yisrael, were prevented from doing so by all sorts of obstacles, and subsequently returned home and sought to have the sales of their property rescinded.[25] These responsa reveal that people did make aliyah and took it very seriously to the point of selling their homes and liquidating their businesses. Second, they reveal that on many occasions, external obstacles thwarted their intent and determination to make aliyah. The nature of these obstacles is not always specified; yet, it is easy to guess that these obstacles involved travelling dangerous routes, inter-tribal quarrels among Berbers, and the like. But whatever their nature, these obstacles were external factors over which the individuals involved had no control.[26]

Finally, numerous other sources (such as reports of tourists and travelers, family records and personal diaries, biographical dictionaries, governmental censuses and other demographic documents, etc.) attest to a continuing presence of Moroccan Jews in Eretz Israel beginning with the latter part of the sixteenth century. These sources reveal that Moroccan Jews immigrated to Israel in all periods and constituted a significant and sizable segment of the old yishuv. Beginning with the end of the sixteenth century, organized Moroccan Jewish communities, known as *adat ha-ma-aravim* were to be found all over the urban centers of Eretz Yisrael.[27]

In general, the tenor of most of their decisions is that residence in Eretz Yisrael even in our days (i.e., in their time) is a great mitzvah. Some of the decisors do not refer to the danger of travel ; others bring up the argument of *sakanat derakhim* only to dismiss it on the ground that the performance of the mitzvah of aliyah will provide protection against any chance of danger.

The only concession they make is where there is sure danger (not just a risk of danger) in which case one may not rely on the protection of the mitzvah. Only one decisor, Rabbi Petachya Berdugo, partly bases his decision not to compel a wife to accompany her husband on aliyah on the consideration of danger to travel.

The bias of the above decisors in favor of Eretz Yisrael is evident not only from their decisions, but also from the very language and the choice of biblical and rabbinic expressions and statements in which they couch their legal decisions. These expressions and formulations reveal a strong attachment to Eretz Yisrael that transcends the legal parameters of the particular issues discussed. The above examples make this quite evident.

I have shown elsewhere that the attitude toward aliyah expressed in these responsa is typical of that of Moroccan rabbis and Morrocan Jews in general. For example, one of the characteristics of Moroccan aliyah in the eighteenth and nineteenth centuries was that it was considered, by rabbis and laymen alike, to be an essential religious duty, to the extent that many fathers included in their will an order to their sons to emigrate to Eretz Yisrael.[28]

NOTES

1   The Moroccan Piyyut constitutes an important branch of Moroccan rabbinic literature. It is a genre of literary creativity that was cultivated zealously by Moroccan rabbis. I have dealt briefly with its messianic and popular aspects in an article, "Poetic and Pragmatic Aspects of Sephardic Zionism," *Focus*, No. 6, Fall, 1975. For a general study of the Moroccan piyyut and an extensive inventory of the major collections of Moroccan Piyyutim, see H. Zafrani, *Poesie Juive en Occident Musulman* (Geuthner - Paris, 1977).

2   I have discussed some typical illustrations of these customs in a forthcoming article, "The Centrality of the Land of Israel in Moroccan Jewish Life," in *Orot Yahadut Ha-maghreb*, being published by the Centre de Recherches du Judaisme Nord-Africain, Bne Brak, Israel.

3   I have traced the history of this aliyah and discussed its distinguishing features in

much detail in an article (*"Yahadut Maroco VeYishuv Eretz Yisrael: Toledot Ha-aliyot Hashonot shel Yehudei Maroco Mehame-ah Ha-16 Ve-ad Reshit Hame-ah Ha-20,"* in *Hagut Ivrit Be-artzot Ha-islam*, ed., Menahem Zohari et al. (Jerusalem, 1981 - Henceforth H. Toledano, *Toledot Ha-aliyot)*, pp. 228-252.

4 These include: various documents bearing on the emissaries from the holy cities of Israel in the Jewish communities in Morocco; reports of tourists and travelers (Jews and non-Jews) who visited Eretz Yisrael and reported their impressions on the various ethnic communities comprising the old yishuv; biographical dictionaries; family records and personal diaries; and governmental censuses and other demographic documents prepared by governmental agencies as well as private individuals. For specific examples of most of these sources, see my article on aliya, *Toledot Ha-aliyot* ... cited above.

5 For an extensive inventory of this literature, see H. Zafrani, *Les Juifs du Maroc; Vie Sociale, Economique, et Religieuse: Études des Takkanot et Responsa* (Geuthner - Paris, 1972).

6 For this aspect of Moroccan rabbinic legal literature, see M. Elon, *"Yihudah shel Halakhah Vehevra Beyahadut Tsfon Afrikah Mile-ahar Gerush Sefarad Ve-ad Yameinu,"* in *Halakhah U-fetihut: Hakhmei Maroco Keposkim Ledorenu*, ed. M. Bar Yuda (Israel; Histadrut Haklalit shel Ha-ovdim, 1985), pp. 15-38.

7 Rabbi Raphael Ankawa (1848-1935) was Chief Rabbi in Salé (1880-1918). He was the first Chief Rabbi of the Supreme Rabbinical Court (Bet-Din Hagadol) following the reorganization of the Moroccan Jewish communities by the French Protectorate authority. He held this position from 1918 until his death in 1935. He was a scion of one of the most illustrious Spanish families in Morocco. His great scholarship and great authority made him the undisputed leader of Moroccan Jewry in his time.

8 Note the use of the strong term *sota* which in the biblical context means a faithless woman and even a suspected adulteress.

9 Note R. Ankawa's unmistakable bias in favor of Jerusalem and its scholars.

10 For example, see R. Raphael Moshe Elbaz, *Halakhah Lemoshe* (Jerusalem, 1901), *Hoshen Mishpat*, secs. 103, 152, pp. 112b, 125a-136a; R. Ya'akov Ben Mordekhay Berdugo, *Shevut Ya'akov* (ms, in possession of R. Shalom Messas), sec. 118.

11 Professor Hayim Bentov, in a recent article on the ties between Moroccan Jewry and Eretz Yisrael, shows that emissaries went to Morocco as early as the end of the sixteenth century, and that already then, Morocco was considered one of the central regions of *shelihut* activity. From other sources we learn that *shadarim* continued to visit Morocco until 1938-1939 when the last emissary, R. Ya'akov Avichzer was in

Morocco. During the eighteenth and nineteenth centuries, the number of emissaries who visited Morocco constituted, relatively speaking, an influx. See Hayim Bentov, *"Kishre Kehilot Eretz Yisrael" in Maroco Viyehudeha Bameot Hashesh-esre Vehashva-esre, Shalem* (Jerusalem, 1992), vol. VI, pp. 335-345: Abraham Hayim, *"Shelihuto shel Abraham Pinto Lemaroco,"* in *East and Maghreb* (Bar-Ilan Univ. Press: Israel, 1980), vol. II, p. 172: Abraham Ya'ari, *Sheluhe Eretz Yisrael* (Jerusalem, 1951), pp. 310, 339-360, 663-678.

12 See Toledano, *Otsar Hagenazim,* (Jerusalem, 1960), pp. 164-196.

13 See Rabbi Shalom Messas, *Shemesh Umaghen* (Jerusalem, 1983), vol. II, chapt. 54, pp. 91-93.

14 See Rabbi Ya'akov Aben Tsur, *Mishpat Utsedakah Beya'akov* (Alexandria, 1894), vol. I, sec. 28, p. 44a.

15 His discussion is published in a work of Novella on the *Shulhan Arukh* by R. Moshe Ben Daniel Toledano, *Hashamayim Hahadashim* (Casablanca, 1937), pp. 30b-31b.

16 His explanation is that according to R. Caro, vows taken with regard to the fulfillment of positive commandments are annullable. Therefore, a vow to go on aliyah or to give charity may be annulled retroactively. But a vow made with regard to certain negative commandments such as a vow not to gamble, though these are only rabbinic prohibitions, may not be annulled. R. Caro's rule in Paragraph 28 deals with such prohibitions.

17 See Rabbi Sha'ul Yeshu'ah Abitbol, *Avnei Shayish* (Jerusalem, 1934), vol. II, sec. 94, pp. 67b-68a.

18 R. Abitbol notes that the two reasons offered by the Tosafot for their opinion: a) the danger of travel, and b) R. Cohen's opinion (see above) are usually understood as two distinct arguments. He raises a number of objections to this reading of the Tosafot, and suggests instead that both reasons are to be construed as one and the same argument; the Tosafot are saying that the mishnaic rule is not binding in our time because of the danger of travel argument, and the reason we do not rely on divine protection is that according to R. Cohen, residence in Eretz Yisrael in our time is not a mitzvah. R. Abitbol finds support of his interpretation of the Tosafot in the Mordechi who attributes both reasons cited by the Tosafot to R. Cohen. Finally, R. Abitbol draws the implication of his understanding of the Tosafot, as he puts it, we disagree with R. Cohen's argument and maintain it is a mitzvah, and therefore the mishnaic rule applies in our time and we do not worry about possible danger.

19 Thus, on the basis of this distinction, R. Abitbol reconciles the seeming contradiction between R. Caro's rule (in *Eben Ha'ezer* 75:4) which repeats the talmudic rule in

absolute terms, and his subsequent statement in the following paragraph (75:5) which sets geographical guidelines as to where the rule is in force and where it is not in force because of considerations of danger, insisting that R. Caro's latter statement applies only where there is sure danger.

20 See Rabbi Petachya Berdugo, *Nofet Tsufim* (Casablanca, 1938), *Eben Ha'ezer*, sec. 25, p. 41a.

21 See Rabbi Raphael Berdugo, *Torat Emet* (Meknes, 1939), *Eben Ha'ezer*, sec. 1, p. 38a.

22 See Rabbi Ya'akov Ben Yekuti'el Berdugo, *Shufreih De Ya'akov* (Jerusalem, 1910, secs. 61-62, pp. 51b-52b.

23 See Rabbi Raphael Moshe Elbaz, *Halakhah Le-Moshe* (Jerusalem, 1901), secs. 6-8, pp. 12a-13a.

24 It is unclear whether the issues discussed by R. Elbaz in responsa 6 ,7, 8, are separate cases or the same case regarding which R. Elbaz changes his decision repeatedly as he learns new details. It is clear though that his main concern is the welfare of the children, which he feels is better served by their going to Eretz Yisrael, unless there are compelling reasons to argue otherwise.

25 In general the discussion in these responsa revolves around R. Caro's rule (*Hoshen Mishpat*, chapt. 207:3) that whenever a sale is made contingent on certain conditions, if the conditions are not fulfilled, the sale is not valid. We have also the principle that the common knowledge that one is selling his property in order to go to Eretz Yisrael is the equivalent of a stipulated condition. In most of these cases, however, the decisors decided against the sellers because the latter did not show any interest or intent to reclaim their property upon their return. Only after the lapse of a long time did they want the sale rescinded. See *Nofet Tsufim*, secs. 22, 133, 282, pp. 85b-86b, 117b-118a, 159a-160a, vol. II, sec. 64, p. 47b; R. Shalom Messas, *Divrei Shalom* (Meknes, 1945), secs. 19-20, pp. 52a-57b; *Shevut Ya'akov*, sec. 119.

26 See my discussion of this particular characteristic of the aliyah of Moroccan Jews during the nineteenth century in my article, *"Toledot Ha-aliyot"* ... , *Me-afyen* 3; pp. 245-248.

27 *Ibid.*, pp. 228-252.

28 *Ibid.*, *Me-afyen* 2, pp. 244-245.

ARCHITECTURE AND VISUAL ARTS OF THE SPANISH AND PORTUGUESE SYNAGOGUE OF NEW YORK CITY

by Ronda S. Angel

I would like to dedicate this paper to the memory Haham Gaon, a great man who truly appreciated the Spanish and Portuguese Synagogue's culture and contributions to our society.

The Spanish and Portuguese Synagogue of New York, Congregation Shearith Israel, was founded in 1654, the first Jewish congregation in North America. Its rituals derive from the practices of Jews from Spain and Portugal from before the expulsion of 1492. Yet the flavor of these rituals is distinctly American, as the ritual objects, as well as the architectural design of the building, reflect American aesthetic sensibility. The American nature of the visual arts of the Spanish and Portuguese Synagogue, together with the Sephardic meaning of the traditions, lend to a service which combines vastly different cultures through an aesthetic medium.

The Spanish and Portuguese Synagogue's history, as well as its architecture, music, and decorative arts, contribute to its position as an American cultural, aesthetic, and religious institution. In this article, I will provide a brief historical context of the arts of Shearith Israel and discuss the present building's visual and cultural characteristics.

LATE NINETEENTH-CENTURY RELIGIOUS ARCHITECTURE

By the late 1880s, the Gothic and Romanesque revival had replaced the Classical as the most popular styles for synagogues. Moorish architecture had become very popular among the German Reform community and began to spread as a stylish form of synagogue architecture.[1]

Arnold William Brunner (1857-1925), the architect of the Seventieth Street building of the Spanish and Portuguese Synagogue (dedicated in 1897), was trained at MIT and was probably the first American-born Jewish architect. He also designed the State Department Building in Washington, the Cadet Hospital at West Point, and the School of Mines at Columbia University, among other buildings. In 1893, he attended an architectural exposition and conference where it was decided that classical architecture was acceptable for secular buildings, but the Romanesque and Gothic revival styles were more appropriate for religious buildings. But rather than adhere to the contemporary trends in religious architecture, Brunner looked to the past buildings of the Spanish and Portuguese Synagogue in order to create a building which would reflect the congregation's history, not the trends of modernity.

The classical architectural history of the Spanish and Portuguese Synagogue begins with its Mill Street Synagogue (built in 1730), with a Gregorian interior and neo-classical references. It continues with the Greek revival Crosby Street Synagogue of 1834 and the Nineteenth Street Synagogue of 1860[2] with the layering of Ionic and Corinthian orders. In his article, "Arnold Brunner's Spanish and Portuguese Synagogue: Issues of Reform and Reaffirmation in Late Nineteenth-Century America"[3] Maurice Berger argues that

> while the Mill, Crosby, and to some extent the Nineteenth Street buildings were designed in the neo-classical styles popular in their period of construction, the Seventieth Street building represents a total departure from contemporaneous synagogue design.

Brunner's concern for history and tradition surpassed the influences of contemporary trends in architecture. In Brunner's own writings regarding the design of the Seventieth Street building, he notes that

> the choice for ecclesiastical buildings now, broadly speaking, lies

between two great styles -- Gothic and Classic. I am unhesitatingly of the opinion that the latter is the one that is best fit and proper for the synagogue in America. With the sanction of antiquity it perpetuates the best traditions of Jewish art and takes up a thread, which was broken by circumstances, of a vigorous and once healthy style (Berger 166).

Shearith Israel resisted new forms of architectural expression for its own synagogue building. Judaism in the late nineteenth century was being pulled in two opposite directions -- toward maintaining tradition and toward assimilation. Placing the Spanish and Portuguese Synagogue amidst this struggle, Berger asserts:

> As a testament to this crucial period, the Spanish and Portuguese Synagogue innately symbolized the great theological issue of nineteenth-century American Jewry -- the polemic between the forces of reform and reaffirmation (164).

Berger goes on to argue that "the selection of a Moorish, Romanesque, or Gothic design, styles popular in the German Reform community, would have suggested acknowledgment, if not outright acceptance, of the Reform influence" (166). In the late nineteenth century, architectural form defined a religious and political affiliation. This had the effect of either welcoming or alienating members of the community, and made concrete the identity of a given community.

Architecture suggests theology and philosophy. It is a form of expression which describes, to some extent, the people it contains. When discussing synagogue architecture from a religious perspective, we can look to the Bible for examples of how much time, energy, artistry, and material resources went into the building of the Tabernacle and Solomon's Temple. These examples of architecture as a representation of a culture, as an art form requiring much planning and artistic expertise, serve as a model to architects of religious buildings. A synagogue not only defines a particular community's philosophy; it also serves as a house of God. What a community considers fit for this purpose is reflective of its theology as well. The choice of architectural design for a nineteenth-century synagogue reflected political, religious, and historical considerations.

The classical style of Shearith Israel describes its ties to ancient traditions and inheritances, as well as its own history as an American synagogue. The services of the Spanish and Portuguese Synagogue are completely traditional; the prayers derive from biblical tradition, religious poetry, and rabbinic writings. In late nineteenth-century America, the hold of tradition was weakening among many members of the Jewish community. Thus, the ancient focus of the architecture of the Spanish and Portuguese Synagogue stresses adherence to traditional Jewish culture and practice. Authority is found in antiquity; authority is found in ancient Jewish tradition; the synagogue is itself a reflection of authority rooted in history. The classical architecture of the Seventieth Street building also maintains the continuum of classical references within the Synagogue's own history.

Also reflective of a Jewish community's philosophy is the interior design of its synagogue. According to Spanish and Portuguese custom, the benches in the Synagogue run laterally along the sides of the building, perpendicular to the Ark of the Torahs. The *Tebah,* or reader's platform and desk, sits in the back-center of the sanctuary, facing the Ark with no object or piece of furniture coming between it and the Ark on the east wall. This serves an aesthetic purpose, emphasizing the clean sweep of the architecture. It also has religious meaning: the lack of interfering objects or benches is said to allow the hazzan's (cantor) or rabbi's voice of prayer to be directed toward the Torah Ark, the most sacred part of the sanctuary, with no intervening barriers.

> As David and Tamar de Sola Pool note in *An Old Faith in a New World,* the liturgy, the ritual, and the music of Congregation Shearith Israel have maintained unbroken the fundamental tradition of Western European Sephardim that was developed during a millennium of life in Spain successively under Visigothic, Moslem, and Christian rule.[4]

The survival of these traditions is echoed in the classical architecture. Even the name of the congregation, Shearith Israel (Remnant of Israel), suggests its ancient roots as part of the original people of Israel. Many of the chants and prayers sung in the services date back to antiquity. However, the Spanish and Portuguese Synagogue is situated in a modern context and has always been involved with contemporary social, political, and educational issues. The ancient references of the Synagogue's art and ritual suggest a place whence to begin to express religious feelings and social imperatives.[5]

ARCHITECTURE AND MEANING:
THE SEVENTIETH STREET SANCTUARY

When one enters the sanctuary of the Spanish and Portuguese Synagogue, one recognizes the large scale and grandness of this interior; yet one is not totally overwhelmed. In contrast, Gothic monumental architecture has the effect of erasing physical presence; it leads one's eyes and thoughts upward, toward high stained-glass panels, toward the point in the arch where both sides of the building merge. Standing in Shearith Israel's sanctuary, one cannot help but be aware of the physical in such a solid and geometrically balanced space.

Though the ornately carved coffered ceiling of the sanctuary is high, its rectangular shape and its symmetry make it knowable. The stained glass, crafted by the Louis Comfort Tiffany studios, like the ceiling, is visible and knowable. Unlike Gothic stained-glass panels, there is no narrative or message to decode in the windows, and rather than seeming to float in a lofty sphere, the windows extend from eye level in the men's section past the top row in the women's balcony. These monumental windows are symmetrical (though variations in the colors in the glass inevitably exist). The parts of the window closest to the ground have earthier tones than do the higher portions which contain more shades of blue and green. The difference in brightness of the upper and lower sections of the windows is probably a result of the exposure of the higher sections to more sunlight, but it is intriguing nonetheless that the division in color -- earth tones/sky tones -- creates the impression of a natural environment even in a highly crafted and manipulated environment.

These windows serve to contain the worshipper's vision within the walls of the sanctuary. The windows are not transparent, nor are they metaphors for a higher message or transcendent concept. Rather, their balanced geometry and muted colors create a boundary, focusing the eyes of the viewer toward the Ark, the Torah, and the prayer book -- the main means for transcendence in this context.

The notions of knowledge, balance, and reason are predominant in the geometry and symmetry of the architecture. Unlike other late nineteenth-century synagogues which incorporate symbols associated with Jewish culture, such as the Star of David, the Spanish and

Portuguese Synagogue limits religious decoration to the Ten Commandments and a Hebrew inscription above the Ark. The inscription, the only overt verbal message in the building, contains the gilded Hebrew letters which mean: "Know before Whom you stand." Though this statement is somewhat paradoxical -- one cannot fully know or understand God -- there is an eternal emphasis on trying to know and attain a greater understanding of religion and one's position in relation to God.

Two of the most pronounced features of the main sanctuary of the Spanish and Portuguese Synagogue are the repetition of leaf and flower motifs and the cross-referential dialogue between the decorative arts and the architecture. The entablature of the building's facade contains intricately patterned designs and laurel wreaths. The pediment also has a laurel motif, and the Corinthian capitols display intricate carvings of vegetation. Flowers and wreaths of laurel are carved on the ceiling supports. The Ark which contains the scrolls of the Torah has a pediment with leaf and flower designs; its center contains a carved laurel wreath from which hangs the *Ner Tamid,* the perpetual lamp.

The candlesticks surrounding the reader's desk serve as a good example of the internal cross-referencing in the main sanctuary. Each brass candlestick represents a carved pedestal on which rests a fluted Ionic column. On top of the column is a goblet-shaped structure which holds a large gas-operated candle. These candlesticks refer to columns of architectural support; only here, they support the representation of a goblet and a light source. The candlesticks suggest a visual equation of physical supports with the support and elevation of the goblet and light. The goblet is a symbol of a ritual sanctification process, and light can be interpreted as spirit, knowledge, and transcendence. These images create a visual metaphor; the practice of the religion will, like a column, support our lives by giving us sanctity, light, and spiritual fulfillment.

On either side of the Tebah, which holds these twelve candlesticks, are large Ionic marble columns that support the women's balcony. Though the predominant order of this building is Corinthian, the juxtaposition of Ionic columns with the candlesticks provides an interesting visual echo of references. Another issue of reference is the floorboards of the Tebah. A bit creaky, these floorboards date back to the floor of the reader's desk of the Mill Street Synagogue of 1730. The notion of walking in our ancestors' footsteps is made literal.

THE LITTLE SYNAGOGUE: A COLLECTION OF RITUAL OBJECTS

Also dating from 1730 are several objects found in the Spanish and Portuguese Synagogue's smaller sanctuary, known, for obvious reasons, as the Little Synagogue. The Tebah and its four surrounding candlesticks, some of the benches, and the Ten Commandments above the Ark, for example, have been in use since 1730. The Little Synagogue is used for daily morning and evening services, life-cycle events such as baby namings, *b'rith milahs* (circumcisions), and small weddings. It is currently also used for women's services and Megillah readings. Like the candlesticks in the main sanctuary, the candlesticks in the Little Synagogue have several references and layers of meaning. These candlesticks are designed with three sections, representing the three ritual objects involved in the *Habdallah* service, performed after sundown on Saturdays to bid farewell to the Sabbath and to usher in the new week. The objects involved are a candle (to show the separation between light and dark, similar to the separation between the weekdays and the Sabbath), sweet-smelling spices or herbs (to refresh one's soul in order to have a happy and productive week), and a cup of wine (to sanctify the separation of the Sabbath from the rest of the week). The candlesticks surrounding the Tebah represent a smaller candlestick, on top of which is a spice box, and finally, at the top is a wine goblet.

These candlesticks are sculpted representations of other ritual objects. They are objects with one function, yet they refer to another function. This clever interplay between function and transformation creates an aesthetic and ritualistic reference for the viewer, who can appreciate both the object's function and its references.

Arthur Danto, in *The Transfiguration of the Commonplace,* discusses Aristotle's observation of the link between imitation, recognition, and pleasure. Danto notes that the knowledge that [the object] is an imitation must then be presupposed by the pleasure in question, or, correlatively, the knowledge that it is not real. So the pleasure in question has a certain cognitive dimension.[6]

The candlesticks surrounding the reader's desks in both the main sanctuary and the Little Synagogue imitate things that they are not. This results in a visual play which involves cognition and recognition in order to get maximum aesthetic pleasure from these objects.

In the Little Synagogue are many ritual objects of historic and aesthetic value. On the wall opposite the Ark hangs a Sabbath Lamp of the Seven Wicks (1730). Hanging on the north wall are two bronze memorial lamps; one (dedicated in 1860, originally as a perpetual lamp) is decorated with flowers and wreaths, and the other (dedicated in 1925) has leaves and Stars of David carved around it. These ritual lamps relate to issues of memory in a religious and cultural context. The fourth commandment, "Remember the Sabbath," suggests the strong link between memory and ritual. The Sabbath is begun with the lighting of candles; the Sabbath Lamp of the Seven Wicks reminds the viewer of the six periods in the Creation and the seventh period of rest (Genesis I). This lamp is used to signify the importance of religious memory. The memorial lamps, on the other hand, serve to preserve cultural and familial memory. These lamps are lit on the anniversary of the deaths of congregants' relatives. A lit memorial lamp in the context of a synagogue conveys the image of continuity of the generations and the communal respect for those who have died. The presence of these different types of lamps brings collective memory and personal memory into the same space.

But the ritual objects in the Little Synagogue do not only preserve the memory of religious commandments and the memory of individuals in the congregation. They also preserve the collective memory of Shearith Israel's origin. Because of the combination of objects and furniture pieces from past synagogue buildings (in addition to the newer objects and windows), the Little Synagogue is like a photo album which can be entered. Each object refers to a different time period in the history of the Synagogue, documenting the ties to ritual tradition and the continuity of a community.

RITUAL OBJECTS OF SHEARITH ISRAEL

Unlike the ritual objects in museums, the decorative arts of the Spanish and Portuguese Synagogue,

> some of which are of high historic and artistic value, are not static museum pieces. They are in use continually, bespeaking a religion that is living, that is lovely and is loved, and that responds to the call of the Psalmist "Worship the Lord in the beauty of holiness."[7]

These objects are not on pedestals with labels next to them; their artistic value is very much linked to their function within a sacred realm. The interconnection between aesthetic beauty and religion is a universal trait of ritual objects. The visual pleasure of religious objects is at once awesome and comforting to the eye; religion is too large to understand, yet its aesthetically pleasing ritual objects can serve to concretize awe.

After Moses led the people of Israel through the Red Sea, he proclaimed: "This is my God, and I shall make beauty for Him" (Exodus 15:2). Rabbis have asked how one can possibly make beauty for the Source of all beauty. They answer: by fulfilling the commandments in the most beautiful way possible. The aesthetic considerations of worship date from biblical times. In this tradition, ceremonial and ritual objects were donated to and purchased by the community to create visually beautiful services and rituals.

Partial-showing in the aesthetic realm is a trait that crosses time and culture. It is evident in the rituals of the Spanish and Portuguese Synagogue. Like the Nazca lines in Peru which cannot fully be seen from a human perspective, or the art work on roofs of cathedrals, one generally cannot see fully every part of the main sanctuary of the Spanish and Portuguese Synagogue. The architecture, though rectangular and clear, has blocking elements in it; the balcony blocks the view directly above or below a person; the reader's desk can block horizontal vision. Though there are no pillars that interrupt the architectural sweep of the building, one can never see without obstruction unless one stands at the reader's desk. Here there is an aesthetic hierarchy; full clarity of vision can only be achieved from the most important point in the sanctuary.

The Torah scrolls are normally hidden behind the doors of the Ark. Even when the Ark is open, the scrolls themselves are covered with silk robes and adorned with silver "bells." The Torah scrolls are invocational objects which are only taken into public viewing at specific times. This partial-showing gives the Torahs aesthetic and ritual power; they become, in their hiddenness, a metaphor of sacredness, and in their display to believers in the Torah, a literal display of sacredness.

In addition to partial-showing, visual indicators in the rituals include the silk cloaks of the Torah scrolls. The color of the cloaks serves as a cue as to the mood of the day. On regular Sabbaths, the Torahs are clothed in red brocade cloaks. On Festivals or special Sabbaths (such as a Sabbath that falls on a New Moon, or the anniversary of the consecration of the synagogue), the Torah cloaks are multi-colored, a sign of festivity. On *Tisha B'Ab,* a day of national sadness, the Ark, reader's desk, and candles are draped in black. Most striking are the Torahs during the High Holy Days, when all of the Torahs, the lining of the Ark, the pulpit, and the reader's desk are draped in white, emphasizing the purity and holiness associated with these days.

Certain bells are used only on specific occasions. The bells which were presented at the dedication of the 1730 Mill Street synagogue are used on the anniversary of the consecration of that synagogue. Another set of bells are replicas of the Liberty Bell. These bells are used on the Sabbath when the verse "You shall proclaim liberty throughout the land unto all its inhabitants" (Leviticus 25:10) is read from the Torah. Myer Myers crafted a set of bells for the synagogue, and these are used on the High Holy Days and other special occasions.

Aesthetic pleasure is very important in the ritual sphere. The ritual objects of the Spanish and Portuguese Synagogue, though, are not merely aesthetic objects. They also serve as visual cues for the viewer and participant; they have communicative value.

The history of the Spanish and Portuguese Synagogue as the first Jewish congregation in North America gives it an aura of authority and traditionalism. Its classical architecture reflects that authority, and ties the history of Shearith Israel to the long history of Jewish tradition. Its architecture and art objects make ritual practices aesthetically, as well as spiritually, fulfilling.

NOTES

1. Maurice Berger, "Arnold Brunner's Spanish and Portuguese Synagogue: Issues of Reform and Reaffirmation in Late Nineteenth-Century America," *Arts Magazine*, vol. 54 n. 6, Feb. 1980, pp. 164-167.

2. Both of these synagogues were designed by Robert Mook.

3. Maurice Berger, p. 165. Page references in the text are from this article.

4. David and Tamar de Sola Pool, *An Old Faith in the New World,* Columbia University Press, New York, 1954, p. 81.

5. The music of the synagogue, I think, is one area where antiquity and modernity meet; the choir sings both ancient melodies and choral compositions written by modern composers.

6. Arthur, Danto, *The Transfiguration of the Commonplace,* Harvard University Press, Cambridge, 1981, p. 14.

7. David and Tamar de Sola Pool, *An Old Faith in the New World,* p. 92.

A HISTORY OF THE JEWS OF BOSNIA BASED ON THE NOTES OF DR. SOLOMON GAON

by Rabbi M. Mitchell Serels
Yeshiva University

Bosnia was of particular importance to the Haham not only because of the location of Travnik, Dr. Gaon's native town but because of Sarajevo, a jewel in the Sephardic crown. After the 1389 Battle of Kosovo, the Ottomans held several border towns. These cities included Vrhbosna, which in 1465 was renamed Sarajevo. Over the next century, the entirety of Bosnia fell into Ottoman hands and became a vilayet (province) of the empire. With the extension of the Turkish Empire, Jews from Spain who had arrived in 1492 were allowed to settle in these various cities. The Turks pacified these areas and increased the Jewish population with the Spanish-speaking Jews, who numerically and culturally overwhelmed their Romaniot coreligionists. By 1565, these Sephardim formed the permanent community of Sarajevo. The Jewish quarter was established at chifut khan near city center. Later a new Jewish quarter was built in Bjelave, giving additional space for the Jews.

Sarajevo became a center for Islamic life. It was the hub of internal trade between the coast and inland, as well as from Italy and Greece. The Turks were excellent warriors and diplomats but relied on the loyal service of the Jews to build the economy of conquered areas. At first, males arrived without their families. These individuals came by 1541 to Sarajevo, but by 1565, the colony consisted only of 10 to 15 families, which formed the permanent part of the Jewish community of Sarajevo.

The Haham was well aware of the symbiotic relationship between the

Jews and the Muslims and wanted to insure that the relationship was properly portrayed. He did not wish that the blemishes be glossed over, but rather the beneficial elements be properly placed in perspective. The Jewish quarter, the Haham felt, was not a ghetto in the classic sense, to which Jews were confined by governmental edict. The seat of Ottoman rule in Bosnia was Travnik. From there the Pasha would visit Sarajevo from time to time or when needed. In 1581 the Bosnian Muslims implored the visiting ruler, Scavish Pasha Atik, to separate their homes from those of the Jews because of noise on Fridays, as well as for fear of the fires which burned on the Sabbath which could create uncontrollable fires. The Turkish ruler agreed to the Muslim request but placated the Jews by building them a new residential Khan. The Jews were allowed to build a small synagogue nearby. Consequently, the separation allowed for independent development and autonomy, beneficial to both groups. In Ladino, the Jews called the center of the area, *el Cortezo*. This concept of the Jewish desire and benefit from the separate residential area is accepted by all historians who dealt with this subject except Maurice Levi. Under Turkish rule, the Ottoman Empire readily provided separate neighborhoods for their millets, the semi-religious ethnic minorities. This residential separation was consistent with ethnic autonomy.

The autonomous governing institution was headed by the Chief Rabbi, who over the years, included Asher Zevulun from Belgrade, Masliah Mujijon, Samuel Benbaroukh, and Rafael Parnaspal. One of the most famous of the Chief Rabbis of Sarajevo was Nehemia Hayon, born in Sarajevo, 1650. Hayon eventually went to Prague where he wrote *Divrei Nehemia* on mysticism (Berlin 1713), *Oz L' Elohim* and *Kodesh Kadashim*, which demonstrated strong Sabbatean tendencies. Hayon's Sabbatean tendencies frequently led to difficulties with the rabbinic authorities in Amsterdam.

The record books starting in 1731, indicate a vibrant, organized community. The book *(Pinkas)* provides a somewhat dry view of the community. By 1779, the Jewish community had risen to one thousand souls. At that time, the Chief Rabbi was Shemtob Zevi. The Dayan was Abraham Dayan, and the spiritual leader of the Ashkenazi community was Joseph Knecht. After Zevi's death, the vacancy was finally filled by David Pardo (born in Venice, 1719), whose father was originally from

Dubrovnik. Pardo founded a number of charitable organizations and built the first Yeshiva in the Bosnian city. The Yeshiva attracted many students from various areas in the Balkans. Pardo authored several books including *Lamnaseah Le David, Mikhtam Le David* and *Hasdei David.* Pardo wrote Hebrew poetry. In 1781, at age sixty-two, Pardo went on aliyah and set the example for Yehuda Alcalay and his proto-Zionism. Pardo died in 1782 at age seventy-three. Pardo's son, Jacob, became Rabbi of Dubrovnik and wrote *Qehilat Yaacob.*

Although the Jews established themselves, and many prospered in Sarajevo, their number never rose above nine-thousand. Ashkenazi Jews arrived in 1687 with the German conquest and later Austrian conquest. Their numbers remained small. From Sarajevo, the Jews moved to smaller cities, such as Travnik (1649) although the Jewish community there never numbered more than a few hundred souls. In 1806 Travnik had twenty-five families; 1808 sixty-adult Jews; 1850 - fifty heads of households; 1879 - three hundred seventy four people. By the 19th century, there were two local Jewish physicians. Jews played an important role in Travnik's business life. A small Yeshiva was founded, the only one in Bosnia outside Sarajevo. Austrian Consul Mittesser, posted in Travnik, continued to report to Vienna on the Jewish community, and monitored its activities. Until the first two decades of the 19th century, the Turkish authority was seated in Travnik. France also posted a consul there and these powers spied on each other. Consequently, the Ottomans used Travnik to feed misinformation to the rival European powers, often through Jews. Mittesser reports that the Jews numbered 4% of the total population of Bosnia.

SARAJEVO PURIM

Days of personal, local or national salvation are often designated as "Purim," after the biblical salvation from the machinations of Haman recorded in the Book of Esther. Sarajevo had its own unique Purim as well. In the early 19th century a native Sarajevan Jew, Moses Hanio, converted to Islam. Hanio joined a Darvish sect under the name Darwish Ahmad. The local Bosnian Muslims considered him a holy man and miracle worker.

Ahmad then tried to eradicate his Jewish origins as an expression of his fanatical attachment to his new faith. He spread lies about his former co-religionists. A Travnik Jew turned to Mustafa Pasha, the local ruler, to force Ahmad to cease his attacks on Jews and Judaism. Mustafa found that Ahmad's membership in the Darvish Cult was not proper and warranted police interference. Ahmad was arrested, tried and condemned to death. The execution was carried out and the Jews felt a respite.

The Muslims, on the other hand, mourned the death of the "Sainted, Mystic Ahmad." They blamed the Jews for lying about a loyal and beloved Muslim. This accusation found a response in the new Pasha, who was sympathetic to the Darvish cult. More a realist, Muhammad Rozdeh Pasha felt the Jews should be punished, particularly with a fine. But with the Jewish Community of Travnik, the seat of the Pasha, a small population, the ruler wanted to obtain greater fiscal responsibility and therefore more money from the larger Bosnian Jewish Community. He arrested twelve prominent Jews from Sarajevo and held them for a large ransom, 500,000 gurus. If the ransom was not paid, the Jews would die. Among the captives was Rabbi Moses Danon who began his tenure in 1815. On assurance of compliance, Muhammad Rozdeh Pasha went to Sarajevo to collect this fortune, to find that the Jews had, with difficulty, raised only five thousand gurus. The Pasha assigned dawn of Shabbat, 4 Marheshvan 1819, as the appointed time for the execution. One man, Rafael Levi, decided to desecrate the Sabbath, in order to save the captives' lives. Realizing that funding limits had already been reached in the Jewish quarter, he turned to the Muslims. Levi spoke to them, cajoled them and cried to them about the Jews. Three thousand Sarajevan Muslims, at sunrise on the appointed date, congregated in front of the palace, in a massive demonstration of public support. Forcibly, the Muslim rioters stormed the jail, uprooted the gates and freed the prisoners. Rozdeh saved himself by fleeing to Travnik. Rozdeh then reported this episode to the Sultan in Constantinople.

The Sarajevan community in turn complained about Rozdeh's rule. The Jews communicated to their fellow coreligionists in the Imperial Capital about the Pasha's blackmail. The Sultan sent a royal investigator, who sided with the population. The Jews celebrated the fourth of Marheshvan as a release from the hands of an astute and powerful enemy, calling the celebration Purim de Sarajevo.

Of the prisoners held for ransom, one stood out in Bosnian Jewish history, Rabbi Moshe Danon. He like many other Sephardic leaders in the area, wanted to emigrate to Israel. A decade after his release and Rozdeh's downfall, Danon left, to fulfill his dream. He died however in June 1830 en route. He is buried in Stolac, whence pious Jews made religious pilgrimages to pray at the gravesite.

A leading lay figure was Dr. Isaac Effendi Salom (1806-1874), the first Jewish physician to obtain an academic title. He graduated from the University of Padua and was appointed a military medic in 1850. He was chosen to be a member of the regional parliament. He, like many other Bosnian Jews, emigrated to the land of Israel where he died. His son, Solomon, replaced him in parliament. Later he and Solomon Yawir Effendi Baroukh served as representatives of Bosnian Jews in the Turkish Parliament.

THE JEWISH LIBRARY

The library of the Jewish community of Sarajevo was of particular concern for the Haham as it represented material studied by the Jews. The 1311 volumes offered for the protection of the Haham represented the sum total of study and intellectual communication between the Jews of Bosnia and the outside world.

The books were printed in a variety of places including Amsterdam, Livorno, Baghdad, Constantinople, Salonika, Belgrade, Izmir, Pisa, Aleppo and Jerusalem, as well as the standard Ashkenazi centers of central and eastern Europe including Vilna, Krakow, Warsaw, Lvov, Lublin, Pressburg, Prague, Odessa, Kovno, Berlin, Vienna, and Budapest, Munkacs, Serai, Sziget, Premysla, Pietrykov, Kishinev, Tiberias, Leipzig, Riga, and Satmar. Also there were prints from newer centers of London and New York, as well as Zagreb, Croatia and Tel Aviv, Florence, Breslau, and Paks.

The collection included standard literature: Talmud and talmudical commentaries; Bible and biblical commentaries; Kabbala and mystical books; Mishna and mishnaic commentaries; codes of Halakha; Prayerbooks of Sephardic and Ashkenazic ritual; ethics and moral literature; mourners' ritual: Piyyutim and Psalms; Homiletics.

The more modern literature included texts for learning Hebrew as a modern spoken language. Since the last books printed were dated from the 1930's, prior to WWII, the books represent the usage in vogue at the period before the establishment of the state of Israel. The library included the works of the poet of Haim N. Bialik.

The Ladino literature included *Historia de los djudios,* by Hershfeld (Belgrade 1891); *Trezoro de Israel* by Jacob Alteras (Belgrade 1890); *La historia djudia* by Isaac Sciaky (Constantinople) as well as twenty-six novels printed in Tel Aviv, Izmir, Constantinople, Salonika and Jerusalem. Dramas include the Constantinople edition of *Los Macabeos* and the Vienna 1922 edition of Shabbetai Gaguine's *Devora* and *La Hija del Sol; Las madres djudias* by Dr. Semach (Constantinople 1913); *Complas de Purim* from Livorno 1902 and Serai 1932 can also be found.

The Haham often stressed the importance of the Sephardic Rabbi Yehuda Hai Alcalay who was the Rabbi in Zemun. Among his congregants was the Herzl family before they moved to Vienna. The Haham viewed Rabbi Alcalay as a proto-Zionist whose influence came to fruition, not only in his own aliya but in Theodore Herzl's political Zionism. The books in the collection included *Shelom Yerushalayim* (Ofen 1840)

Works by Abraham Kapon: Kapon was a favorite teacher and poet of the Haham. The Haham chose to quote two of Kapon's poems in his acceptance speech for the Principe de Asturias Award in 1990. Kapon's *El Angustiador* was printed in Serai in 1914. His *Shibat Sion* was printed in Serai in 1921 as well as the 1839 Viennese edition and the *Darqei Noam* of 1839 in Ladino.

The oldest book in the collection is listed as a 1599 edition of *Sefer Haarukh* by Yehiel di Roma, printed in Basel. There is also a 1647 Verona edition of *Ein Yaakob*.

The volumes of responsa represent both Ashkenazic and Sephardic authors including:

> I. Castro (Livorno, 1777); Benzion Cuenca (Jerusalem, 1901); I. Zilberstein (Buczacz, 1915); I. Pardo (Salonika, 1781); M. Mayoukas (Salonika, 1799); Eliyahu Hazan (Livorno, 1879 and

Alexandria 1907); I.B. David (Constantinople, 1760); Azaria Castelnuovo (Livorno, 1868); Jacob Burla (Jerusalem, 1882); and N. Fried (Munkacs, 1913).

There were also eighty copies of volume I and one hundred copies of volume II of the homiletical works by Abraham Romano published in Jerusalem under the title *Abraham Abraham*.

The books represent the connection of Sarajevo Jewry with the lands of the old Ottoman Empire as well as the old Austro-Hungarian Empire. The material is vast and eclectic, combining traditional learning with pre-Israeli Hebrew language and history. There are translations into German, English, Ladino, Croatian, and French representing the polyglot nature of Sephardim.

The Haham left behind two mini-cassettes in which he had dictated the initial ideas to his secretary Carole Santana. The Haham felt that he, as a product of Yugoslavia, could properly express the history of the Jews there. Dr. Gaon was active in the Association of Yugoslavian Jews in America. He knew, studied with and admired Dr. Isaac Alcalay, the late Chief Rabbi of Yugoslavia prior to World War II. Dr. Gaon also left several pages of notes which remain in the archives in the Sephardic Reference Room at Gottesman Library of Yeshiva University. This article is not only dedicated to the Haham and his scholarship but is based on his notes. The notes cover only the Ottoman period.

Most Travnik Jews were originally from Sarajevo. The Haham traced his family to Vittoria, Spain on his father's side. His mother was from the Pinto family. Pinto is a small town outside Madrid and famous for chocolate and storks. The Haham was worried about the impending deterioration of the situation between the various ethnic groups in Bosnia. He feared, now in hindsight justifiably, that there would be death and destruction. When in 1990, he received from Crown Prince Philip of Spain, the Premio Principe de Asturias de la Concordia, the Haham altered his prepared text to include a hint to the need for other people to put aside old ethnic hatred and distrust and to look to find peaceful means, to coexist as Spain and the Sephardim had learned. Unfortunately his words were not heeded.

Dr. Gaon often viewed himself as a "Turk" or a "Serb." He could speak and read Serbo-Croatian. He did not want any ethnic group Croat, Serb or Muslim to be portrayed as the sole savior of the Jews nor the sole persecutor of the Jews. Dr. Gaon preferred a balanced view. His parents however, had been killed by Croats. He was aware that the Mufti of Jerusalem had raised a Muslim Brigade to fight alongside the Axis. Yet the Jews in Turkey, a largely Muslim country, were protected and well treated. The Haham was certain that individuals, not people, should and eventually would be judged.

The Haham sided with those who felt that the formation of a distinctively Jewish area in Sarajevo was beneficial and therefore not Ghettoization. While he believed that people should learn mutual respect and the means to live together, the Haham also felt that ethnic solidarity and observance of religious law were enhanced by having a unique area. Consequently, Ghettoization should not be viewed as a form of Ottoman anti-Semitism which he felt was minimal, but rather an expression of Ottoman belief in separate and autonomous development for recognized ethno-religious groups.

The Haham did not present the opposing idea that the Ottomans decided to segregate Jews as infidels. However, because the complaint was raised by Muslims, the Jews were separated to insure tranquility for the Muslim faithful, thereby limiting by legal procedure where the Jews could live. Oddly enough, those few Jews who remain in Sarajevo today are highly respected by the three ethnic groups because the Jews tend to the medical and pharmaceutical needs of all wounded.

The Haham received the copy of the list of the Sarajevo Jewish collection to interest him in obtaining a safe haven for the library. The Haham was able to obtain the Judaica collection of Dubrovnik for exhibit and safe keeping in the Yeshiva University Museum. The Croatian Government later sued to have the artifacts returned to Croatia which now claimed rule over Dubrovnik. The U.S.A. courts ruled that the Yeshiva University Museum should retain custody of these treasures, for the time being.